P9-CQM-332

A PREFACE TO
POLITICS _____

A PREFACE TO POLITICS

THE SPIRIT OF THE PLACE

FOURTH EDITION

David Schuman
University of Massachusetts, Amherst

Bob Waterman
Gonzaga University, Spokane

D. C. HEATH AND COMPANY
Lexington, Massachusetts   Toronto

For the interest of our readers, we list the sources of the quoted material found on the following pages.

Page
61, 93   From Studs Terkel, *Working: People Talk About What They Do All Day and How They Feel About What They Do* (New York: Pantheon Books, Inc., a division of Random House, Inc., 1974).

188–189   From Perry Miller, *Errand into the Wilderness* (Cambridge, Mass.: Harvard University Press, 1975).

241,   Reprinted with the permission of Farrar, Straus & Giroux,
269,   Inc. from *The Electric Kool-Aid Acid Test* by Tom Wolfe,
287–288   copyright © 1968 by Tom Wolfe, copyright © 1967 by the World Journal Tribune Corporation.

259, 263   From R. D. Laing, *Knots* (New York: Random House, Inc., 1972).

273   Lyrics of "Friendship" by Cole Porter. Copyright © 1939 Chappell & Co., Inc. Copyright renewed. International copyright secured. All rights reserved. Used by permission.

Copyright © 1986 by D. C. Heath and Company.
Previous editions copyright © 1981, 1977, 1973.

All rights reserved. No part of this publication may be reproduced or transmitted in any form or by any means, electronic or mechanical, including photocopy, recording, or any information storage or retrieval system, without permission in writing from the publisher.

Published simultaneously in Canada.

Printed in the United States of America.

International Standard Book Number: 0–669–07552–3

Library of Congress Catalog Card Number: 85–60978

"I was never allowed to do anything for myself so I never learned to do things. The world doesn't seem quite real. If you don't do things then things are never quite real.

—R. D. Laing and Aaron Esterson

"free men and women never need be told of their good fortune . . . repressed men and women do not need to be told of their repression."

—Larry Spence

"The galley slave sticks to his oars."

—Samuel Beckett

CONTENTS

REINTRODUCTION:
THE AMERICAN DREAM IN DIFFERENT ACTS OR, THE MORE THINGS CHANGE, THE MORE THEY STAY THE SAME

. . . you think this is too horrible to have really happened, this is too awful to be the truth! But, please. It's still hard for me to have a clear mind thinking on it. But it's the truth even if it didn't happen.

—*Ken Kesey*

Imagine a world in which things constantly change while remaining the same. Imagine that there are important differences between years, yet there are even more important similarities. But, and here's the catch, those similarities are rarely seen or mentioned. The similarities form a silent context for whatever goes on, and that context provides the basis of meaning for what we do.

To rewrite this book is an exercise in sorting out what has changed and what has remained the same since the last writing. That gets complicated because I have changed and the world has changed, and one thing I have to do is figure out how a changed me looks at a changed out there. I have to do the same thing for what has stayed the same, stayed the same.

I literally look different; I now wear glasses sometimes and contacts sometimes. The world changes before my very (four) eyes.

There is a fact of American politics (and American life) that too often overwhelms us and obscures an important lesson. The fact is this: Issues change from time to time; politicians, favorite pastimes, and certainly fashions change at an increasingly fast rate. That is *not* a lesson; that is a fact.

The lesson, which is all too often ignored, is this: Each generation generally responds to the same underlying tensions and themes. To know the themes is to help your chances of knowing about American politics.

In a shorthand way, let me offer three generations' responses to American life. It is easiest to do with examples from movies.

The first movie, the old one, is *Easy Rider*. The heroes were two drug dealers. Big stuff in the sixties. They were apparently without families and without homes. They rode big motorcycles, had long hair, and wore dirty clothes.

All *statements*.

They were, it seemed, "anti" almost everything established, and were practicing a kind of small-time capitalism in a corporate society.

The film is, in part, a travel picture. We see the characters travel through beautiful country, stop and see beautiful communal life, party, and the like. We see them stop in small towns and big cities. We see them travel a little on acid.

Near the end of the movie, in a quiet scene, one of the easy riders had a sense something was missing. They had, in his words, blown it.

The other one was happy

In the last scene they were both killed.

Come the eighties and we have yet another bike movie. Of course, this is a new generation; so this bike movie has to do with a bicycle. The title *Breaking Away* is an interesting name for a movie in which travel is not a theme. Actually, we do see our hero bike fifty miles in one scene; he goes from one city in Indiana to another city in Indiana. The other long trip—this one is two hundred miles—is done on an oval track.

Literally going in circles.

The hero has a family and friends. At first he is happy pretending to be an Italian. (Breaking Away?) He is happy with his friends. (Breaking Away?)

His parents are unhappy with all of this.

Our hero does not use bad language, stay dirty long, or seem to hold grudges. During the whole movie, he kisses one young woman one time. Maybe twice. He shaves his legs once, there is one big fight, and many people eat pizza often.

All *statements*

Do not be fooled. He is a hero. With limited help from his friends, he wins the big bike race. He goes to college. His father (a used car salesman) begins to ride a bicycle and to have pride in himself. His mother gets pregnant.

In the last scene, our hero, as a college freshman, meets a French exchange student, and likes her. He begins speaking French.

Each movie, in its way, is good. Each movie, for our purposes, tells us about what to expect.

Breaking Away is an Indiana-1980s-Waltons. The point seems clear enough. This generation is ready to get back to the American Basics: clean living, close families, optimism, a college education, modesty, pride, and so forth. This generation will live out—or act out—the dreams of its parents. And, if this is the best of all worlds, its parents will be reformed by it.

It seems the title of the film is accurate, in a strange way. People want to break away not from the traditional liberal/capitalist values; they want to break away from the last generation. No more protests. (Big ones anyway.) No more rebelling. (Not big rebellions, anyway.) No more mess. No more wandering. No more insecurity.

Given the, at best, very mixed results of the last generation, that seems reasonable.

After thinking about it, and consulting with those people I trust and admire, I came to the sad conclusion that there was no wonderful movie which captured this time. I was going to squeeze a movie in because it made some kind of orderly sense. There was a kind of symmetry which appealed to me. So much for that; there was just no movie.

Two things did appear which seem to be appropriate examples of the mid-eighties. First, there is Michael Jackson. Here he is, working on his act since he was just a babe in arms. He has this amazing talent. Great voice, great dancer. His face is a monument to good genes and surgical talents. The man made an album which has sold 35 million copies so far; a video which is popular; and a video about how *that* video was made which was popular.

Last year, he earned about forty million dollars. Bigger bucks may be in his future. Why not. He is talented.

Michael Jackson is at the cutting edge of any MBA program. He has worked hard, he has made himself into a marketable product, he has marketed himself very well. He *is* the bottom line to a generation which looks closely at the bottom line. But, with all of that talent, it seems that there should be something more than that. Let me offer an example.

His song *Billy Jean* is about a young woman and a young man who is wrongly accused of being the father of her son. The woman is not treated in a very attractive way, and the man escapes by disappearing into thin air. None of that is troubling. After all, the theme is a real one to many people.

No, the catch is this: Jackson uses the music from *Billy Jean* to sell a soft drink. It is hard to understand the emotions of a song which is at once about possible paternity and selling Pepsi Cola. It is clear that what we have are two traditions at work here. The first is the bottom line tradition in which making money is good music to the artist's ears. In that tradition, Pepsis and parenthood finally get down to dollars and cents. Michael Jackson, in many ways, is at the top of this generation. He is supertalented, he works hard, and at his core he is merely a marketable product.

The second tradition has to do with music. Music has carried whole generations to explore different things. Rock and roll opened up America in many ways; the Beatles did too. Traditional folk music has been wrapped up in the anti-slavery movement, in civil rights, in union politics, in revolution. So far, Michael Jackson—the cutting edge—is a part of none of these aspects of the tradition.

And nobody seems to care much, which is the real point.

I can do it another way. Several years ago, while eating dinner, my oldest daughter and I had a talk. She was telling me about the wonders of disco, how it was the greatest thing ever, and how it would never die. I made a very big bet with her that she was wrong. (I was right, but have yet to collect.)

When my second daughter was in the seventh grade, a few

years ago, she decided that punk was the only thing to be. I offered to have her hair died purple. She refused, but assured me that someday everyone would be punk and have purple hair.

Had my daughters been right, then this generation would now be at a disco. They would have purple hair and be wearing chains. I do not see that at all.

My oldest daughter is studying for her college boards. She is trying to figure out which college she wants to go to. Her plan is to go into business. My other daughter has very pretty brown hair and wears things that go with her pretty blue eyes. She was on the honor roll her first year in high school.

That, I believe, has a lot to do with what this generation is. In many ways, it is like one of the generations I grew up in. I grew up once in the 1950s and once in the 1960s (I guess I was a slow learner). This generation is much like the fifties, only with computers and birth control pills.

I am convinced that for every clean and quiet generation, there seems to be a dirty and rowdy one. If you are uneasy with what you are expected to do and to be, know that your turn will come.

Put differently, if you really believe you have found the answer to traditional American questions, the next generation will tell you that you are wrong. Today's disco is tomorrow's hoola hoop; today's president is tomorrow's Richard Nixon.

Put differently still, the underlying issues—like individualism, friendship, and bureaucracy—remain virtually unchanged. Each generation simply puts on a different mask to face them.

No matter what goes on, there are certain things that seem to be true. For example, James Madison[1] quit changing and revising *Federalist* No. 10 some years ago. It seems reasonable to assume that the *Federalist* No. 10 that was printed in the first two editions is the same one that will appear here. Bureaucracies have just gotten bigger, organizations have become more complex, science is more powerful, and the military is able to kill us more times over. And, with regularity, people keep trying to be elected to some office or another, and other people keep encouraging them by voting.

---

[1] Good old Madison. My friend Ken Mayers was more than amused when he pointed out that the heart of the real-world-of-selling-America is called . . . Madison Avenue.

The basic undercurrents of our culture are still powerful, and what was true a few years ago is true today. The critique then is the critique now.

This generation does not have the kind of exciting news of the *Easy Rider* days. It is hard to get really worked up about acid rain or a big budget deficit. Those things are invisible; being drafted to fight a war was visible. Here we are, in the midst of so many important things, almost none of which we can see or get excited about. Why not just go to business school and think about yourself?

Why not be a marketable product and make forty million dollars next year?

Of course there is terrible unemployment, we are polluting ourselves to death, and discrimination is still an everyday fact. But those are *hidden* things. Not news. Not dramatic. They are just facts without much reality for us.

They're just there.

No more marches. Sit-ins. Non-negotiable demands. Up against the walls. Day-Glo. Hippies or revolution. The Movement moved. Tom Hayden wears a suit, and Jerry Rubin is now "totally into himself" (at least he has finally admitted it). Blue jeans are now designed by Gloria Vanderbilt.

All kinds of different ways of trying to come to terms with America have come into being. While a lot aren't strikingly unique, these ways have distinct characteristics of this generation. This generation? What does *that* mean?

The older brothers and sisters (and I mean blood ties) were people who belonged, if not participated, in long hair when it was a political statement, dope when it was national news, and war— in it or against it. They dropped out, and all that.

This generation saw the hurt and the fun and some of the successes and failures. Apparently, they disapproved and/or they wanted an identity of their own. It was their turn to come to terms with America. "Generation gaps" apply almost as well to successive generations as to the space between parents and children.

The eighteen-year-old turns his or her back on the twenty-eight-year-old. The classes in business are now over-enrolled. God has made a comeback. One suspects people even wash behind their ears. Change, indeed. Hair is short; success is "in."

But, of course, we all get tugged by a lot of the same forces; and, because of all the big and obvious things—like language and schools and TV—we have much more in common than we often admit. We're a whole lot alike. That is the truth of it. Our environment, physical and cultural and mythical, seeps in and affects us all. In real ways we are where and when we live.

If we want to do it right (makes more sense than to want to do it wrong), if we want to be smarter and better than we are, part of what we have to do is understand how others have dealt with their times. Clear but bad advice may be helpful, even if it is said as good advice. Part of what older generations should do is to put their knowledge into forms that younger generations might learn *something* from. The other part is that younger generations should try to listen.

The other day I read this fact, which seemed true enough: No eighteen-year-old has ever been forty years old, but every forty-year-old has been eighteen years old. There is a big problem, one that is difficult to answer. What the fact assumes is that the forty-year-old, because of having had more experience, knows more than the eighteen-year-old. In certain things, that may well be true.

This also may be true: The forty-year-old may have twenty-two years more wrongheaded thinking than the eighteen-year-old.

It's sometimes hard to know.

But there are some things that seem right. For example, given all we know, with an amazing amount of hard work and good intentions and clean hands and a pure heart and all that—given all those things—sometimes we get lucky and get a little smarter and better.

Besides, there are some things that can't be the truth even if they did happen.

—Ken Kesey

THANK YOU AGAIN ____

In most acknowledgments, people are thanked, editors praised, and a husband or wife is offered a written hug in the last paragraph. This acknowledgment will be like that, but not yet. To begin with, most of the people who helped with the other three editions are far away; they are simply not around to talk with, or to trade jokes, ideas, books, or troubles with.

What I am interested in acknowledging—in a sense—is a place. The writings of the various editions of *Preface* represent a kind of American pioneer movement. Only backward. It began in the West, in Berkeley and then Seattle, and moved East, to Northampton, Massachusetts.

Certainly the temporariness of the places is very American.

Normally, houses are not acknowledged, nor are the towns in which they are located. I am not certain why. Around the corner from us, on one of our jogging routes, is the home of a former mayor of Northampton and President of the United States: Calvin Coolidge. Neither Barbara nor I draw any particular political inspiration when we pass the house. There was not then, nor is there now, any charisma surrounding Silent Cal.

Down the street from the house is the site of the church where Jonathan Edwards once spent time preaching about a hell full of fire and brimstone. The old church burned down. Now, the new Edwards Church is across the street from the junior high school Tama attended.

When she went to this particular junior high—which is as American as the Edwards Church—there is a surprising amount of violence, drinking, and drugs. Practice, I guess, for high school. The students are already "tracked." Practice, I guess, for college . . . and the rest of life.

That was four years ago. The junior high has been converted into condos and Amy went to a junior high where some of the classes were held in mobile homes. Yuppies now live in the old school.

Why acknowledge this not very large, nor very famous place? So what if we get three major networks, an educational channel, and major movies from Hollywood two months late? The fact of the matter is this: Northampton is home for a lot of people. In its small ways, in the texture of its neighborhoods and friendships, in its shared winter storms and its concern about asparagus blight (no kidding), a lot of life gets defined.

This edition cannot help but reflect these things. It is also influenced by the family, and my graduate students, and the undergraduates I meet. There are Ben's tennis teachers, and my tennis partners. There are the local politicians who do seem to get inspiration from Calvin Coolidge and seem driven to say remarkably silly things. There is the small town gossip.

Acknowledge, acknowledge. Somehow, all of that is part of the book.

More immediately important—aha, here it comes—are the summer seminars and Barbara. Annually, and sometimes more often than that, we get together with Larry and Maya Spence, and Bob and Olivia Waterman. They are remarkable times.

This version of the *Preface* owes much to Bob Waterman. He not only added particular parts, but has added perspective to the whole. It is fun to talk with him and to read what he has to write.

The family, like the town, refuses to let me escape into the merely academic since important matters of everyday life are much more compelling. That is a gift beyond measure.

David Schuman
A hot summer day
Northampton, Massachusetts

FOCUS _____

David and I have talked about the ideas in this book for years. It occurred to me, while teaching from the Third Edition, that there were ways in which the book could be made a better teaching book. As we discussed the changes, our informal talks became a more formal collaboration.

At the end of each chapter I will re-emphasize the idea which pulls together the essential points being made. The purpose of these Focuses is to remind you of the main point made in each chapter and to assist your study, thought, and reflection about the material. After reading the focuses, you will want to check back over the chapters to confirm whether you understand the particular unity that has been emphasized. If you discover discrepancies between my formulation and your own thinking, reconsider your understanding in light of my suggestion. If discrepancies still linger, formulate a main point that better captures the meaning of what you have read.

At the end of the book these chapter points will be put together into an overview of the entire argument. You also will want to rethink your understanding at that time until you see the way each part fits into the comprehensive point of the book.

For example, and to anticipate the overall argument, the book is written from the viewpoint of the American citizen in 1985.

Today's citizen seldom has experience with direct exercise of political power and usually does not believe that she, he, or fellow citizens should have such a privilege or right.

In contrast, the citizen of the United States who lived in a township around 1800 believed that he did have the right to directly participate in government. No campaigning or other electoral activity was necessary before using legislative and executive power. The citizen merely had to show up at the town meeting in order to have voice and power in the enactment of local laws, to be a legislator. At the same meeting the citizen also might have been selected for one of the nineteen local administrative posts filled by ordinary townsmen for a one-year period.

Although the sheer size of the American population in the 1980s no doubt makes difficult substantial political activity by every citizen, the book argues that numbers of people are not the primary obstacle. Much more important is the way we habitually think about politics and government in the United States at this time. The goal of the book is to have us reflect upon our assumptions, or "myths" as they are called, so that we can see that we have lost part of our political heritage through habit rather than because of insurmountable objective factors. In this regard, it might be helpful to think of the book as being written by crusty, old-fashioned Americans of the early 1800s who, when visiting our century, discovered that their descendants voluntarily had relinquished the political initiative which they had undertaken regularly. You can imagine the anger. In order to discipline and make constructive use of that anger, this book was written.

Bob Waterman

THE SPIRIT OF
THE PLACE

"*The world doesn't fear a new idea. It can pigeon-hole any idea. But it can't pigeon-hole a real new experience. It can only dodge. The world is a great dodger, and the Americans the greatest. Because they dodge their own feelings.*

—*D. H. Lawrence*

"*An important book is one which reads us, not the reverse.*"

—*W. H. Auden*

The title *A Preface to Politics* seems easy enough to understand. It is an introduction to politics. While that is certainly accurate, it is merely accurate and in the long run does not tell us all we need to know. To begin to read this book with the idea that it will be a simple account of the popular notions of politics (Congress, the presidency, the Supreme Court) would be to begin with a whole set of misconceptions.

Politics is more—and often different—than just what television and the print media tell us. To truly understand politics, it is necessary to understand the country in which it takes place. To understand American politics, it is important to understand as much of America as possible. We need to know how we think about things, and why. We need to know our ideological biases, and how that carries out into our everyday activities.

In order to know about American politics, it becomes necessary to take very little for granted. The most common activity or event may tell us about who we are, and may give us a clue to our politics.

The book, then, is full of everyday events and thoughts. It is full of our biases and speculations about what those biases might mean. This *Preface* is about The Spirit of the Place (a phrase taken directly from D.H. Lawrence, for those of you interested in such things), and it is meant to be discussed. I am convinced that to understand our politics we must look to our surroundings, and to understand that it is necessary to study and talk about it.

It is, I believe, in everyone's best interest to understand about textbooks in general, and this one in particular, in some detail.

TEXTBOOKS: GENERAL AND PARTICULAR

It seems sensible to begin by saying something that most people already know if they have taken the time to think about it. These first pages have to do with textbooks whose purpose is to introduce people to political science and to politics. To understand some of these attempts is to begin to understand how uninviting—and in some cases how misleading and dangerous—these attempts *may* be.

Anyone with reasonable intelligence and enough courses in political science can outline an introductory textbook.

First, there is the secret language to explain. This means that at least one chapter must be devoted to defining terms. "Politics is . . . ; science is . . . ; therefore, political science is . . ." That is fine. It certainly *seems* reasonable to expect people who use the same language to have similar words mean similar things. So, our ideal textbook strains toward purity of definition. It strains toward standardization.

On with the text. After definitions—after laying the parameters—there seem to be at least four things we must try to do. First, we should give examples of the system proving that it is good or bad—*but giving tacit support in either case.* Second, we must give as many "facts" as possible. Third, perhaps we should include a couple of case studies to make the whole thing more "real" and appealing. Finally, we should consciously integrate material from other fields to show the interrelationship of all the social sciences.

Worthy aims, all.

There are, of course, little things that ought to be done. We might discuss how a bill becomes a law, and/or how power is spread less or more evenly around, and/or how elections count. We should, of course, find an appropriate quote from old Abe Lincoln. If we can manage to do this, and work up a teacher's manual with true-false questions of medium difficulty, then we will have succeeded in writing a standard—and possibly even successful—textbook.

These elements a text doth make.

It seems difficult to fault our ideal/typical textbook, because it sounds so reasonable, so obvious, so normal. It is what was, what is, and what always will be. Basically, there is nothing terribly wrong with the notion of an introduction to a field—nothing wrong, that is, unless it goes unquestioned. Certainly we should know about the political system, be introduced to "facts," and involve ourselves with word definitions. All these things may, at some point, be critical to the student. Nevertheless, there is work that must go on before this begins. The investigation of the obvious may *not* be the obvious place to begin. There are questions that are logically prior to the "facts" of the empirical world. Let me try to explain.

Built into our typical text are assumptions about politics, about the system, and about knowledge. Our book would be correct if we were agreed on the ultimate "truths" of the empirical facts of the "real world." If we could agree not to question these "truths" and not to question what they meant or whom they benefited, then such a book would be a fine one. We would have to agree that politics was pretty well limited to elections and representatives, that it was generally an activity that was neither noble nor had any immediate effect on our lives.

There is, of course, no good reason to accept these assumptions. Politics, in a real sense, affects everything we do. To begin to understand politics, we must begin by understanding the range of politics and the power of ideology. To look at politics in this manner is to open up a whole series of problems—problems that do not seem to be political but really are. Politics—in spite of what we have been taught to believe—may have something to do with how we think about happiness or with why we seem to be lonely. It may have a great influence on how we view each other, or on how we react to rules, or on what we think is important. For certain, politics is more than voting, and to understand it requires much more than trying to integrate the social sciences.

What I want to argue is that what you do means something, that your actions are connected with what you believe—or were taught to believe—and that these actions are important for at least two reasons. First, most of our learned behavior supports the status quo, supports what is. Our political system and, in fact, Political Systems, are geared to self-survival. This is achieved, in no small measure, by teaching the people who live under that system to support it. No great news in that. Second, our behavior is important because it defines who we are. If you act like an ass, but think like a saint, you are still an ass.

The task of this book is immodest: to begin to explore how we think and act, why such behavior is political, and what all that might mean.

There is little reason to assume that all I write is true. Of course it is not. Politics is often unsure and sloppy, a lot like life. To write a textbook—indeed, almost any book—using only those things we can all agree upon would be as boring as it would be useless. To begin to understand politics is to begin to understand how we got to where we are—as individuals and as groups of individuals and as a society. This has to be incredibly complex, and must be made up of many different truths.[1]

There is an order to this book, an effort to explain a position and then to explore it. A "model" of politics is contained in the initial chapters. Simply stated, this is an attempt to understand the kind of individual our system tries to shape; how that individual is taught to look at the world (how he or she knows what he or she knows); and what kind of societal structure is constructed in

---

[1] There are many problems an ordinary text deals with that are not covered in this book. The most obvious example is the set of problems (complicated by racial bigotry) minorities face in a nation. In a sense, this book concentrates on the problems of those who have lived in America for any length of time and who have been socialized—or victimized—by our particular ways.

the image of that individual. These chapters are most clearly understood after the others have been read.

In an important sense, the rest of the book deals with the texture of a person's life. It attempts to explore some of those problems that seem to require only natural, everyday, commonsense answers, but that actually deserve much closer attention. Somehow, we all live in groups and seek to be free, but we do these things without thinking about what they mean or about how we have been taught to understand them.

We must understand the *context* of our actions, both from the outside in and from the inside out. We must begin to be aware of the transactions between our selves and our society.

We will begin with what we know best—ourselves. Every one of us is the system, we have it in our heads, and we act it out in our everyday lives. To learn about the system is to learn about ourselves—and, of course, the reverse. To think about making the one better, we must know about both and about how they are related.

It at least doubles what we have to know; it may well more than double what we may be capable of doing.

WHEN? _____

Perhaps in time the so-called Dark Ages will be thought of as including our own.

Sometimes you just want to sit down, sigh, and wish you knew how you got where you are. After another sigh, another question occurs: Just where are you?

Don't look at me, I don't know. It is possible to pinpoint the century we're in. We may learn more than we want by just knowing that much.

As Friedrich Nietzsche wrote and grew older and his thought matured, he became more aware of what great limitations societies placed on individuals. His work became a chronicle of repressions and restraints; of the loss of a person's creative energy in the modern state.

So he developed an image of an individual who understood what was happening—a kind of superman—who was condemned to the sad realization of the blandness of the current state of affairs. The superman wandered Europe telling those he met the horrible truth of their lives. Far from being a Germanic conqueror—an Aryan goose-stepping in formation—Nietzsche's truthsayer did not seek conquest, but rather education. He took no pleasure in victory, but rather shared the individuals' pain of loss.

Zarathustra lived on the mountaintop for ten years. He then came down full of wisdom and joy, knowledge and sadness. He walked the earth with his destructive yet creative message.

Freud lived in Vienna and did his work seated silently behind a blank screen. His message was to a whole different point.

Think of the world as it was in 1850—and then make it more fully developed. The industrial era was a fact. It won. Governments and industries and societies were fully involved in becoming much bigger and more complex. The way to handle complexity was to organize it; the way to handle people was to make them fit into organizations.

There were, of course, some pretty obvious losses.

For example, as roles became more explicit, more specialized, the range of human activities became more limited. The paradox is a nice one: As the whole society becomes more complex, the individual in the society has been forced to become more simple. As the industry produced more and faster, the individual produced greater volume but fewer things. The world was working, but the people in it seemed to be breaking down. Even Victorian morals weren't doing their job in keeping society stable and people stable.

If the aim of Nietzsche was to go beyond the present by understanding the past, Freud's aim was to help people adjust to now . . . to make it work. What Freud worked with was each individual; each of us living in his or her own little world. Freud knew we were more than we appeared to be. He listened to our words and tried to understand our dreams. He made myths for us to believe.

Freud wanted to save people by understanding them—he wanted to understand by quietly listening to someone talking on a couch.

When Nietzsche wandered, Freud sat; Nietzsche spoke, Freud listened and took notes; Nietzsche defied—Freud was paid to befriend:

Nietzsche died in 1900.

Welcome to the twentieth century.

1

POLITICS AS EVIL PEOPLE

Although I know very little of the Steppenwolf's life, I have all the same good reason to suppose that he was brought up by devoted but severe and very pious parents and teachers in accordance with that doctrine that makes the breaking of the will the cornerstone of education and upbringing . . . in so far as he let loose upon himself every barbed criticism, every anger and hate he could command he was, in spite of all, a real Christian, and a real martyr. As for others and the world around him he never ceased in his heroic and earnest endeavor to love them, to be just to them, to do them no harm, for the love of his neighbor was as deeply in him as the hatred of himself, and so his whole life was an example that love of one's neighbor is not possible without love of oneself, and that self-hate is really the same thing as sheer egoism, and in the long run breeds the same cruel isolation and despair.

—*Hermann Hesse*

. . . and the past not uncommonly takes a while to happen, and some long time to figure out.

—Ken Kesey

"Although the past may not repeat itself, it does rhyme."

—Mark Twain

POLITICS: WHO, WHAT, HOW

There are all kinds of traditional questions in politics. The more a person knows about history and political thought, the better the chance to sort things out. While there are constant themes in American politics, every generation gets engaged in its peculiar and particular variations.

We are, it seems to me, engaged in some serious Who, What, and How questions: Whom should I sleep with? What am I going to breathe? How am I going to earn a living?

I do not want to give the impression that these are all of our problems. There is, for example, a whole series of problems that revolve around trying to be sane in an insane world; but those are best backed into. Beginning with insanity (which is an every-morning starting place if you pay attention to the news—or even if you think about the day ahead) seems too depressing when being introduced to politics.

Can you imagine—first a knock on the door, then a deep rumbling voice saying: "Hello, I'm the world. Guess what? I'm way out of control."

No, that is just too depressing. Better to begin with Who.

Who

Of course it does seem a little off to think about politics beginning in bed. For most people in America, until the last ten or fifteen years or so, Whom should I sleep with? was a fairly simple question. A person tried to find someone of the opposite sex to fall in love with, marry—and as things happen—sleep with.

Where are the politics in that?

As Americans learned (as all those closets opened), the first question might easily be: Which sex do you want to sleep with? Or, if it is too difficult to make up your mind, do you enjoy both equally? There are more choices: choices of number, choices of color, choices of married or unmarried. There are pregnancy choices and abortion choices.

And (this is the one choice that is totally offensive to me) there is the choice simply of technique, or emotion, or some combination.

The fact is that there are whole *political* movements built around almost every aspect of this Who question. And I mean the voting, lobbying kind of politics that is familiar to us. People win or lose elections, get jobs or get fired sometimes because of whom they like to sleep with.

How have we come to have a political stand while lying down? What does that mean?

What

The What am I going to breathe? question is straightforward enough. Progress, that driving force of so much American life, has somehow gotten us to the point of killing the world in pursuit of a more comfortable material existence.

We have now learned that much of our manufactured environment—from automobiles to spray deodorants to nuclear reactors—puts something into the air which is very bad for us. We know that spray deodorants do it on a more regular basis than reactors, but that one wrong "puff" of radioactive stuff can be a fairly serious problem.

No one, or to be more precise, no one I know, is really against smelling good or using electricity for all kinds of things. But that is only part of the matter. The other part is that one of the great unintended consequences of all times seems to be that our own production is making the world unsafe to live in.

A political problem? How can that be?

It is reasonable to expect that, as a country, we should be able to regulate any number of things in the "national interest."

"Aha," the shrill, harsh voice of Political Science says, "define national interest. There it is, in print and in quotes, as if it means something. Well, what does it mean?"

The truth of the matter is that there seems to be no agreement on the specifics of our national interest. Books are written about it, governmental commissions are formed to define it, politicians always believe they understand it, and newspaper editorials often proclaim it. What they all have in common is their lack of success.

There are some things we can say in general. For example, there seem to be rules about people killing other people; there are rules about people or people-made things killing everybody. We are, after all, guaranteed liberty as well as life, not to mention the pursuit of happiness.

If that is so, what kind of politics—what kind of national interest—allows this slow death to go on?

What you breathe turns out to be an unlikely but wholly valid political problem.

How

This third question, How am I going to earn a living? is a nagging one, but one not always of immediate concern to most college students. While you may think of school as job training, the fact is that school is a career for only a few of us. Also, in important ways, working does not belong in the category of politics.

After all politics is, well, politics. It has to do with armies and Congress and electing mayors and Presidents. Politics is voting, not getting a job.

That, of course, is the myth.

Working (according to the same myth) has to do with personal ambition and talent and whom you know and what you are paid. Working is all wrapped up in the American Dream of Horatio Alger, making it, rugged individualism, white collars, professions, status seeking and status getting, and the like.

Jobs are private (but possibly prestigious); politics is front-page public (but faintly dirty).

Somewhere in our consciousness we know that is not quite right. After all, government is politics and government is in the job business. More people are employed by government than by any other employer. One out of six people working, works for the government.

While the regulation of the economy is anything but a science, certainly prosperity in general and many jobs in particular are affected by governmental decisions. If the decision is made to raise interest rates, less money is loaned, fewer things are bought, fewer things are manufactured and, as this keeps going, the one thing to rise will be—da da—unemployment. What happened to the public/private myth?

Think about it: You could be bright and able and energetic and selling apples on a street corner during the depression of the 1930s. You could be bright and able and energetic and fighting in Vietnam in the 1960s and early '70s. You could be bright and able and energetic and collecting unemployment in the 1980s because of shortsighted energy policies, inflation, and economic stagnation.

It is, to be blunt, nonsense to misjudge the effects of government and politics, and to think that working is a sign of personal triumph or failure.

What's going on here?

MADISON. . . . AS THE AVENUE

At the end of this section, there will be an extraordinary piece of political literature. It was written by James Madison in order to explain and argue for the adoption of the Constitution of the United States. As you will see, it is a political fix.

The claim I want to make, following those curious political issues and the vision of Madison, is that there are ways in which our politics require certain things of us. The things, it turns out, are less than inspiring.

We are a myth-driven people. We have the myth of making it. The idea of the little engine that could, no matter how high that mountain, if we just keep on chugging we will get to the top. Each of us as an engine. Each of us with our own mountain. Each of us dragging our past, our baggage, up the heights.

Each American putting away: "I think I can, I think I can."

The trick is that we are compelled to do it alone. Each by ourself. Later, we will look at our romantic past. We will look at

H. D. Thoreau and living at Walden Pond. Now *there* was a real American. Writing a journal about living alone in the wilderness. It is the dream: a house on the lake, and a little peace and quiet. (It is an American myth: Thoreau kept rewriting his diary until it was good literature, and then went to his mother's house for dinner every Friday night.)

We can go farther back. Here come the Puritans, to set a moral example for the world. Goodness knows that we are a self-righteous bunch. Can you imagine that, as the native Americans were here living at peace with the land, some moralistic religious people came here to establish a colony so virtuous that it would shame all of Western Europe into a kind of religious renewal?

Western Europe did not seem to be impressed. In fact, not all of the second generation Puritans were impressed. They began moving out, moving West. That movement has become another part of our collective background. It seems that the four things we can count on are these: death, taxes, leaving home, and moving on.

We settle only to become unsettled and go to resettle. And we do not do it in groups of friends, or by neighborhoods; no, we either do it alone or do it a family at a time. We do it to get more, to get better, to get it faster. Maybe we do it sometimes just because it's in our blood.

From the Puritans on, there have always been enterprising Americans. There was a whole country to fill-in. Lots of land. There were fortunes to be made. While the how-to-do-it has changed (the only way forty acres will make you rich today is if it happens to have oil or gas underneath it), the fighting for a fortune is a part of the air (polluted it turns out) we breathe.

Now, we either want our own business, or want to be at the top of a very big business. There are those who pay for their college education by selling drugs; there are others who dream of hitting on "the" idea and making millions: MacDonald's and You. Either way, we are capitalists.

We hold to these images. We believe in them, no matter what the realities may be. We are self-righteous, mobile, capitalists: We act on our myths. There is nothing at all wrong with that, only if you are willing to look behind them, see the basis of the myths, and admit that myth and data don't always have much in common.

Beneath all of this, grinding away at so much of how we think and what we do, is the idea of individualism. We seek it, depend on the idea that we are unique, and will not hear arguments to the contrary. We are a nation of One's, and the political consequences are powerful. There is passage in a book by J. P. Donleavy that concerns a young man who is very kind to many people. He says, ". . . at a distance, people look different but when you talk with them all become the same." Have you thought about your conversations lately?

Politically, we were set up for just such a thing. We were set up to believe we were unique (alone), heroic (lonely), making it (embattled), and privileged for the opportunity. Politically, of course, this is nothing short of a formula for keeping each of us speechless and powerless.

You can scream all you want to at the frontier; you can make as many threats as you want on your lake front home; you can move anytime you want. Who cares? People with power could certainly care less.

So, fellow citizens, we swallow our myths whole, and come out hungry for companionship, politics, and even a little power.

How did we get into such a fix?

One logical place to begin to understand how we came to be how we are is to go back to James Madison, and his *Federalist* No. 10. A background of the paper seems in order.

James Madison attended the Constitutional Convention. For a number of reasons, he stands out. It is Madison who informs us of that convention; he kept a literate and intelligent diary of the convention debates. More importantly, along with Alexander Hamilton and John Jay, he wrote a series of papers defending the Constitution for the citizens of New York State. The papers—*The Federalist Papers*—are brilliant propaganda that do much to explain the Constitution. The following is *Federalist* No. 10, in which Madison writes about our citizens' relationships with each other, what they should be, and how they should be handled.

Two suggestions: Read it at least twice—once for what it says and once again for what it does not say. Omission is important (especially if one knows what to look for).

Among the numerous advantages promised by a well-constructed Union none deserves to be more accurately developed than its

tendency to break and control the violence of faction. The friend
of popular governments never finds himself so much alarmed for
their character and fate as when he contemplates their propensity
to this dangerous vice. He will not fail, therefore, to set a due
value on any plan which, without violating the principles to which
he is attached, provides a proper cure for it. The instability, injustice, and confusion introduced into the public councils have,
in truth, been the mortal diseases under which popular governments have everywhere perished, as they continue to be the favorite and fruitful topics from which the adversaries to liberty
derive their most specious declamations. The valuable improvements made by the American constitutions on the popular models,
both ancient and modern, cannot certainly be too much admired,
but it would be an unwarrantable partiality to contend that they
have as effectively obviated the danger on this side as was wished
and expected. Complaints are everywhere heard from our most
considerate and virtuous citizens, equally the friends of public and
private faith, and of public and personal liberty, that our governments are too unstable, that the public good is disregarded in
the conflicts of rival parties, and that measures are too often
decided, not according to the rules of justice and the rights of the
minor party, but by the superior force of an interested and
overbearing majority. However anxiously we may wish that these
complaints had no foundation, the evidence of known facts will
not permit us to deny that they are in some degree true. It will
be found, indeed, on a candid review of our situation that some
of the distresses under which we labor have been erroneously
charged on the operation of our governments; but it will be found,
at the same time, that other causes will not alone account for
many of our heaviest misfortunes, and particularly for that prevailing and increasing distrust of public engagements and alarm
for private rights, which are echoed from one end of the continent
to the other. These must be chiefly, if not wholly, effects of the
unsteadiness and injustice with which a factious spirit has tainted
our public administrations.

By a faction, I understand a number of citizens, whether amount-
ing to a majority or a minority of the whole, who are united and
actuated by some common impulse of passion, or of interest,
adverse to the rights of other citizens or to the permanent and
aggregate interests of the community.

There are two methods of curing the mischiefs of faction: the one, by removing its causes; the other, by controlling its effects.

There are again two methods of removing the causes of faction: the one, by destroying the liberty which is essential to its existence; the other by giving to every citizen the same opinions, the same passions, and the same interests.

It could never be more truly said than of the first remedy, that it was worse than the disease. Liberty is to faction what air is to fire, an ailment without which it instantly expires. But it could not be less folly to abolish liberty, which is essential to political life, because it nourishes faction than it would be to wish the annihilation of air, which is essential to animal life, because it imparts to fire its destructive agency.

The second expedient is as impracticable as the first would be unwise. As long as the reason of man continues fallible, and he is at liberty to exercise it, different opinions will be formed. As long as the connection subsists between his reason and his self-love, his opinions and his passions will have a reciprocal influence on each other, and the former will be objects to which the latter will attach themselves. The diversity in the faculties of men, from which the rights of property originate, is not less an insuperable obstacle to a uniformity of interests. The protection of these faculties is the first object of government. From the protection of different and unequal faculties of acquiring property, the possession of different degrees and kinds of property immediately results; and from the influence of these on the sentiments and views of the respective proprietors ensues a division of the society into different interests and parties.

The latent causes of faction are thus sown in the nature of man, and we see them everywhere brought into different degrees of activity, according to the different circumstances of civil society. A zeal for different opinions concerning religion, concerning government, and many other points, as well of speculation as of practice; an attachment to different leaders ambitiously contending for pre-eminence and power, or to persons of other descriptions whose fortunes have been interesting to the human passions, have, in turn, divided mankind into parties, inflamed them with mutual animosity, and rendered them much more disposed to vex and oppress each other than to co-operate for their common good.

So strong is this propensity of mankind to fall into mutual animosities that, where no substantial occasion presents itself, the most frivolous and fanciful distinctions have been sufficient to kindle their unfriendly passions and excite their most violent conflicts. But the most common and durable source of factions has been the various and unequal distribution of property. Those who hold and those who are without property have ever formed distinct interests in society. Those who are creditors and those who are debtors fall under a like discrimination. A landed interest, a manufacturing interest, a mercantile interest, a money interest, with many lesser interests, grow up of necessity in civilized nations and divide them into different classes actuated by different sentiments and views. The regulation of these various and interfering interests forms the principal task of modern legislation and involves the spirit of party and faction in the necessary and ordinary operations of the government.

No man is allowed to be a judge in his own cause because his interest would certainly bias his judgment and, not improbably, corrupt his integrity. With equal, nay with greater reason, a body of men are unfit to be both judges and parties at the same time; yet what are many of the most important acts of legislation but so many judicial determinations, not indeed concerning the rights of single persons, but concerning the rights of large bodies of citizens? And what are the different classes of legislators but advocates and parties to the causes which they determine? Is a law proposed concerning private debts? It is a question to which the creditors are parties on one side and the debtors on the other. Justice ought to hold the balance between them. Yet the parties are, and must be, themselves the judges, and the most numerous party or, in other words, the most powerful faction must be expected to prevail. Shall domestic manufactures be encouraged, and in what degree, by restrictions on foreign manufactures? are questions which would be differently decided by the landed and the manufacturing classes, and probably by neither with a sole regard to justice and the public good. The apportionment of taxes on the various descriptions of property is an act which seems to require the most exact impartiality, yet there is, perhaps, no legislative act in which greater opportunity and temptation are given to a predominant party to trample on the rules of justice. Every shilling with which they overburden the inferior number is a shilling saved to their own pockets.

It is in vain to say that enlightened statesmen will be able to adjust these clashing interests and render them all subservient to the public good. Enlightened statesmen will not always be at the helm. Nor, in many cases, can such an adjustment be made at all without taking into view indirect and remote considerations, which will rarely prevail over the immediate interest that one party may find in disregarding the rights of another or the good of the whole.

The inference to which we are brought is that the *causes* of faction cannot be removed, and that relief is only to be sought in the means of controlling its *effects*.

If a faction consists of less than a majority, relief is supplied by the republican principle, which enables the majority to defeat its sinister views by regular vote. It may clog the administration, it may convulse the society, but it will be unable to execute and mask its violence under the forms of the Constitution. When a majority is included in a faction, the form of popular government, on the other hand, enables it to sacrifice to its ruling passion or interest both the public good and the rights of other citizens. To secure the public good and private rights against the danger of such a faction, and at the same time to preserve the spirit and the form of popular government, is then the great object to which our inquiries are directed. Let me add that it is the great desideratum by which this form of government can be rescued from the opprobrium under which it has so long labored and be recommended to the esteem and adoption of mankind.

By what means is this object attainable? Evidently by one of two only. Either the existence of the same passion or interest in a majority at the same time must be prevented or the majority, having such coexistent passion or interest, must be rendered, by their numbers and local situation, unable to concert and carry into effect schemes of oppression. If the impulse and the opportunity be suffered to coincide, we well know that neither normal nor religious motives can be relied on as an adequate control. They are not found to be such on the injustice and violence of individuals, and lose their efficiency in proportion to the number combined together, that is, in proportion as their efficacy becomes needful.

From this view of the subject it may be concluded that a pure democracy, by which I mean a society consisting of a small number of citizens who assemble and administer the government in person, can admit of no cure for the mischiefs of faction. A common passion or interest will, in almost every case, be felt by a majority of the whole; a communication and concert result from the form of government itself, and there is nothing to check the inducements to sacrifice the weaker party or an obnoxious individual. Hence it is that such democracies have ever been spectacles of turbulence and contention, have ever been found incompatible with personal security or the rights of property, and have in general been as short in their lives as they have been violent in their deaths. Theoretic politicians who have patronized this species of government have erroneously supposed that by reducing mankind to a perfect equality in their political rights, they would, at the same time, be perfectly equalized and assimilated in their possessions, their opinions, and their passions.

A republic, by which I mean a government in which the scheme of representation takes place, opens a different prospect and promises the cure for which we are seeking. Let us examine the points in which it varies from pure democracy, and we shall comprehend both the nature of the cure and the efficacy which it must derive from the Union.

The two great points of difference between a democracy and a republic are: first, the delegation of the government, in the latter, to a small number of citizens elected by the rest; secondly, the greater number of citizens and greater sphere of country over which the latter may be extended.

The effect of the first difference is, on the one hand, to refine and enlarge the public views by passing them through the medium of a chosen body of citizens whose wisdom may best discern the true interest of their country, and whose patriotism and love of justice will be least likely to sacrifice it to temporary or partial considerations. Under such a regulation it may well happen that the public voice, pronounced by the representatives of the people, will be more consonant to the public good than if pronounced by the people themselves, convened for the purpose. On the other hand, the effect may be inverted. Men of factious tempers, of local prejudices, or of sinister designs may, by intrigue, by corruption, or by other means, first obtain the suffrages and then betray the interests of the people. The question resulting is whether small or extensive republics are more favorable to the election of proper guardians of the public weal; and it is clearly decided in favor of the latter by two obvious considerations:

In the first place, it is to be remarked that, however small the republic may be, the representatives must be raised to a certain number in order to guard against the cabals of a few, and that, however large it may be, they must be limited to a certain number in order to guard against the confusion of a multitude. Hence the number of representatives in the two cases not being in proportion to that of the two constituents, and being proportionally greater in the small republic, it follows that, if the proportion to fit characters be not less in the large than in the small republic, the former will present a greater option and consequently a greater probability of a fit choice.

In the next place, as each representative will be chosen by a greater number of citizens in the large than in the small republic, it will be more difficult for unworthy candidates to practice with success the vicious arts by which elections are too often carried; and the suffrages of the people being more free will be more likely to center in men who possess the most attractive merit and the most diffusive and established characters.

It must be confessed that in this, as in most other cases, there is a mean, on both sides of which inconveniences will be found to lie. By enlarging too much the number of electors you render the representative too little acquainted with all their local circumstances and lesser interests; as by reducing it too much, you render him unduly attached to these and too little fit to comprehend and pursue great and national objects. The federal Constitution forms a happy combination in this respect: the great and aggregate interests being referred to the national, the local and particular to the State legislatures.

The other point of difference is the greater number of citizens and extent of territory which may be brought within the compass of republican than of democratic government, and it is this circumstance principally which renders factious combinations less to be dreaded in the former than in the latter. The smaller the society, the fewer probably will be the distinct parties and interests, the more frequently will a majority be found of the same party; and the smaller the number of individuals composing a majority, and the smaller the compass within which they are placed, the more easily will they concert and execute their plans of oppression. Extend the sphere, and you take in a greater variety of parties and interests; you make it less probable that a majority of the whole will have a common motive to invade the rights of other citizens; or if such a common motive exists, it will be more difficult for all who feel it to discover their own strength and to act in unison with each other. Besides other impediments, it may be remarked that, where there is a consciousness of unjust or dishonorable purposes, communication is always checked by distrust in proportion to the number whose concurrence is necessary.

Hence it clearly appears that the same advantage which a republic has over a democracy in controlling the effects of faction is enjoyed by a large over a small republic—is enjoyed by the Union over the States composing it. Does the advantage consist in the substitution of representatives whose enlightened views and virtuous sentiments render them superior to local prejudices and schemes of injustice? It will not be denied that the representation of the Union will be most likely to possess these requisite endowments. Does it consist in the greater security afforded by a greater variety of parties, against the event of any one party being able to outnumber and oppress the rest? In an equal degree does the increased variety of parties comprised within the Union increase this security? Does it, in fine, consist in the greater obstacles opposed to the concert and accomplishment of the secret wishes of an unjust and interested majority? Here, again, the extent of the Union gives it the most palpable advantage.

The influence of factious leaders may kindle a flame within their particular States, but will be unable to spread a general conflagration through the other States. A religious sect may degenerate into a political faction in a part of the Confederacy, but the variety of sects dispersed over the entire face of it must secure the national councils against any danger from that source. A rage for paper money, for an abolition of debts, for an equal division of property, or for any other improper or wicked project will be less apt to pervade the whole body of the Union than a particular member of it, in the same proportion as such a malady is more likely to taint a particular county or district than an entire State.

> In the extent and proper structure of the Union, therefore, we
> behold a republican remedy for the diseases most incident to
> republican government. And according to the degree of pleasure
> and pride we feel in being republicans ought to be our zeal in
> cherishing the spirit and supporting the character of Federalists.[1]

In many important ways, *Federalist* No. 10 gives away most
of the plot, a plot we have accepted with almost no reservations,
accepted almost unknowingly. As it seems to have worked out, we,
bright and brave college students; we, bright and brave future busi-
nessmen and women; we, Americans, really do not like or trust
each other very much. At least we are not supposed to. We do not
relate to each other well enough to make mutual decisions. *Federalist* No. 10 is the story of mistrust. Madison speaks of the rab-
bleness, of the potential evil doings of public meetings and
democratic practices. He poses the essential question: How can we
trust government to the people when we have no faith in them?

People, self-serving, self-centered, selfish people, are the raw
material for our state. We are encouraged to be a private, materialistic people. We are essentially an uncommunitarian, antipolitical
people who may act differently in spite of—certainly not at the
urging of—the state. Harsh words, these. Let me try to explain.

Madison knew something that we must learn. He knew that
there was a close connection between how people relate to one
another and the structure in which that relationship takes place. It
is important to understand Madison's argument in different terms.

If the problem is how to create a system that will continue
regardless of the basic inability of citizens to rule themselves, the
answer is deceivingly simple. Structure the system so that its citizens
will become mired in a self-grabbing, self-gratifying way of life.
Make it so that petty people, materialistic people, will be allowed,
whether acting singly or in small groups, to go about the task of
robbing the poor, robbing the rich, robbing the consumer, or even
building a better mousetrap. Madison, in all his political wisdom,
worked it out so that we could pursue our own private, material

---

[1] *Federalist* No. 10 can be found in various places. Clinton Rossiter edited a complete
version of the Federalist papers, and Bobbs-Merrill has reprinted some of the papers
individually.

interests. The plan was not a stupid one; for certain, it has had lasting effects.

Have you ever seen a fairly large group of children "playing" on a playground? There are balls and bats and fields and courts and sandboxes and toys. Here, these young citizens of the future grab and kick and cry and fight over the toys, or over the games they are to play. Sometimes groups form and play their own game— are able to play their own game—but sometimes they just make nasty remarks to other groups. The critical element in the playground is that the whole hassle is pretty harmless. The children are being looked after, taken care of, and ultimately directed by adults. Theirs is a choice of what to do in the sandbox. If Madison is correct, that is good training for the system, good practice for the future.

The point is obvious: Do we make decisions of any more importance than what toys we are going to play with? Houses, cars, boats, big motorcycles, little pills—what difference does it make? Face it, we are playing by their rules on their playground. The strategy of *Federalist* No. 10 is to divide and make politically impotent; it does and we are.

IS IT SO? (AS IN: SAY IT ISN'T SO.)

Metaphors are helpful, no doubt about it. One is able to get many cuts into reality by using metaphors. But, the sandbox will get us just so far. We need to see if there are some real-life examples of our claimed political impotence.

What about all of those countries to the south of us? What about Russia? What do they have to do with each other and with each of us?

The government in power now (Ronald Reagan is the current Commander-in-Chief) believes that to keep the United States as it is, then communism must be kept out of the Americas. That means out of Central America, that means out of Granada, that means out of our sphere of dominance.

The threat of communism is so intense to this person, that lesser evils are tolerated . . . and even supported. So, the news is full of terrorism from the right-wing and terrorism from the left-wing of these countries, and we support the right-wingers. It is as if terror, and torture, and the absolute loss of freedom is all right as long as the communists do not support it.

You and I cannot do much about this remarkably unthoughtful policy. I can be angered, you might even be drafted, but neither is very effective.

What our policymakers seem to have forgotten is that we began this particular government with a revolution. For its time, it was more liberal than most. Our policy is self-defeating. We force revolutionary movements in Third World countries to seek the aid of communists by failing to recognize that some of our best friends seem to be dictators.

But, every time the president gives a speech about fighting communism (the Russians), we are made to feel very patriotic. The flag is waved and we salute. It is just the right thing to do.

Or is it?

Maybe flag waving is not the place to persuade. How about the price of energy? The price affects how comfortable our body is, how we get around, prices of the things we buy, and so on.

Between the first edition of this book, and this edition, there have been several different presidents, and two major "energy crises." With each crisis, the price of energy has gone up. What was $3 a barrel in the early 1970s got to be $38 a barrel in the early 1980s. As I write, the price had dropped to $29. (A drop in the bucket, if you will.)

One would think that at least a couple of things might have happened in the last ten years. First, people would try to save on their energy costs. It happened. We got small cars, tight houses, and familiar with carpooling and buses. Second, government would have an energy program. Well, it happened and it didn't.

The government decided to have a reserve, so it has been filling big holes in Louisianna with oil. Then, it decided to support "synthetic" fuels. Lots of trouble there. It is expensive to produce, and two results are that it might flatten the state of Colorado, and release poisons into the air.

Of course, the government could have chosen to carry on a careful and lasting insulation program. Insulation neither flattens nor poisons.

The government chose synthetics. Then the world overpro-
duced oil and gas. Then we had a warm winter and the price fell.
The synthetics program stopped. Big cars which use lots of gas
came back, and if I had any extra money I would invest in oil stocks
so that I could keep up with prices come the next crisis.

Isn't the government foolish?

Aren't we suckers?

It is no great insight that the government makes decisions and
we willingly or unwillingly have no say. But there are two points
which produce tension and which seem important to suggest.

The first point has to do with the faith each of us has in each
other and in the country. The fact is that the United States is just
not all that bad. Neither are we. There are some freedoms and a
lot of material things to make life easier. Even many of our public
officials *seem* to have good intentions. (At least they are not *obviously* evil and awful.)

The second point, and the one that is not easy to live with, is
that the faith we have gets systematically abused. Our power is the
power to react, not to act. So what if we have nothing personally
against people in Central America, or are against synthetic fuels?
So what?

Given the fact that we can control neither information, debate,
nor decision making, we are essentially powerless. Without power.
Power-less.

No power.

Of course, that is the way it was set up to be. Built right into
our political structure and our ideology is the dynamic that we
should be grateful with what little we have; built right into it is the
pressure to forget that there is much more than we have the right
to do. Our myths support our powerlessness. Each of us discovers
it in his or her own way, but the important fact is that each of us
discovers it.

The idea of a political state built on the evilness—and, hopefully,
the powerlessness—of its people sounds pretty silly. It should. Regrettably, to consider what students are taught about the system is
to consider just such thoughts. The following questions are quoted
from a very reputable textbook.

1. "How is it possible to maintain a real equality of influence and power over government?" (In other words, won't a minority of people gain power?)

2. "If everyone is to have an equal say, how can the decisions of government be made with sufficient knowledge and expertness?" (How can we expect "ordinary citizens" to understand?)

3. "How can a popular government act vigorously, speedily, and decisively, particularly in crises?" (Citizens are just too slow.)

4. "How can a system of popular government ever cope with . . . larger groups . . . tyrannizing smaller groups?" (We count on the worst in people coming out.)

5. "Can a system really operate with the consent of *all?*"

These are not abstract questions but live issues. . . . In one way or another every popular government must surmount these problems. . . .[2]

There is no doubt but that these are hard questions. While not exactly in the same class as "Have you stopped beating your wife?" they are close. At the root of these questions lies an unarticulated, seemingly reasonable bias: How do we form a popular government in spite of the weaknesses of people? Look at those five basic questions and at what they assume about you: that, among other things, you are probably not able to understand the complexities of government; that you will probably get more power than others if you are able; and, finally, that if you have the power, you will tyrannize others.

The beauty of it all is that we have been taught that *we* are not like that—but that *they* are. The self-protective mechanism is simple: "If others were only as good as I, then I could begin to act as kindly and generously and good as I really am." Score another one for Madison.

---

[2] Robert Dahl, *Pluralist Democracy in the United States* (Chicago: Rand McNally & Co., 1967), pp. 10–11.

CROSSING OURSELVES

In *Federalist* No. 10, Madison wrote about factions. The notion of factions has had a noble history in our political thinking. These groups of active citizens have formed the basis of many theories of politics in the United States. The most powerful of the theories is called pluralism, which we will come back to later.

In another chapter, there will also be a more complete discussion of social science and of group theory. I want to introduce the topic here in order to give you a sense of some of the underlying meanings of our interest groups—of our factions.

In a Standard Textbook on American government by James Q. Wilson,[3] there is a chart showing the percentage of people belonging to "interest groups" in five Western nations. Basically, the United States is compared to Great Britain, Germany, Italy, and Mexico. The percentages show conclusively that more Americans belong to interest groups than do the people in those other countries.

The reason that is wonderfully good news, according to the theory, is this: It is because of "the greater sense of political efficiency and the stronger sense of civic duty among Americans."

Let me tell you the logic of it all. We all join interest groups. Each group grows in number and therefore grows in strength. The groups then pressure the proper governmental agency or official. In that way, our interests are taken care of.

While the shortcomings of the theory (and they seem to outweigh everything else) will be dealt with later, there is an emotional reality that is important to understand now.

There is a name for this theory of factions, for this theory of interest groups. The name sounds fairly nasty: cross-cutting cleavages. The name has merit as one of the most descriptive in political science. It is, in truth, on the cutting edge of theory.

The theory, to repeat it in a little different way, is that society is broken up into competing groups. It is clear that groups vie for power. It is equally clear that often there are power struggles within any particular group.

All of the cleavaging leads to at least two things. First, a kind

---

[3] James Q. Wilson, *American Government,* (Lexington, Mass: D.C. Heath, 1983).

of hyperactivity that may lead to a great deal of canceling out of each other's activity. Second, and more important, it leads to political stability. We each have a small amount of power that gets dissipated in many different groups. To put it in the language of Madison, factions fight factions and the whole is undisturbed.

At the level of the political system, and if the political system is the most important thing, then a theory that aims for stability seems sensible. While it is normal to think those cross-pressures work out best with groups, it is important to remember that those cross-pressures are aimed at each of us. We are the target, you and I. It is here we can see the cleavage part of the theory.

Each of us gets cut up in our own cross-pressures. We are taught to believe in our own self-interest, in our own ineptness, in our own evilness. The theory is a powerful one because we get trapped in ourselves and are not given much of a sense that there is something beyond the selfish pursuits of our very own interest.

And we are cut up by it.

How can we join one group that will lobby for less governmental bureaucracy and regulation, and another group that will lobby for tighter regulation or even dismantling of nuclear reactors? Cross purposes. How can we be members of a group that is for lower taxes and another that is for better public education? Cross-cutting. How can we be for a "strong" country and be against the draft and military spending? Hum.

We have a political arrangement that turns each of us back on himself or herself. Much is missing from the theory of groups that represent people, not the least of which is a citizenry active in politics. We are urged to be unpolitical and private, alone to tend to our wounds.

When we read Madison we read a truly amazing version of who we are. He was able to visualize a mechanical way of creating a nation-state in which the distrusted citizen could appear active yet remain virtually powerless. In many ways that is the unkindest cut of all.

As it turns out, we are much like our parents. Maybe there are style differences: drugs, dress, and the like; but the basics are similar. We know we must train ourselves to be private, to get ahead, if we are to fit into this land of the free. So, we go to college to learn a trade, to become a professional, to prepare to be rich. Education for increased earnings. Education in how to live a life geared to privacy. We must learn to listen to and follow directions well. We must produce when told.

The structure of college is the structure of society, and the ends are the same. We go from class to class, learning truths contradicted by truths. We write our own exams and our own papers. Those who can best compartmentalize truth, who can learn most of what they are told, and who can do so alone get prizes. To excel is to be super-average. To excel is to be rewarded materially.

That is like the state and our parents. We all agree on ends and on how they are to be judged and rewarded. We understand— at a subtle, sophisticated gut level—why the state protects its property. Our institutions and our ideology are geared to similar principles. In important ways, we agree with what is. We agree to mistrust ourselves with our own ruling, we agree to judge ourselves, in large part, in terms of what we buy, and we agree on the basic rules of materialism, "capitalism," corporate wealth, and the like. James Madison would be proud.

Some problems are obvious. Because we mistrust others, we have lost control of all those things we might have in common. Every issue, every topic, every decision that might include all of us, is denied most of us because we have so little faith in the ability of people to make political decisions. Let us review what the Federalists, as exemplified by Madison, believed:

1. People could not be trusted to rule themselves. Indeed, the only thing worse than a few people trying to rule themselves was many people trying to rule themselves.

2. The morality of the system was in almost no sense public. Morality was a private thing, a commodity of the individual based on self-interest.

3. Citizenship was based upon an individual's remaining private. The system depended upon materialism, self-seekingness, and self-interestedness, and the citizen became trapped in this self-view.

4. The system was created by people of the Enlightenment who

believed that if only the right (read *rational*) set of institutions were discovered, then the system could run indefinitely, in spite of people.

BUT ME?

Built into what the America of Madison means is that each of us acts in certain kinds of ways. We are, in truth, often threatened folks. It is, after all, a way to relate to the world we've come to know and—I mean this—to love.

I guess you don't hear it anymore, but for quite a few years there was a phrase used in politics that never failed to tickle me. To a then young lad like myself, it sounded like a cumbersome, slow-moving, and slightly terrifying beast. It was, of course, *creeping socialism*. My impulse was always to look around to see if it was near, to prepare to stomp that dreaded creep right into the ground.

As it turns out, neither socialism nor capitalism was much to get excited about, but that's not the point.

In too many instances we seem subject to a lot of similar sounding evils. While we've learned what to like and dislike about socialism (creeping or not), we've had trouble identifying other things. The world, for an uncomfortably large number of people, is a threatening place. Think of a day in college—grades, money, popularity, professionalism, sex, roommates, etc.—to better see the fear.

School is spring training for life.

Why are you in school? Just what are your motives? In an amazingly optimistic way, let's start our list with something nice. It is possible that people go to college to gain wisdom. Or (less grand and noble) we fear ignorance; or (more accurate probably) we don't want to appear stupid. That, of course, is the top of our list—the most impressive of our motives.

Why the hell are you in school? For future money? Maybe. For a wife or a husband with a college degree? Maybe. 'Cause your friends or parents silently (or not so silently) demanded it? Could be. Just a terrific set of reasons. But they are, in the end, not the most important or interesting topics. What counts—at least two things that count—are what you see and what you do.

We know, as one of those "facts," that a college or a university can put you through changes. Personal changes, value changes, social changes, which you will probably like, and which are for the good. It has been known to happen before. There is even a kind of secret history of people who have gotten wiser and better, and who started that process in school. In spite of a whole lot of mindless effort and action, learning can and does go on. It is a learning that has to do with serious and important questions.

But two things seem to get in the way: students and teachers.[4]

We are painfully aware that there is a very good chance that any class you walk into will be fairly shallow, uninteresting, and destructive to your good mood and desire to learn. After all, the university is peopled by those who have, in a strange way, done the very best in the most ordinary way.

More precisely, if we learn from example it is important to remember that people in the university are often malignant forms of what is normal and ordinary. That a person made good grades and got high scores on standardized tests means nothing more than this: a person made good grades and got high scores on standardized tests.

There are an amazing number of other reasons why teachers aren't good at teaching, but what I wanted to say was they are mostly just normal—malignantly normal.

Students aren't much better, in some cases. What has always been most curious to me are those who *know* what's wrong; who *know* their compulsions, and who are so "sophisticated" they laugh at themselves.

We announce our anxieties about grades or money or whatever—we then explain why the anxieties are silly and talk about how we are "stuck" with them. After this formal announcement we then go about being anxious, unhappy, unpleasant, or the like.

That kind of self-analysis doesn't really do much good. In fact, it is often little more than a self-delusion that we "smart" people

---

[4] I am not even strong enough to get into administrators at this point. They, like the rest of us, are a problem.

do. It works in a wonderful way: As we make fun or ourselves in sophisticated ways (but still act out those myths we are supposed to act out), we just make fools of ourselves. We're simply much less witty and insightful than we think we are.

So we all walk around threatened by one thing or another. We are forced to miss many things—like an education in college—because we fear either looking for the truth or looking at ourselves. Every time we step back or turn our head or close our eyes to those things, we have only ourselves to blame.

Being threatened is another way of saying we are afraid, and that is another way of acknowledging the force of the system in which we live. If we can go to school and be scared enough to avoid being educated, what chance do we have when we go outside of college and try to do good?

If you're scared now, you're on your way to becoming a dynamite citizen.

Politics

But we must understand more than what the Founding Fathers wrote. We must go beyond their words and even our own actions. We must begin to get at what was not said. We must try to figure out what the world of James Madison lacked.

What Madison excluded, what he feared and so eloquently attacked, was politics. Those things shared, the things we have in common, to him were not best served institutionally. The idea of community is not mentioned—only the idea of "interests." If politics were a science, then there could be a fairly accurate definition of those things political. But regrettably for accuracy, politics seems to be beyond the precision of science and the impurities of language. The best that can be done at this stage is to discuss a few of the concepts involved in politics.[5]

Before that, I would be remiss if I failed to do a couple of

---

[5] For various but obviously related discussions of politics, one might see Max Weber, "Politics as a Vocation," in Hans Gerth and C. Wright Mills, eds., *From Max Weber* (New York: Oxford University Press, 1958); Hannah Arendt, *The Human Condition* (Garden City, N.Y.: Doubleday & Co., 1959); and Sheldon Wolin, *Politics and Vision* (Boston: Little, Brown and Co., 1960).

things. First, there is a whole American political tradition which James Madison fought. He was a federalist and wanted the adoption of the Constitution. The anti-Federalists (and there are studies which indicate that they were in the majority) did not trust the centralized government, and were much more democratic. They are part of our not well-enough-remembered political past. To quote William Carlos Williams: "Memory is a kind of accomplishment." A good kind, I trust.

Earlier, I suggested that you read Madison twice: Once for what he said and once for what he did not say. Did you read anything about annual, direct elections? a confederation of small republics? rotation of office? or accountability to constituents? He failed to suggest that, and a lot more. Now, what about politics?

Politics, to overgeneralize, is the activity by which people live together. It is the process of adjusting aims and activities between you and others: the one and the many. Aristotle believed that it was society's highest form of activity. It was, he thought (and I believe rightly), through citizenship—through people deciding how to act and then acting that way—that an individual could develop his or her capabilities to the fullest. Through this participation, people helped define themselves.

This definition implies much. It is meant to make politics have something to do with morality. What is implied is that politics means taking a stand, being passionate about something, defining what you believe to be right or wrong, good or bad, and then acting on that belief. It is not an easy kind of activity, especially when one is taught to reject just such propositions. But it seems to me that politics involves the inner tension of trying to figure out—and then doing—good in a world where we do not know what good is and where no choices seem clear-cut.

Politics, then, is something profoundly human, something with its roots in morality and its sources of action in a deeply felt inner tension.

Through political action, the individual becomes responsible. To either destroy or check the power to act is to destroy an individual's capacity to do good. By destroying the personal responsibility for power, one destroys its moral roots. It is precisely this kind of equation that Madison failed to acknowledge. We are denied the possible joys of making joint decisions yet seem to be responsible for the actions of others. Politics includes the possibility of sharing happiness or unhappiness—but not so the Federalist state.

Finally, there must be some place for politics to take place. Politics needs an arena, a public space. There must be arenas, in terms of issues and ideas and even physical space, where citizens can come together and work out courses of action. Space is both psychological and physical. Thus far, our only public space is the ballot box, which is neither public nor really space. There is always the idea of going into the streets, or of sitting in a building, or of bombing monuments. Those are only the choices of how to create space, a problem that is ahead of where we are now. To deny the citizen a public space is to suffocate political activity. That is very close to the precise state of our political life.[6]

But we have a tradition, a view of ourselves that denies us the opportunity to share. Certainly we give something to charity, or buy Girl Scout cookies, or avoid littering. But we do not involve ourselves in those decisions that control our lives. Madison talks about dividing power, pitting it one against the other; he talks about the selfishness of people, pitting them one against the other.

We are structured not for cooperative acts but for private ones; we are given a form of government that calls not for the best in people but only for the minimum in them. What we must realize is that we are living a self-fulfilling prophecy: that by founding a government geared to selfishness, we can maintain it only by being selfish. By participating within the structure, we are acting out Madison's belief that we are unworthy.

Let me try it another way. You might read this and think: "It's a privilege to live in America. Thank your lucky stars you don't live in Russia, or wherever."

The underlying sense of that line of thinking, it seems to me, goes like this: Thank my lucky stars that I am (or may be) privileged—and I better be a good person (citizen) or it will all be taken away from me. Who am I, after all, to say my government is wrong?

The point, I think, is that since it is a privilege to live in the

---

[6] Hannah Arendt, *On Revolution* (New York: Viking Press, 1965), discusses the idea of political space and why it does not exist in the United States.

United States, we each have the freedom to be politically active. We have, if you will, the privilege to go beyond our limited sense of what we are allowed to do and enter into creative forms of political activity. The point of the privilege is not to be thankful and docile, but to pursue what needs to be done. This will become more clear in Chapter 5.

To repeat, Madison outlines a life alone; a life of technical skills, or savings bonds, and of mini-vans that carry our hopes for happiness. A common life without community, a public life without politics, and popular decisions without people.

What I am arguing is that our basic view of humanity condemns us to an autistic public life. We are powerless over ourselves. We are mute. We consider ourselves an evil people condemned to a life without trust, without power, without politics.

> I know a place where you can sometimes sing along with yourself ... "Row, row, row your boat, gently down the stream ..."— and just when you get to your merrily—merrilies, the echo comes in "Row, row, row ..." right on cue. But you must be careful in choosing your key or your tempo ... because an echo is an inflexible and pitiless taskmaster: you sing the echoes away. And even after you have left ... you cannot help feeling, for a long time after, that any jig you whistle, hymn you hum, or song you sing is somewhere immutably turned to an echo yet unheard, or relentlessly echoing a tune long forgotten. . . .
>
> —Ken Kesey

Focus One

The main point of Chapter 1 centers on two questions: What does our government want from us? What should we as citizens want from our government? The answers to these questions are tied to criticisms of how we Americans think about politics. The dynamic works like this: The government wants stability and support from its citizens; as citizens, we should express support by seeking stable governmental encouragement for our own grass-roots political activity. Today the government gets most of what it wants from us; we as citizens receive stability but seldom get active official efforts or new institutions which foster

citizen use of political power at the local level. The
relationship between government and citizen is one-sided:
the American political system has created a widely quiescent
democratic citizenry while the citizens find direct access to
political power very difficult.

The assumption behind this dynamic is that governmental
institutions should provide the populace with arenas for
exercising political initiative and judgment. One can then
conclude that the government does not serve its citizens
well. In other words, citizens deserve political opportunities
in addition to the right to vote periodically and to run for
office.

Nonetheless, the American citizenry is not a particularly
discontented lot. The chapter argues that a pervasive
attitude of mistrust is the reason why the one-sided
relationship between government and citizen works as
felicitously as it has in the United States. Citizens distrust
government and each other with political power; they
distrust politics in general. This attitude of mistrust
discourages citizens from cooperating actively in politics and
from demanding that government foster local participation
in direct exercise of power. Furthermore, by making the
connection to Madison's *Federalist* No. 10, it is easy to
assert that citizens mistrust each other because they view
each other as primarily self-interested in politics. The feeling
is as deeply rooted in our American past as it is widespread
today. Although we believe self-interested behavior is
"natural" for human beings, the suggestion was made that
this belief is a "myth"; that is, an assumption which we do
not have to emphasize as strongly or centrally as we do.

Since some apprehension about misuse of political power
seems realistic and prudent, is the preceding suggestion
naive? On the other hand, is criticism of the "myth" not
only futile, but potentially dangerous? What does the critic
want or does he want nothing? Is the argument that of a
nihilist? A gainsayer?

Recall that I imagined in the initial *Focus* that the book
was written by early-American townsmen who became
angry at what they saw when visiting our century. Imagine

now that the first source of anger is the disappearance of
the townships, the replacement of their open political arenas
with professional local and municipal government, the
removal of the ordinary citizen from positions of political
authority. Without political spaces within which to balance
mistrust with morally rooted and humanly responsible
political action, the inactive contemporary citizen has no
direct experience with political cooperation and creativity.
Instead of wanting nothing, these American critics reflect
about the attitude of mistrust in order to remind us that we
rightfully might demand that government make the re-
creation of grass-roots political arenas a prime goal of
American domestic politics. For the moment, put aside the
objective problems of whether townships could be re-
created in a form appropriate to present day realities, that
is, be adapted to modern, urban, industrial life. Instead,
consider whether you would look upon the establishment of
such places as desirable for yourself and your fellow
citizens. If, after genuinely considering the possibility for a
moment, you hesitate because you are uncertain about the
trustworthiness of your fellow citizens, you may at least
conclude that the first point of the book was well chosen. A
major cost of mistrusting others politically is hesitancy
about creating a local public arena also open to oneself.

2
POLITICS AND KNOWLEDGE

*T*hus science is much closer to myth than a scientific philosophy is prepared to admit. It is one of many forms of thought that have been developed by man, and not necessarily the best. It is conspicuous, noisy, and imprudent, but is inherently superior only for those who have already decided in favor of a certain ideology, or who have accepted it without ever having examined its limits.

—Paul Feyerabend

"But even worse was the way he talked about science—in which he did not believe. . . . It was a belief, like any other, only worse, stupider than any; the word science was the expression of the silliest realism, which did not blush to take at their face value the more dubious reflections of objects in the human intellect; to pass them current, and to shape out of them the sorriest, most spiritless dogma ever imposed upon humanity. Was not the idea of a material world existing by and for itself the most laughable of all self-contradictions?"

—Thomas Mann

Truth is always in poetic form; not literal but symbolic; hiding or veiled; light in darkness. Yes, mysterious. Literalism is idolatry of words; the alternative to idolatry is mystery. And literalism reifies, makes everything into things, these tables and chairs, commodities. The alternative to reification is mystification.

—Norman O. Brown

Knowing and being are opposite, antagonistic states. The more
you know, exactly the less you are. The more you are, *in being,*
the less you know.

—D.H. *Lawrence*

KNOWING THINGS

All of us act as if we know things. Moreover, we act as if we know
how we know things. Every society is built, in great measure, on
a method of knowledge gathering, on a way of knowing things.
This is normal enough, but what does it mean? How much do we
really understand about how we know things, about why a fact is
a fact, and why knowledge is knowledge? What if our approach to
knowledge is more closing than opening, more confining than
freeing—in essence, more mechanical than human? What if our
"facts" are unclear, misleading, or false?

In an important way, this chapter is simply an extension of the
first. We now know something about Madisonian people, about
ourselves. In this chapter, we will consider how we look at the
world, what we know, and how we know what we know. To know
about knowing is to begin to fill out our knowledge of politics.

The Madisonian person is, in a sophisticated sense, scientific.
Put most simply, the link between the two is materialism; the link
is an extraordinary reliance on the reality of objective things. We
have a notion of what is real, of how to analyze reality, and of
what that analysis means. It is that method—commonly, but mis-
takenly called science—and its accompanying myths that form the
basis of this chapter. It is "evil" people in a scientific, material,
objective world who will be our main concern.

In essence, our society's knowledge gathering rests on what
has been called (and I believe correctly) the myth of objective consciousness. It is the kind of myth that needs to be looked at in
pieces, as well as a whole, to be fully understood. For a start we
might say that the myth of objective consciousness assumes that
the only "facts" in the world—the only things that are real—are
those things that are apart from us. According to this myth, things
have a reality if we can perceive them objectively.

A fact is a fact, in and of itself. Without help. A rose is a rose.

All that, simple as it is, sounds reasonable. Certainly it is what we have been taught. Indeed, it sounds so right that we rarely examine the assumptions upon which it rests. We think that all facts are objective things, but we fail to realize that we tie facts with moral codes. We seldom see that the result of our myth of objective consciousness may be trauma-filled. Yet the myth fills our lives in many ways—ways we are often unaware of.

The myth makes scientists of us all—we become counters; the more sophisticated of us, statisticians. We add and subtract reality. We use our fingers and toes, calculators and computers, to find facts, facts that become truths. This is our style: precise, calculating, objective.

Certainly, there are those who will object to what is being said. It would be foolish to deny that this style has led to a great many things. After all, somehow those numbers are able to make airplanes fly and bridges span, and offensive and defensive missiles project. Science does produce a kind of magic; but the problem is more complex than that. To quote Theodore Roszak, "If we believe there is some place to get and if we believe it is important to get there very, very fast—despite the dangers, despite the discomforts, despite expense, despite the smog—then the automobile is an impressive piece of magic."[1]

The tension is obvious enough: Objectiveness is the stuff of science; but is it the stuff of politics?

SCIENCE: REAL AND TRUE AND ITS APPLICATION

Science, in its approach to knowledge, in its gathering of it, and finally in its view of what is real, is little more than a value system of impressive proportions. To get at these values, we must get at the elements that make up science. We must study what it studies, approach it in a critical way, and try to make a judgment about the

---

[1] Theodore Roszak, *The Making of a Counter Culture* (Garden City, N.Y.: Doubleday & Co., 1969), p. 259. For an interesting work on the nature of scientific discovery, see Thomas Kuhn, *The Structure of Scientific Revolutions* (Chicago: University of Chicago Press, 1962).

reality it produces. We might begin by clarifying objective reality, and then go on to the method of science.

It is important to realize that what is being discussed is not an isolated phenomenon that may or may not be personally interesting to me.[2] Again to quote Theodore Roszak: "Objectivity as a state of being fills the very air we breathe in a scientific culture; it grips us subliminally in all we say, feel and do. The mentality of the ideal scientist becomes the very soul of society." He continues to say that the stuff of this soul is objectivity and that the belief in objectivity becomes myth:

> The myth of objective consciousness is to cultivate a state of consciousness cleansed of all physical distortion, all personal involvement. What flows from this state of consciousness qualifies as knowledge, and nothing else does . . . . [Scientific knowledge] is a verifiable description of reality that exists independent of any purely personal considerations. It is true . . . real . . . dependable. . . . It works.[3]

It is real. Better yet, it is concrete. Yes, science is just what we can believe in because it deals with the real world, and if there is one thing we have learned to agree on, it is the real world. Of course, that is part of the myth—that we *think* we know what the real world is. Let us not accept that we know what the real world is, let us not accept the definitions that underlie science. It seems reasonable to begin to understand the myth of objective consciousness by trying to understand the term "real."[4]

What I would like to argue is that it is no easy thing to know what is "real." To say that what one sits on is a real chair does not tell us quite enough. Are other kinds of chairs "real," or are they false? If we worked at the silly example of the chairs long

---

[2] For example, see Floyd Matson, *The Broken Image* (Garden City, N.Y.: Doubleday & Co., 1966), or Abraham Maslow, *The Psychology of Science* (New York: Harper & Row, 1966).

[3] Roszak, *The Making of a Counter Culture,* pp. 208, 216. To skip ahead a bit, objective consciousness is the consciousness of the corporate liberalism of the Pentagon.

[4] This is taken in large part from J. Peter Euban, "Political Science and Political Science," in Philip Green and Sanford Levinson, eds., *Power and Community* (New York: Vintage Books, 1970), pp. 3–59.

enough, we might get to the point of knowing exactly what was included in, and *excluded from,* the phrase "real chair."

When we go from chairs to the "real world," everything gets more complicated. Maybe the "real world" consists of only those things that one can see, touch, or count. If that is so, and scientists as well as most social scientists would have us believe that, then we should know something about that reality.

To believe solely in the scientism of our time is to believe in a fairly static and, to me, fairly boring state of affairs. To begin with, the bias is clear: If the scientist studies the "real world," then presumably the rest of us study the "false world." They have hard "facts," we, soft; indeed, they have facts, we, only values. The scientific method, as we all know, insists that all of its experiments be repeatable and that all of its hypotheses be verifiable.

Think about a world in which everything that is true (could there be a "true fact"?) must be able to happen again and again and again. If that is what "true" is, and if it comes from things that are real, then "real" is nothing more than what we already have. To put it differently, to accept the scientist's vision of reality is to accept a world in which change is neither probable nor perhaps even possible, and is certainly not desirable.[5]

Part of what I would like to argue is that politics is an art, a practice, a part of life that is beyond the validations of the scientific method. Maybe an example will help make my case more clear. Scientists build reality carefully, finding those "facts" in the "real world" that are "true" and making them into hypotheses that are potentially verifiable. Simple enough—just find enough truths, find enough facts, and one can build a real world.

Several years ago, someone studied how people voted in Congress.[6] What he wanted to do was to build a model that would predict how each legislator would vote. The work was impressive, sophisticated science. There were numerous tables and charts and

---

[5] Thomas Kuhn, in *The Structure of Scientific Revolutions,* discusses what changes in views have occurred and how they can happen.

[6] The following figures suggest a very complex model found in Michael J. Shapiro, "The House and the Federal Role: A Computer Simulation of Roll-Call Voting," in *The American Political Science Review,* 62 (1968): 494–518.

models of the most advanced type. Correlations were made and statistically things were at an important level of significance. With all this work, the author was correctly able to predict how each member would vote 87 percent of the time. Pretty impressive—87 percent.

Of course, an 87 percent correct prediction rate is not all that impressive. As an unsophisticated (methodologically, that is) student, you could predict outcomes almost that well. By knowing whether a legislator was a Democrat or a Republican, you could accurately predict his or her vote 84 percent of the time. The point is simple enough. The politics of the Congress takes place in that 13 percent of the vote that cannot be predicted. Most of the really interesting votes concern precisely those issues that are in doubt, those issues on which Republicans and Democrats do not vote a straight party line.

In part, I am suggesting that to be successful in science, one must necessarily be limited to very ordinary, repeatable events. To have a social science is to think in rather limited, sometimes unimaginative ways. To use the word *science* implies too little: Maybe we should consider more carefully the "unreal world."

A WARNING AND A SUGGESTION

Before the attack on science continues, at least three things should be made clear. First, just because a person is a scientist, or a social scientist, there is no obvious reason to believe that he or she is a conservative son-of-a-bitch who is hopelessly involved in wasted effort and useless endeavors. That would be foolish. All I am trying to argue is that the world in general, and politics in particular, is much more complicated and involved than science is able to comprehend. Second, I am *not* suggesting that we, personally, are the source of everything; or, more precisely, that what each of us thinks is right, or that what we say is accurate, or even that what we do is *not* good simply because *we* think, say, or do it. To ignore science entirely would be about as bright as to accept it entirely.

Finally, I am using the popularized notion of science. What it is, really, is a technique and not science at all. A good deal of our troubles come from misunderstanding just what real scientists do.

Still, I will be talking about our images initially. Just be warned that things are not always what we believe them to be.

What I would like to suggest now and to explore later is the idea that the distinction between objective and subjective reality may not make sense.[7] Indeed, one does not make sense without the other. A more reasonable formulation of the world might be this: The interaction between our conscious selves and the world—the relationship between the objective and the subjective—makes what we know as reality. This view implies that science and objectification are simply less significant, less accurate ways of dealing with the world than is the more unconventional, and yet well explored, phenomenological view.

SCIENCE: COMPARTMENTALIZATION, OBJECTIFICATION, AND "POLITICAL" STYLE

We are problem solvers, we Americans. We think about something, analyze it, and then do it. We think of all the different ways we can do it, but we rarely consider the reasons for what we do. Values? Ethics? We God-fearing citizens get these every Sunday. But we practical people are mostly "manual"-oriented: how to repair a Rabbit, how to survive the coming crisis (whichever one it happens to be), how to make a killing in the stockmarket, have thinner thighs, a flatter stomach, a better job, and on and on. What I want to suggest is that this emphasis on technique is a natural by-product of the emphasis that science places on method; moreover, that somehow we get divided—method from feeling, parts from the whole. To describe the techniques of science may help clarify the point.[8]

---

[7] This approach is called phenomenology, and was first explored by Edmund Husserl around the turn of the century. It was furthered by his student Martin Heidegger. Phenomenology is extraordinarily difficult to read, but there are explanations of it that do make sense. For example, one might read the introduction to William Barrett and Henry Aiken, eds., *Philosophy in the Twentieth Century*, vol. 3 (New York: Random House, 1962).

[8] Kenneth Keniston, *The Uncommitted* (New York: Dell Publishing Co., 1965), p. 254.

To begin with, we are taught that everything is a problem (therefore, solvable) and that each problem is to be analyzed. So we do. We analyze. We take our lives or our problems or our relationships and break them down into manageable parts. We seek units of analysis. We make components; we compartmentalize. We ignore the whole. We dissect; we cut up; we make small.

What happens is clear. We have the impulse to *reduce* complex things to simple ones. Science urges us to devalue the rich—which we find difficult to understand—so that we can get to the common— which we might easily understand. We sacrifice the unique. To quote Kenneth Keniston: "Theories of learning frequently proclaim that human learning is essentially no different from animal learn- ing—that Michelangelo in his studio is to the cheese-seeking rat merely as the large computer is to the small."[9] We are intellectual dis-integrators. For the most part, we perceive only pieces of problems.

The obvious way to go about problem solving is by counting and comparing. We measure, we total, we add up the sum. Then we can *compare reality* and see *which* is the most, *which* is the best. Quality is too difficult to measure, or to compare; but horse- power, income, and grade averages are not.

And all the adding depends upon what one thinks reality is. To count depends upon those things that are external, that are objective. It is firmly rooted in the metaphysic that individuals must always turn outward, never inward. Insight is worth nothing if it cannot be made tangible. Science shuns the invisible: magic, art, religion, love. By doing so, we split our knowing from our being, our knowledge from ourselves. To do that enough is to be crazy. People who are able to divide themselves well are often considered successful; people who do not do it well are diagnosed clinically as schizophrenics.

"Crazy" is a later topic. For now I would like to argue that this gathering, quantifying myth of objective consciousness gives us an odd perception of anything public, of anything that should be political. We have a public style of numbers. A politics of volume.

---

[9] Ibid., p. 256.

For example, each week we were given the number of people killed in Vietnam. Body counts, they are called. It is instructive to think about what they mean.

To look back on that war is not very happy. While the obvious lessons of what war does have been repeated and repeated, it seems important to look at *how* we learned about what was going on. Where one starts helps explain just where one can expect to go.

So that you do not think we are out of that way of thinking, there is always the recent study by the Department of Defense on the probability of a limited nuclear war. The study concluded that we could *win* that war because the numbers were in our favor. We, of course, would lose tens of millions of people, but the Russians would lose more. How could you disagree? The numbers just do not lie.

There is something very natural about the affection we all have for quantity. Of course, as we think more carefully about it, the affection is not at all natural but is like many other things . . . it is learned. Let me give you an obvious and gross—but very real—example. It is about a friend of mine and his son.

One day the son came home from elementary school very upset. He was good in math but had gotten a bad grade. His parents sat down with him and tried to figure out what was wrong. The problem revolved around a series of questions like this:

> There are two piles of pennies. In one pile there are 1,000 pennies, in the other pile there are 100 pennies. Which would you rather have?

In every case the boy chose the *smaller* number. When asked why, he explained that he really did not like pennies very much. They were, after all, dirty and not worth very much. So, given the choice, he would take less rather than more. A clear value choice. His parents understood the argument; so they went to talk with the math teacher.

The math teacher was having none of that thinking. Math, the parents were informed, was an exact science. There was one right answer to any single question, and everyone knew that more had a higher value—that more was, by definition, better.

The mind boggles at the overwhelming wrongness of the teacher, but that is not quite the point. The point is, we are *taught* to believe in these ways. We not only learn certain skills, like math, but we learn a whole ideological way of dealing with the world. In the end we may forget our fractions or geometry or whatever, but the informing ideological bias stays and stays.

It has staying power, in part, because it is not taught but is always simply assumed. It is difficult to examine as it is rarely articulated. It remains at the root of things, and as such remains very difficult to uncover.

With each fact, there is an implied value. As Americans were reported to have killed more Vietnamese than Vietnamese killed Americans, we were led to believe at least three things: (1) God was on our side; (2) we were better fighters than they; and (3) we were winning the war. However, this turns out not to have been the case. All we know for certain is that these figures—these objective "facts" of the war—cannot be trusted, that they do not tell the whole story, and that they are absolutely incapable of conveying what is really happening. By objectifying reality, an effort is made to reduce war and killing to numbers and to measure success in columns. Surely insane. But we kept getting facts—real facts from the real world—and were led to believe that there were related values.

All this, of course, sounds foolish. We know that the examples are a bit overdrawn, and are probably wrong—somehow. It is offensive to think that we can be given a list of numbers and then be expected to find meaning and social value in them. Upon reflection, it is an outrage to believe that those numbers represent anything meaningful, except perhaps to an individual who is insecure personally and must relate impersonally; who is less interested in understanding the "why" of values than in being almost wholly dependent upon material worth.

The point is *not* that facts are useless ingredients in any moral argument. Facts and values are dependent upon one another. Each helps to inform and define the other. The point has to do with *which* "facts" we look at, study, and are given, and *what* we imply from them. The point is that for us—Madisonian people in a scientific, objective world—more is better than less and that we regularly make qualitative judgments from quantity.[10]

The sad truth seems to be that the example offers a fairly clear vision of the world we inhabit and provides insight into the way we view reality. The scientist is closer to truth than the magician—at least, that is what we are taught to believe. But we must question our knowledge.

Is it possible that there is a kind of knowledge that is not objective but that is nevertheless real? Must we measure everything—ourselves and our environment—in material terms? Can there be a better kind of politics that is related to a more inclusive kind of knowledge? Can there be an "us" that responds to a less gross ethic? What kinds of questions can we ask that will lead us to a different, and maybe better, set of answers?

SOMETHING ELSE

> *I suppose it is tempting, if the only tool you have is a hammer, to treat everything as if it were a nail.*
>
> —Abraham Maslow

In a simplified way, the dynamic has been suggested that objects are facts, that lots of facts seem to imply values, and that these values appear to indicate moral worth. The conclusion, stated just as simply, is that there is a kind of insanity in that view. It seems to me that we must begin to understand ourselves as makers of both fact and knowledge, as makers of both value and morality. To make the world more understandable, indeed to recapture some personal power and meaning, we must think in terms that supersede the coldness of rationality and the sterility of science. It is necessary to go back and seek an explanation.

At the base of every social system—and ours is no exception—there is a series of rules that most people follow. Many of the rules

---

[10] For a full description of the psychological process involved, see Murray Edelman, *Symbolic Uses of Politics* (Champaign-Urbana, Ill.: University of Illinois Press, 1964).

are not obvious, but nonetheless they are remarkably binding. For example, most of us either do not know why we are in college or are here just because it seemed the thing to do. Either our parents wanted us to go or all our friends were doing it. More self-consciously, we are here to find a wife or a husband, or so that we can get a good job when we graduate.

In all these cases, we are getting ready to fit into the system. We are following its laws, obeying its rules. But what if our arguments have been correct, what if these laws are based on a reality that really is not human? It is unpleasant to think that the system is based on a kind of magic that can produce cars more easily than it can handle human cares; that spends more on bombs than on little babies; and that is tuned more to the values of quantity than to the good of humanity. The argument, so far, has led us to the point of generalizing that to have a basic view of the world as being only objective can produce the kinds of rules and laws that function not to help people in particular, but only to produce more material reality.

Our politics are as sterile as our reasons for being in college or our experiences in high school or—in all too many cases—our own lives.

There are thinkers who believe that knowledge is the result of more than objective reality, more than those things we can touch. They argue that knowledge is the result of the interaction between the object and the individual; a kind of mingling of the "what is" with the "what might be"; the personal and the impersonal; and I and the thou. Let us begin with two individuals who meet and talk. They are strangers who view each other with what we know as typical insecurity and fear—two Madisonian people in our modern world. Each views himself or herself as "I" and the other person as an "it." There is no real exchange of anything between them. Each has his or her own little social act, own game to put on the other. Both become dehumanized, both objects. People become things; politics becomes impersonal and impossible.

What seems necessary is to begin again. Objective reality is not the only place to begin, and science—when you get right down to it—is science. Just as there is knowing and knowing, so there is science and science.

What our sciences have to teach is truly amazing. Part of what is truly amazing is that they don't teach us what we generally expect them to.

Just see.

SCIENCE AND SCIENCE

Now it's time to further an understanding of nature's order by reassimilating those passions which were originally fled from. The passions, the emotions, the affective domain of man's consciousness, are a part of nature's order too. The central part.

—*Robert Pirsig*

One of the critical political tasks ahead of us is to understand that life is at least as strange as science fiction if we do it (life) the right way—maybe even stranger. Before you argue that I have misunderstood, that "strangeness" not only does not seem a critical task but certainly *is not* a critical political task, let me try to explain myself.

Science fiction and similar kinds of fantasy can be interesting and instructive and even good escape. There are lessons to be learned from "Star Trek," *Star Wars*, and *Dune*, and what passes for the future on TV and in the movies. But an amazing amount of "science" "fiction" is pretty lightweight stuff. Fun for sure, and certainly a way to play, but it is generally just a logical extension of what we have and know.

Science fiction *is* instructive for showing ourselves as we are. It often looks strange because, if you happen to be in the mood to see it, much of what we do *is* strange. We worship gods and machines and things; we kill others and our earth and ourselves; we do marvelous and wondrous things for no reason beyond the fact they are right. In the end, it all makes only a very limited amount of sense—at best—and our science fiction really doesn't do much to help us. It's a lot like angel food cakes: I never pass it up—it's good and light and fluffy, but all I get is a good taste in my mouth and a pimple or two.

What I want to recommend is that it makes sense to understand the world in a way and do life in a manner that puts the particular "fantasy" of science fiction in the limited box where it belongs.

It seems necessary to take seriously the multiplicity of meanings of any event or of "facts." We are faced with a curious situation in the twentieth century. It is our legacy, in part, to be emotional heirs to a kind of despair and ultimate meaninglessness, which has been powerfully argued for the last hundred years or so. Until that time, there were the twin assurednesses of religion and science. Philosophers took on religion and, in many important ways, seemed to have won. We know that by the turn of the century, scientists had begun to make the theoretical breakthroughs that forever removed science from the realm of Truth with a capital T, and removed it from Certainty.

With Einstein's theory of relativity, you literally had to triangulate your position in the universe just to know where to hang your hat.

It is misleading and a cheap shot to say that because there is no certainty, then everything is relative. In a technical sense, that may be a fact—but that does not necessarily make it true for us. There are categories, concepts, and human convictions that do not easily fit into the casual name-calling style of being "relative."

Multiple meanings mean multiple meanings. The trick is that each of us—at some preconscious, inarticulate place—has a sense of the rightfittingness of the world.

To know about knowing is to begin to know why we see what we do, why we ask the questions we do, why we may be "right" and why those who disagree with us may also be "right." We must both look and act as well as look at looking. Things must mean *and* mean.

Let me try to sort that out.

FALSE STUFF, IF WHOLLY BELIEVED

Between cockroach and codfish there were only structured differences—their substance was the same and this substance itself was a lie.

He saw the entire Universe wheeling, made of a fine
shimmering pattern, a lie of such grand and incredible artistry
his own vain dream of political empire collapsed—the White
House was a doll house played in by childish fibbers. He left
the University that morning, disappearing without forwarding
address, becoming a nameless wanderer.

—William Kotzwinkle

The effort of this section is not to say all science is wrong. (In
"correct" writing, I'm told no one should begin a paragraph *that*
defensively. The truth is, I simply don't want people to misunderstand that point.) What I want to show is that there is an
amazing amount of stuff that science either cannot deal with, or
mishandles, or ignores, or tries to destroy. If possible, I would like
to begin to work us out of the binding myths of science. That work
will include some stuff that will make something between limited
and no sense to you.

That's all right. Work at it, think hard about it, but relax. None
of us, after all, really understands.

This is the order to what follows. We will consider science,
our heads, what things might just possibly be, and some of the
implications of change. Put differently, fiction is stranger than life—
but not very often.

It makes sense to go about knowing in several different ways.
Since I'm convinced and will argue that there are intensely individual
aspects to how we see the world, it would be foolish to believe one
argument would satisfy all folks. One could say, quite rightly, that
if there is a "system" in our country, at its base it is a *system of*
thought. The genius for politics—or the villainy of it—is located,
at first, in our heads. It is how we see and structure our world. Our
system of thought may well be our first unnatural act.

That is one way to begin our argument. Better, we could begin with a man described by his biographer as possessing "authentic magic": we could start with Albert Einstein. Read this: ". . .
Einstein's physical intuition, though not infallible, had certainly
stood him in good stead. *All science is based on faith.* The many

strange developments that we have already seen . . . should have convinced us by now that great science is not built on cold logic."[11]

As we have seen, our science wants us to believe in a predictable universe. Not only is that bad life, it is even wrong science. The logic of the argument about how to get from predictability to chaos is fun; it is also useful to know.

The classic function of science is to "discover" those few elementary laws from which the universe may be built up by pure deduction.[12] This, as we know, comes from the careful following of the scientific method. The method, in shortened form, is (1) stating a problem, (2) stating a hypothesis to explain the problem, (3) designing tests for the hypothesis, (4) predicting the results of each test, (5) conducting the tests and observing the results, and, finally, (6) making conclusions from the results.

Fair enough. We are taught to believe that if the same results occur each time a particular test is given, it may be a "law."

In repeatability we trust.

But, this is simply what we have been told science is about. The facts seem to indicate that this is not what scientists do at all. It is science for popular consumption; it certainly does not produce the kind of social knowledge that we need to help improve our social conditions, our social lives, or our own selves.

What we are not taught are all of the problems with this method, or with the method's relationship to the truth. Einstein: "Evolution has shown that at any given moment out of all conceivable constructions a single one has always proved itself absolutely superior to the rest."[13] Let's accept that, and then look at what we have just accepted. In essence, we are accepting the idea that truth, in part, is a function of time.

---

[11] Banesh Hoffmann, *Albert Einstein: Creator and Rebel* (New York: The Viking Press, 1972), p. 193.

[12] As an aside, the Greeks invented classical reason, but they knew some of the limits of its usefulness. For example, they listened to the wind and predicted the future from that. The way most life is, that is as reasonable a way as any. See Robert Pirsig, *Zen and the Art of Motorcycle Maintenance: An Inquiry into Values* (New York: William Morrow & Co., Inc., 1974), p. 171.

[13] Pirsig, *Zen and Motorcycle Maintenance*, p. 115.

No pretense about it. Something is true, in measure, because we are *who* we are, and live *where* we live, and exist *when* we exist. Those are odd kinds of criteria for truth.

But there's more. The scientific method is great, in those physical things to which it can be applied, only *after* the problem has been stated *and* the hypotheses have been formulated. The part we never seem to remember is that there are an infinite number of hypotheses for any given phenomenon. The whole basis of the scientific method rests on our own imaginations. We make up problems and tests and truths; we base our science on our myths.

Again, Einstein: ". . . the concepts and fundamental principles that underlie [theoretical physics] are free inventions of the human intellect, [and they] form the essential part of a theory, which reason cannot touch."[14] When we get to the nub of the most central of our sciences—theoretical physics—we see a group of people who believe in something more basic than logic, who often think in terms of beautiful pictures and of how they believe the physical world *may* be.[15]

The heart of science is not Reality, but one or another Myth.

We may do the argument another way. Even if you don't know or understand the details, you probably know that there is Euclidian and non-Euclidian geometry. For that matter, there are several of the non-Euclidian kind. What is interesting (are you listening, hard-core-science-types, you left-over believers in the absoluteness of science?) is that these geometries contradict each other.

All of them, as it turns out, are "right," but some just happen to be more convenient than others. To quote: "Geometry is not true, it is advantageous."[16] That, at one level, is just outrageous. With little trouble, we can get to the same outrageous point with math as we did with the concepts of physics the math is used to "prove." Mathematical solutions have a harmony, a beauty, an

---

[14] Hoffmann, *Albert Einstein,* p. 170.

[15] In 1916, a distinguished astronomer reported on Einstein's general theory of relativity. In part, he wrote, "Whether the theory ultimately proves to be correct or not, it claims attention as being one of the most beautiful examples of the power of general mathematical reasoning." Ibid., p. 129.

[16] Pirsig, *Zen and Motorcycle Maintenance,* p. 264.

elegance to them, and are often chosen for those reasons. It seems that our most hard-core, hard-science, high-powered magicians are seekers not of truth, but of beauty.[17]

What is astounding is that we keep the myth of scientifically verifiable truth. The system in our heads may be systematically wrong-headed.

If one pushes science, if one sees the way hypotheses multiply until there are too many to keep track of and too many to test, if one sees that scientific "truth" keeps changing at an increasing rate, and that the half-life of truth keeps getting shorter and shorter, or if one sees that underlying the basic principles of science are people's senses of beauty, one can come very close to seeing the obvious: The most impressive product of modern science is antiscience.

By understanding the work of our science, we can understand our world as chaos.

REAL STUFF

William James tells us that the world "is a turbid, muddled, gothic sort of affair, without a sweeping outline and with little pictorial nobility."

Terrific. Start with knowing about knowing, and end up with the idea of chaos. You want facts and you get beauty.

Think of it this way: When you are working out how you know what you know, and reality, there may be no simple answers. Equally possible, there may be no complex answers. There are ways to get into all of this, and what seems necessary is to sketch at least one way *other than* science.

Let me be specific about a thing or two: I am not suggesting that theoretical physics be our model for politics. All I want to argue is that if we are really hung up on the Truth of our science, we may as well admit to ourselves that some time ago science admitted its fundamental relationship to magic. Equally important, human lives and events are much more complex than "physical" events. Trying to live a day, much less a lifetime, with some meaning

---

[17] I think I like them better for that.

and social "goodness" makes discovering elementary particles of the universe seem like a piece of cake.

To get on with the topic, we will take up just where we find ourselves, what that might mean (or *not* mean, in this case), and how we can begin thinking about it.

We live in a world that quite literally never stops. While myths and often social institutions stay fixed for limited times, our world just keeps changing. Reality, in part, consists of all of the "facts" of our existence, *plus* relationships, functions, motives, ideologies, and the like.[18] Reality, to put it a little differently, simply keeps becoming. Jean Paul Sartre writes: "For us, truth is something which becomes, it *has* and *will* have become. It is a totalization which is forever being totalized."[19]

We are what we were and what we will be in situations that will not stay set. As we will see, we became creators and definers in the context of our times and our surroundings.

The world in which we find ourselves—and now I'm talking about the physical world, the one science "deals" with—may well be, in its essence, just stuff. Basic, primal stuff. No few basic particles from which to create or recreate the world. Stuff. The stuff in our head is the same as the stuff of a desk, a car, or a flower.

Our universe, if we care to look deeply enough, is fundamentally chaos. The argument goes further. Each of us begins from that general chaos; we sort things out and make distinctions that help make sense of the world and that allow us to have some communications with those around us. We try to understand—more to the point, often we invent—the world around us. We learn to do well at it, but we fool ourselves if we believe we tap into anything more ultimate than our own myths—our own ghosts, as Robert Pirsig would say.

---

[18] To quote William James, "Life is in the transitions as much as in the terms connected; often, indeed, it seems to be there more emphatically, as if our spurts and sallies forward were the real firing line of the battle, were like the thin line of flame advancing across the dry autumnal field . . . Mainly . . . we live on speculative investments, or on our prospects only." *Essays in Radical Empiricism and a Pluralistic Universe* (New York: E. P. Dutton, 1971), pp. 46–47.

[19] Jean Paul Sartre, *Search for a Method* (New York: Random House, 1968), p. 30.

Part of what I want to warn about is that we should be careful of what we take as "given." For example, we know that there are many people in the world who really do see ghosts of one kind or another: old friends, dead relatives, supreme spirits. We have just a terrible time seeing those ghosts. But fear not, we have our own ghosts. We can, for example, "see" the law of gravity, which is a ghost many others simply cannot envision. In any lived day one ghost is no more real (or false) than the other. After all, when we finally admit it, the world is relative and we really don't even know which way is up.[20]

Here we sit, in the midst of chaos, ultimately understanding that even the "basic" split between the objective and the subjective is a distinction we make. Please don't misread that. It was written to say that, originally, everything simply *is,* and we continually add meaning to it. That does *not* mean everything is subjective or objective, but rather, just is.

And each day, each instant, we are confronted with objects and actions and events. Confronted with much more than we can deal with or sort out or make sense of. Much passes us by—or, we pass by much—because our world is cluttered and chaotic. We memorize whole lists of things (a pen is a pen, a desk is a desk), which helps us in the world a great deal. However, we are left with two critical points: what we do choose to consider, and how we put it together.

In the messy world, we are constantly experiencing, and that experience immediately becomes a part of our past. From that past, we choose to recall parts, grant meaning to those parts because we pay attention to them; and we give them added meaning by thinking about them the way we choose to.

Nothing—no part of our experience—has self-evident meaning.[21] Once we are conscious of something, we add meaning to it. Not only that, we *get* those meanings from our surroundings. The

---

[20] It makes sense to try to imagine a good, scientific "law." So far, I've come this close: What goes up must come down, most of the time, if we just knew which way was up. I'm attracted to the law for its preciseness.

[21] For much of this, see William James, *Essays in Radical Empiricism.*

myths of our society, the values of our parents and peers, the kind of day we're having, all contribute to how we make sense and meaning of the events around us. We make meaning *within* in the context of meaning; we make history *within* history.

That is half of it, the choosing-of-the-events half. The other half has to do with how those events are arranged in our heads. There are scientists (maybe they are really pseudoscientists) who would have the inside of our heads look something like a great pyramid—things (blocks) arranged neatly, in a hierarchy, in a way that reflects the way *they* arrange the world on paper.

Life and learning, for those scientists, are a matter of stacking up reality in a prescribed order. I suspect that when some people speak of the building blocks of knowledge, they aren't speaking figuratively at all.

A way to think of the world that seems more useful—even more accurate—is to envision the arrangement of the events of our lives as a mosaic, not a pyramid. Each of those events, those happenings, those striking elements finds a place in our mosaic; each finds a place in our understanding of the arrangement of the world.

But the events, the tiles, of our mosaic are just part of our reality. Equally important is the glue that holds the tiles together—the relationships that place events in order in our heads.[22]

In important ways the key is in those relationships—in that glue. Much of how we do our arranging has to do with what we are taught both to see and to value. The more rigid we are about our reality, the more fixed the relationships, the less likely we are to change, to rearrange. We all know someone—a friend or relative or teacher—who just cannot "see" something very obvious to us.

In politics (more accurately, in our common business) we run into that non-seeing, that "blindness," all the time. People who have bought into the myths so deeply, who have set their mosaic so firmly, that change for them seems out of the question. Later, there will be a chapter on voting, which is, in a way, a tile in *your*

---

[22] The eloquence of Einstein: "I am grateful to destiny for having made life an exciting experience so that life has *appeared meaningful*" (emphasis added); or, "Approached rationally that fear [of death] is the most unjustified of all fears, for there is no risk of any accidents to one who is dead or not yet born. In short, the fear is stupid but it cannot be helped." Hoffmann, *Albert Einstein*, p. 261.

mosaic. My guess is that it is a tile well set, and that whatever age you happen to be, you will resist rearranging your mosaic *even* if you agree with what I say.

If we arranged chaos in a pyramid based on *firm scientific data,* then change would really be incredibly difficult. We would probably have to replace one huge edifice with another. No wonder that damned hierarchy is so tough to get rid of; not only is it taught to us as Truth, it is taught in a way that makes it replaceable only with another Whole System. That, in short, is bunk.

In a mosaic, change is still difficult but certainly possible. With it, we can rearrange, "see," play a little with the facts of our life. I am not saying that fundamental change (whatever that means) is an easy thing, but it is possible.

Our—or any—culture constantly provides patterns of commonly held relationships. We just know what is expected of us, either in a classroom or drinking beer or being in a serious discussion. From the pattern of our speech to the pattern of our political and economic system, we are silently (and sometimes not so silently) given directions on how to put our act together in fairly particular ways. We are told of the "proper" relationships of events.

The world is chaos and we're forced to make meaning out of it. But it's more complicated than that. We want to be members of society, and society tells us how to order that chaos while being chaotic itself. How do we live in a way that satisfies both ourselves and our society, and still remember the chaos?

We must continually consider a world of multiple truths and realities, and ongoing social-political-economic truths and realities, all of which help us form powerful and interrelated facts. To keep the tension and chaos close at all times is tough but really necessary.

All of that, it seems to me, provides the conditions of optimism.

It is about time we do a little "politics." We can do it in laundry-list fashion. If some of the tasks of politics are living together in a way (1) in which important decisions are decided in a collective way, (2) in which each of us has both responsibility and power when it comes to actions we each take, (3) in which dignity and justice and excellence are alive with meaning for decisions made—if these are some of the tasks, then it seems fairly obvious that we have to rearrange the way we know the world.

Since our world is not set, does not rest on any ultimates, does not rely upon scientific methods to be verifiable—since our world is in constant motion and is given shape by each of us individually as well as collectively—then our job is nothing short of this: We must re-form and re-inform ourselves, and then work to have our society reflect that re-formation.

All of that doing and redoing is political. It is, in its essence, the basis of politics.

I am convinced that each of us has a sense of how the world fits together in a good—and beautiful—way. That sense, or picture, or whatever, should be the touchstone of our mosaic.

There is no reason to believe that each of us will share the same sense of the rightfittingness of the world. Not only that, there *is* reason to believe that these differences will not be simply matters of taste or beauty, but will extend from our moral values to how we wish to arrange ourselves organizationally, to what we understand as politics.

As the monolith of our scientifically socialized heads, and then society, begin to break up, we should look forward to an America of united states or cities or towns or neighborhoods or blocks. A place where we can begin with our own self-conception of the way the world looks best; a place to join like-others to create an environment in which that sense can be worked out; in which we have a duty to be our best selves because the whole community will depend on it.

If we are creatures of myth, it makes sense to take it seriously and choose to live with the myths of our choice.

One could, I suppose, imagine whole groups of people who choose to think of themselves and others as evil, who will base their reality on the science of a hundred years ago, and who will wholly believe in the myth of objective consciousness.

How weird.

OF HUMAN (LANGUAGE) BONDAGE

I would like to change the focus in order to put what has been said in a little different light. In this section, the focus will be the person doing the wrong-headed kind of science which has been described.

The discussion is based on a fine book by Larry Spence titled *The Politics of Social Knowledge*. What follows is my shortened version of just one of his arguments.

The point is this: The person who uses this kind of popularized version of science is not practicing science at all. In fact, this person is not producing knowledge, but is producing myth. In order to see this more clearly, it is necessary to see the different parts of the argument.

In all communications (don't worry, we will get to the point in due time) there are at least two levels. The first level is what actually is said or done, and the second level is the context in which that takes place. We can take the example given by Gregory Bateson. Bateson has us imagine two animals. Then he has us imagine that one animal bites the other. That is the first level, and from it we really know nothing. Finally, we imagine that these animals are playing, and immediately we know that the bite is nothing more serious than a little nip.

What is important to remember is that the context (often unstated or invisible) is critical to the meaning of what is said or done. That is the background we must know.

Back to the person doing research. What this person does is divide himself or herself from the context of what is being studied. He or she denies personal experience and knowledge in order to be "objective." The person looks upon an event from a separate, exclusive, and polarized position.

Spence says that this is heroic research. The heroic researcher stands outside of life itself, and asserts "a general, contextless knowledge of social order." By dismissing the context, the meaning of the findings depend absolutely upon what the investigator says the meaning is. The heroic researcher makes the context of findings the myth that he or she has created.

If Spence is right that a worthy task of the social sciences is "the prediction of the effects of social contexts on human capacities for adaptation and the control of such contexts" (and I think he is) then heroic research will never get us there. We, in fact, can never become unbound from their talk, as we never know about the context in which they put their facts.

Heroic research is the research of political and social power, not necessarily the research which leads to social knowledge. For Spence, heroic research is not science.

POLITICS AND KNOWLEDGE: A TIE

Classically, one is supposed to state what is about to be said, then say it, then tell what has just been said. In a funny way, that is what I'm about to do. Let me repeat in different words and a little more to the point.

In order to challenge the amazing accumulation of facts lying between us and significance—the world of projected death in a nuclear war to grade points—we must know ourselves and our actions well enough to teach and learn from others. An I-thou relationship is, in many ways, revolutionary politics.[23]

The burden of the argument is clear: How one understands knowledge and how one does politics are interrelated. If by knowledge we mean only those things that are objective, then we may never have politics—but only an *elite* of science, a mythology of numbers. We will be organized as a bureaucracy, and each of us will be reduced to a statistic of the state. Ours will be a well-ordered, rational world where rules replace revelation.

It is important that we become seriously involved in the search for social knowledge. To do that, several things must change. For example, we must be aware, and be able to describe the context in which speech and action take place. We must no longer be heroic researchers, taking ourselves out of our own experiences and trying to control others by the making of myths. Heroic researchers produce mystification; the job of good social science is to help develop practices that will better serve the needs of all of us.

---

[23] There are certain things I am fairly clear about. For example, I believe consciousness raising is one of the more pompous, elitist, arrogant concepts around. Either you *are* conscious (I think that includes *all* of us) or you're not. People are conscious of different things, and we can fight about what's best . . . what our choice happens to be. But *levels* of consciousness builds in an amazing bias that translates out—more often than not—White Middle Class Vision Is Best.

It may be best for the white middle class, but fairly silly (or much worse) when given the weight of some incredible psychological law.

When thinking about research, it is necessary to rethink what we mean by objective. From now on, being objective should not be the practice of excluding but the practice of including things. Larry Spence believes that this new objectivity should be based on "our immersion in, observations of, and participation with the human and structural elements of the context."

Spence takes this to the very core of investigation: the hypotheses. He writes: "If our hypotheses seem to be outrageous . . . let them be based on the felt terrors and joys of our lives so that by means of them we may learn something that we can use to improve, here and now, the quality of life." What I want to add is that the multiplicity of hypotheses should be related to the multiplicity of aesthetics alive in the world.

In order to do research which will improve our world, it is important not to be heroic and believe that there is only one right way. It seems to me much more honest and accurate to bow to the multiplicity of right ways, and acknowledge the beauty of many aesthetics.

Given that, good social science is a real possibility.

Knowledge is neither entirely objective nor rational. We must insist that those who lead share their knowledge with us; moreover, that those who lead follow us as we share our knowledge with them. One task of political science is to make clear as many different ways of living as possible. Henry Kariel has written that by "postulating functions which have the effect of shifting our perspectives, we expose previously unseen institutional forms. We perceive a new reality—lives *not* lived (or not lived decently) because of decisions not made. When the empty space in which potentialities might have been realized is bared, we become aware of our losses."

> *Weakness is true and real . . . faking only proves weakness is real, or you wouldn't be so weak as to fake it. No you can't fake being weak. You can only fake being strong.*
>
> —*Ken Kesey*

Focus Two

This chapter argues that division of knowledge exclusively into objective and subjective dimensions without recognition

of the third alternative of rightfittingness misleads us when
we think about politics. Rightfittingness—an evocative
concept novel to the discussion of political knowledge—was
explained as a triangulation from the objective-subjective
dichotomy. It synthesizes some elements of each with new
elements to create an independent third perspective. In
everyday language, rightfittingness also could be called
judgment: a determination reached through the human
capacity to make up our minds based upon our feelings in
response to what we know about the objective world of
things and other people. For example, a person may judge a
house "right" after consideration of several feelings about
its objective characteristics—such as joy about the
craftsmanship which went into it, disappointment about the
layout of the kitchen, and so on—based on that individual's
idea of what is best for that person and the world.
According to the notion of rightfittingness, the house is
judged right because it will encourage that person to be his
or her best self, and enable that individual to be that best
self with family, friends, neighbors, and acquaintances. Out
of the houses available in the world, this is the chosen one
because it fits rightly or best with who that person is.

The chapter argument asserts that rightfittingness is based
on a person's deep moral roots as well as on transitory
emotions. Also asserted is its connection with a person's
careful thoughts about how the world should be and how
that particular person should fit into it. Because
rightfittingness fits a person together with the world, it also
must take prudent account of the world's existing
arrangements in order to know what might be changed and
what must be accepted as given. Rightfittingness, then,
combines moral roots, thought about what should be, and
prudent calculation about power into a compass for giving
direction to human action.

Politically, a central question for rightfittingness, as
suggested in the previous Focus, is whether a person feels in
his or her deepest being that participation in elections
suffices for citizenship or whether one wants the

opportunity to debate and exercise political power more
directly. Nineteenth-century American townsmen knew that
voting was only one and not the primary element of their
public life. In the language of this chapter, they believed
that living together politically meant dealing publicly and in
a dignified way with the rightfittingnesses of themselves and
other people as they were shaped and made apparent in
public meeting. Because the town meetings gave the
nineteenth-century Americans the opportunity to hear,
confront, and persuade the judgments of others, the
townsmen were willing to take on the chores of politics,
including adminstration. The townsmen were drawn
regularly to political activity because it gave an almost
objective reality in laws and public agreements to their
deliberated sense of collective rightfittingness; that is, as
they legislated and instructed delegates, they went on
formal, public record about what was right and wrong
politically in their world; what should be changed and how;
what enjoyed or endured. In doing so they had to reveal
things about their interior selves and their identities because
they endeavored to justify their public stands with reasons
connected to their political beliefs and moral convictions.

   At first glance town-meetings look like only a
burdensome task which interrupted more productive
activities and leisure time. No doubt the meetings were
burdensome and would be today. But on second thought,
they also are the few occasions when one's considered
opinions count to the community as a whole. Since one
directly is helping to conduct the common business, one
becomes essential to the history of the community, perhaps
known for what one says and does. This possiblity of public
reputation, together with the joy of living out
rightfittingness, reportedly has been the central attraction of
political life in the past. (See Hannah Arendt, *On
Revolution* and Machiavelli, *The Prince.*)

Since the objective-subjective dichotomy reduces political opinion to mere preference, it obscures the stabilizing and directive role rightfittingness can play in political matters, especially when diverse people are able to deliberate to a common public conviction, thus allowing people with different rightfittingnesses to act and live together effectively. The dichotomy is misleading for politics because political agreements are neither scientific truths nor mere subjective feelings, but the results of political actions. These agreements are the best that diverse human beings can do in the political realm. They can keep a diverse nation of people together in a civilized manner generation after generation despite whether they agree about the truth or have the same feelings.

This chapter is nonpartisan; it advocates a role in politics for rightfittingness that is general rather than any single political ideology or viewpoint. It assumes that political discussion will be immensely more fruitful when citizens in public arenas discover their own rightfittingnesses and give attentive respect to the genuine rightfittingnesses of other people. The ideal is a variety of individuals holding differing political viewpoints who, in addition, are able to agree on a basic constitution for their community or nation, a basic framework that will encourage them to be their best selves together with other people. That goal certainly was the aim of the ninteenth-century townsmen and their predecessors of the revolutionary and constitutional eras in the United States. In other words, while the word *rightfittingness* is a new one, the idea behind it and its political ramifications have deep roots in the American past.

3

POLITICS AS RULES:

THE ENEMY AS ORGANIZATION

As he struggles in this jungle, every position he's in, he's terribly lonely. He can't confide and talk with the guy working under him. He can't confide and talk to the man he's working for. To give vent to his feelings, his fears and his insecurities, he'd expose himself. This goes all the way up the line until he gets to be president. The president really doesn't have anybody to talk to, because the vice presidents are waiting for him to die or make a mistake and get knocked off so they can get his job. . . .

The executive is a lonely animal in the jungle who doesn't have a friend. Business is related to life. I think in our everyday living we're lonely. I have only a wife to talk to, but beyond that . . . When I talked business to her, I don't know whether she understood me. But that was unimportant. What's important is that I was able to talk out loud and hear myself—which is the function I serve as a consultant. . . .

I have a goal. I want to end my life in a home for the aged that's run by the state—organizing people to fight 'em because they're not running it right. (Laughs.)

—Studs Terkel

"We have modified our environment so radically that we must now modify ourselves in order to exist in this new environment."

—Norbort Wiener

Robots have no future. They merely have a past that has not yet occurred.

—Robert Boguslaw

If how we think of the nature of people means something to politics and to our personal lives, and if how we view the world and knowledge means something, then it seems pretty obvious that the way we organize is also important. The way we organize ourselves and the accompanying ways in which those organizations dominate our behavior are the concerns of this chapter.

One way to begin to understand the effects of organizations, to understand their ideology, is to look at a concern central to political science: power. One of the debates of scholars of American politics is who has power: Who Rules? Do The People Rule, or An Elite, or Elites? The optimists say "The People" rule, the pessimists, "The Elite." Personally, I think either position may well be optimistic. If someone is in charge, if someone has power, if someone has control, then that someone can be changed. To believe that one or a few or many have power is to have faith that human beings are making decisions about the future. That is optimistic.

What if, ultimately, nobody is in charge?

The whole idea that no one is in charge, that we have a tyranny without a tyrant, is an unhappy one.[1] It is an idea tied directly to large organizations and how they work. To begin to understand how large organizations operate, to understand the rules by which they operate and the rules they impose on our world, is to begin to recognize that a large organization is greater than the sum of its human members.[2]

There is a tendency, a very natural one, to believe that because people work in organizations, organizations are simply the reflection of all those people. Such a tendency ignores the point of this chapter: that a large organization may easily set the rules for our society, and those rules will be geared toward organizational—not

---

[1] For an excellent discussion of this, see Hannah Arendt, *On Violence* (New York: Harcourt, Brace & World, Inc., 1969).

[2] Probably the most clearly spelled out statement of why organizations act as they do is to be found in James Thompson, *Organizations in Action* (New York: McGraw-Hill, 1967).

human—ends. That may be a description of our reality. To understand what it means to be involved in this kind of reality, this kind of societal/governmental machinery, is to understand what it means to be little more than a small cog in an impersonal machine—a cog that is interchangeable with other cogs, one that wears out and is replaced with no loss to the machine.

Before describing and analyzing large organizations, it might be useful to make this point: To understand what is going on, we cannot ignore the study of large organizations; they exist, they are "real," and they seem unwilling to go away.

ORGANIZATIONS AS A HISTORICAL "FACT"

It is my intention to argue that many problems facing us today are related to the size and workings of complex organizations. Right now, all I want to show is that to look at history and the dynamics of organizations is to understand that these problems will increase with time.[3]

It is not news to be told that from the middle of the last century to now, organizations in America have become bigger and more complex. Indeed, *bigger* and *more* seem the dominant organization themes. *Bigger:* According to one investigator, "The American Telephone and Telegraph Company controlled 'more wealth than is contained within the borders of twenty-one states.' "[4] *More:* "The A & P chain, which had some 5,000 stores in 1922, had added 12,500 more by 1928."[5] *Bigger* and *more:* In 1903, when Ford Motor Company produced its first car, it had 125 people employed, and authorized capital of $150,000. It took Ford six months to conceive and produce the first automobiles. In 1964, when the Mustang was introduced after three and one-half years' preparation, Ford had assets of $6 billion, employed 317,000 people, and

---

[3] This discussion draws heavily on Robert Presthus, *The Organizational Society* (New York: Vintage Books, 1962), and Kenneth Dolbeare and Murray Edelman, *American Politics*, 3rd ed. rev. (Lexington, Mass.: D. C. Heath, 1979), pp. 23–24.

[4] Presthus, *The Organizational Society*, p. 71.

[5] Ibid., p. 72.

spent $9 million on "Engineering and Styling" costs and $50 million on tooling costs for the new car.[6]

The history of growth—of industrial consolidation and mergers—means that we are all becoming more involved in big organizations and bureaucratic conditions. The facts are these: Large organizations are more likely to survive than smaller ones, and people are now likely to be employees, not their own bosses. To quote Robert Presthus: "Huge capital resources, experience, and good will enable established firms to survive. Failure rates support this interpretation, showing that small firms have a very high failure rate, while big enterprises rarely fail. In time such a pattern probably increases concentration."[7]

What about now, and is everything still big? General Motors Corporation takes in more money than all these states combined: New York, New Jersey, Pennsylvania, Ohio, Delaware, Massachusetts, *plus* the five other states of New England.[8] General Motors has three times as many people working for it overseas as does the U.S. State Department; it has a tanker fleet half again the size of Russia's; it has $17 billion in assets.

That is big.

And big dominates: Three companies control the aluminum market (Alcoa, Reynolds, and Kaiser); three companies manufacture more than 95 percent of automobiles (General Motors, Ford, and Chrysler); three companies produce more than 75 percent of steel (U.S. Steel, Bethlehem, and Republic); and one company produces more than 90 percent of telephone equipment (Western Electric).

Even banking is big and centralized. More than 26 percent of all commercial and industrial lending by U.S. banks in the 1970s was done by only nine banks. Not only that, of those nine, six were associated with the Rockefeller-Morgan group.

---

[6] John Kenneth Galbraith, *The New Industrial State* (New York: Signet Books, 1968), pp. 23–24.

[7] Presthus, *The Organizational Society*, p. 74.

[8] The source of these statistics and those in the paragraphs that follow is Dolbeare and Edelman, *American Politics*, pp. 23–24.

This means, in part, that we are all a part of it; ours is an organizational environment.

Eighty-five percent of us are directly involved in the organizational apparatus and are susceptible to an organizational ideology. It is an ideology of impersonality, rules, interchangeability, and productivity. The history of organizational growth seems to indicate the following: *What we have Now is an extension of What Was; What Will Be will be a bigger and more Now.*

We must begin at the beginning and try to understand what bureaucracies and large organizations can do and might do.

BUREAUCRACY

> *There was only one catch and that was Catch-22, which specifies that a concern for one's own safety in the face of dangers that were real and immediate was the process of a rational mind. Orr was crazy and could be grounded. All that he had to do was ask; and as soon as he did, he would no longer be crazy and would have to fly more missions. Orr would be crazy to fly more missions and sane if he didn't, but if he was sane he had to fly them. If he flew them he was crazy and didn't have to; but if he didn't want to he was sane and had to. Yossarian was moved very deeply by the absolute simplicity of this clause of Catch-22 and let out a respectful whistle.*
>
> *"That's some catch, that Catch-22," he observed.*
> *"It's the best there is," Doc Daneeka agreed.*
>
> —Joseph Heller

Most automobile manufacturers, certainly the Department of Defense, and any Big State University qualify as bureaucratic organizations. In each, there are few at the top and many at the bottom, the leaders and the led, those with positions of power and those without. The point of a bureaucracy is that those at the bottom feed information to those at the top, and those at the top give orders to everyone. Information up, orders down—that is the simple story of bureaucracy. It makes sense in a perverted kind of way. But that is getting ahead of where we are.

The first point I want to make is that when you are dealing with a bureaucracy, there is at least one vital lesson to learn. The lesson is simply that information is the stuff of power—the stuff to control organizations.

People who study organizations seem to be fascinated by charts and graphs. They are, in fact, picture drawers. So, to illustrate the "information is power" point, picture the following. You're a student at Big State U., and something bad has happened. The administration has somehow messed up your record. You expected to graduate in June, but now the computer printout card from the registrar says that you lack units. That rude news could mess up your plans to go to Europe, to hitch across the country, or to retire to a villa; so you decide to see someone about it. Where would you go?[9]

Begin at the top of the organization chart. At many universities, there is a board of regents, or a board of trustees, which has a great deal of power. One could try to go to them, but common sense suggests that that would be a wasted trip. Below the regents, there might be a president, a chancellor, some vice-presidents, and some vice-chancellors. But again, they seem a bit too high up. Theirs are problems of millions of dollars or whole faculties or new buildings or doing politics with state legislatures and huge private corporations. None of these is of direct relevance to a person who simply wants to graduate.

Next on the chart, next down, is an administration of deans and assistant deans and various divisions and an incredible number of secretaries. Lower yet but a little more accessible are department chairpersons, vice-chairpersons, administrative assistants, undergraduate faculty advisors, undergraduate secretaries, faculty, junior faculty, graduate students, and, finally, undergraduates. Where does one go? Whom does one see?

Reasonably, one should see a secretary. The business of the secretary is to know, to have information about how things work,

---

[9] The story of school as bureaucracy is an oft-told one. In my opinion, one of the best and most complete analyses of the problems confronting the student and the university in contemporary society is found in Sheldon Wolin and John Schaar, *The Berkeley Rebellion and Beyond* (New York: Vintage Books, 1970).

to know whom to call to find out important facts. In an important sense, secretaries are everyone's best friend in beating the bureaucracy. While deans and presidents, faculty members, and graduate students pursue a variety of goals, the secretaries help human beings with the workings of the organization. Characteristic of bureaucracies, those at the bottom of organizational charts—the very individuals who are in direct contact with the public—are those members of the organization with the least formal power.

To repeat the point of the story: Information is power.

Government as Bureaucracy

> *"No, you can't go home,"* ex-P.F.C. Wintergreen corrected him. *"Are you crazy or something?"*
> *"Why not?"*
> *"Catch-22."*
> *"Catch-22?"* Yossarian was stunned. *"What the hell has Catch-22 got to do with it?"*
> *"Catch-22,"* Doc Daneeka answered patiently . . . *"says you've always got to do what your commanding officer tells you to do."*
>
> —*Joseph Heller*

This section of the book is the one that comes closest to dealing with what is traditionally considered the governmental process. While it does not exactly deal with "How a Bill Becomes a Law," Congress and the president and the Pentagon are mentioned.

The fact to begin with is this: The government is a large-scale bureaucratic operation, and the military is really a bureaucrat's bureaucracy. It is big, hierarchical, bathed in the national interest, and seemingly unbothered by the national debt.

Buried in the Pentagon bureaucracy are advocates of different kinds of weapon systems, different models of missiles, different kinds of training for assault forces. It is in someone's personal interest—career interest—to be tied to some project that will cost billions of dollars and require the services of hundreds of thousands of people.

Periodically we see advanced weapons advocated by various Pentagon personnel. We are familiar with the BMs of our offense and defense. We have the ICBM (intercontinental), the SLBM (from submarines), and the ABM (the anti-ballistic ones). We now even have MIRVs—which have the capacity to take a one-shot missile and to multiply it.

Put differently, we have enough nuclear stuff to blow up the world.

Yet we seemingly always have the same problem: There is never enough of the right stuff. We need more. The Russians are always building more weapons, and few of us are willing to go unprotected. We are to be protected—you must remember—by bureaucrats.

They are anxious to protect us. There is intraservice fighting about which projects to push. There is interservice fighting to see who gets to go before Congress. There are big companies that attach themselves to the appropriate bureaucrat to fight for *their* new weapon. All of this is in the national interest . . . and in someone's particular interest as well.

We can see this with almost any issue.

Let us take a "hypothetical" decision, one that involves a great deal of money for a group of individuals but that has little effect on the lives of most of us. The example selected involves the decision by Congress to build the B1 bomber. The B1 bomber was supposed to replace the B52 as our strategic bomber. As I write this, the decision was made not to build the B1 . . . well, not to build very many of them, at least.

The Pentagon as Bureaucracy

It is easy to start with the Pentagon, with the U.S. Army, because it represents the most obvious, the biggest, and possibly the most "ideal" bureaucracy anywhere (with the exception of other armies and maybe the Catholic Church). A word about the Pentagon.

Every few years, new people are put in charge of the military. If a bureaucracy is a pyramid, then every so often the top of the pyramid is lopped off and a new top put on. The president appoints civilians to head the armed forces, which is probably a good plan. One problem, an obvious and big one, is that the civilian head of the military never knows a great deal about the defense establishment. Further, the leaders are wholly dependent on the bureaucracy in gathering information that might be beneficial to the military.

At some point, well before the public became aware of it, the military was working on ideas for the B1 system. A task force, probably headed by a major or a general, was in charge of the research. That individual's future, in many ways, became linked with the future of the B1. The more successful the B1 could be made to appear, the more necessary for the sake of our air defense it could be shown to be, the more the offices would know about it and consequently the better off he would be. As the B1 project grew, that somebody's importance would grow.

The dynamics of this revolved, in *part,* around certain important issues. First, there were the environmentalists' arguments that the high-flying bombers would muck up the ozone layer. (The military reply was classic: "Make no mistake about it," said one official, "I am just as much concerned about the environment as the Sierra Club." But it is not to worry says the military . . . most of the time the B1s would be on the ground.) Second, the cost. The first prototype models were said to cost more than their weight in gold. As of now, a production model will cost $337,000,000. Third was the issue of nuclear warheads. If B1s carried them, there would be one-third more in our arsenal—13,000—more than the number of cities on the face of the earth.

But we are really dealing with bureaucratic questions. The military would have no great desire to make public any information that reflected badly on the B1. Also, when a new secretary of defense was named, there would be a huge effort on the part of the military to sell him or her on the B1 program. Information in a bureaucracy goes up; information in a bureaucarcy is power. In other words, why wouldn't the new secretary of defense be convinced that the project was worthy of billions of dollars and millions of working-hours? The B1 means institutional growth, glamor, and stability.

Finally, the dynamics indicate that a bureaucrat in one bureaucracy will seek out a counterpart in another to help promote a similar goal.

The B1 case helps us to understand an interesting process. One part of the process is how a bureaucratic aim becomes a sacred aim. Frightening but true. Moreover, in this particular case, there were those in the military who were opposed to the B1. Yet the fighting that went on was kept mostly *within* the organization itself. The military, as represented by the secretary of defense, presented only those "facts" to the public that favored the B1. One can wonder aloud why political decisions are made from private debates.

CONGRESS

On to Friends of the Bureaucrats—this time the Congress. Congress is set up so that it is possible for an individual to get more, rather than less, power. It helps for an individual to work hard and to follow the rules and to be intelligent. But it helps most to be reelected over and over and over again. The longer a congressman or congresswoman lives and continues to be reelected, the more power will be accumulated.

Almost as foolproof as that.

Congress, like any complex organization these days, is set up to produce specialists. This means that committees are formed, and then each committee is broken down into subcommittees. If a legislator or senator is interested, he or she can become a specialist, an expert in an area, and control the information having to do with that area. The longer the person lives, the more powerful his or her word becomes on matters in the area of specialty.

The late Senator Robert Kerr of Oklahoma illustrates the point. Kerr was all those things we have talked about: hard-working, rule-following, long-lived, and often reelected. After some years, he became Chairman of the Subcommittee on Rivers and Harbors. That God had provided Oklahoma with so few rivers and harbors mattered little in the logic of the Senate. Kerr was a Senior Senator, and Rivers and Harbors was a powerful subcommittee. Every river dredged or harbor built or dam constructed went through Kerr's subcommittee. Kerr could get these projects for any state—for any senator—but in return he could expect favors. A dam for a vote on an important matter, or some such calculation.

A committee is important in the Congress in part according to the monies it controls. The Appropriations Committee is more important than a subcommittee of the Governmental Operations

Committee. Power in committees often revolves around expertise in expensive projects.

The point should now become more clear: There were individuals in Congress who would benefit politically if the B1 were passed. Its passage would mean more control over more expensive projects. It could mean more bargaining power with other members of Congress. It is precisely this group of people that became allied with its counterparts in the Pentagon, with all those individuals working on the B1, supporting the B1, and selling the B1 to their leaders and to the nation.

The interested legislators and military people found help from those individuals in "private" industry who worked on war-related goods. To learn just how much of the economy is supported by building goods for the armed forces is to learn how effective this industry is as a pressure group. Its Washington operation is generally very well financed, has much experience, and is able to supply information to those individuals in Congress who are considered friendly.[10]

There is an informal rule of politics that organized groups are more effective than unorganized ones. Certainly what is known as the Military Industrial Complex is a very well organized group. To conceptualize it another way, think how easy it would be to gather an effective group of people from industry, the Pentagon, and Congress to work for the B1. They could virtually control the public's access to information about the B1. Think how difficult it would be to gather anti-B1 forces. At best, it would be a group of strangers with no obvious connection to important sources of information, no money with which to publicize or pressure Congress, and no ongoing organization.

There are all kinds of "fictional" stories we could offer. Pretend our democratic country financed a very huge and expensive bunch of spies. Make up a name. Call them, say, the CIA.

Pretend they made mistakes (like not even hinting at the Tet offensive or the 1973 Yom Kippur War) and spent time figuring out how to kill "enemy" Heads of State. Just pretend.

---

[10] One might see Robert Heilbroner, "Military America," *The New York Review of Books,* July 23, 1970; or Seymour Melman, *Pentagon Capitalism.*

What about the person in charge of the House Oversight Committee—Lucien Nedzi—who knew those things? Simply construct
an iron curtain called "national security" so we citizens need not
worry about problems of "our" interest. Nedzi keeps his mouth
shut.

What about William Colby, head of the CIA? His idea was
that in order to answer the questions the Congress and the Rock-
efeller Commission asked him, he should tell the truth. Only one
solution: Fire him for being too "candid."

But that wouldn't really happen here.

This would: Bureaucracies need bureaucracies. The CIA is an
amazing example.

In the Senate hearing about the CIA, it was learned (read *revealed*) that the Russians, by using antennae on their missions in
the United States and by using orbiting satellites, can spy. (Something—if not Body—really is up there looking at you.) The Russians
monitor and record thousands and thousands of telephone conversations carried by microwave.

It turns out we're doing the same thing in Russia.

What's interesting is that we could jam the Russian interception
of our microwave communication. Of course we don't because then
they would jam ours in Moscow. Bureaucracies need bureaucracies.
The CIA needs the KGB. They do, after all, see the world in the
same way.

Information is power in a bureaucratic world, and bureaucrats
from different organizations share knowledge if they share a common aim. What we must understand now is just what kind of style
bureaucratic politics has, what the bases of its decisions are, and
what the built-in limits of its organizational structure are. What
underlies, what motivates, the actions of a bureaucracy?

BUREAUCRACY: THE IDEOLOGY

Ideally, a bureaucracy is a hierarchy, with few at the top, many at
the bottom. Those at the top—ideally—have the authority to make
decisions; the others have the responsibility for carrying out those
decisions. As we know, information from the outside world comes

in through the bottom and is sent up the organizational ladder if it seems important. Decisions stem from this information.

A bureaucracy is supposed to be a human machine. Each position in it is defined, described as to function, and limited in its freedom of action. The position becomes standardized; as a piston does only the work of a piston, so a clerk does only the work of a clerk. When either malfunctions, it is replaced.

The human machine is geared toward productivity. It must produce something, and that something must be measurable. Whether it is measured in terms of profits, sheer quantity of goods produced, or number of diplomas granted, the output of a bureaucracy must be able to be measured. So the basis of information for a bureaucrat is objective reality. What is objective can be counted, and that is precisely what bureaucracies are good at. It is very important to understand that bureaucracies are too gross, too inexact, too unsubtle to comprehend quality. Huge organizations like our bureaucracies function "efficiently" and are capable of understanding that functioning only in terms of how many in how short a time and at what material cost.

Like any machine, a bureaucracy works best when it is well insulated from the outside, well protected from different elements. In a real sense, bureaucracies are afraid of the outside, afraid of the public sector. Paranoid, if you will. So they grow. They keep trying to occupy more space and to control more sectors so that their internal workings will be protected. The larger a bureaucracy grows, the more the world will look like a bureaucracy. The more the world is like that, the greater the likelihood is that more decisions that should be made publicly will be made privately and that the criteria used will suit organizational demands rather than societal ones. The style is production oriented, paranoid, and private.

The dynamics of the B1 fit this style. So does the style of the CIA.

THE FUTURE

When man invented the machine, for which there is no external model in nature, he invented it in his own image. The machine

*does not come from nowhere—it mirrors man's mechanical
head.*

—Philip Slater

There is a logic to large, complex organizations that we must understand. In question form, it is this: If a bureaucracy is a human machine (and, therefore, vulnerable to human mistakes), wouldn't it be better to develop machines that would eliminate many of those mistakes? This kind of thinking has led to a technology and an organizational style with implications far beyond organizational efficiency.

Large organizations are coming to rely more and more on the centralization and standardization of information gathering. This is particularly true in the case of the military. As the technology, as computerization, becomes more central to an organization, that organization begins to change its operations. To quote Judy Merkle:

> Because the computer does not process general information in the same subconscious manner as human commanders, and because errors are incredibly costly, computer technology forces an immense clarification of thought and a precision of action in preparing computer inputs. The rules governing the operation of organizations and the decision process must be determined, the routine business must be separated from functions requiring human judgment, and the procedures for computerized functions must be laid out before actual computer calculations. In creating a man-machine network to process information, more and more effort must go into the precise definition of organizational requirements. . . . Technology has not merely merged with organization theory, it has become organization theory.[11]

Thus, as technology begins to control information, it begins to change the world to fit its categories. "The core technology," continues Merkle, "because it is computerized, has no means of handling ambiguity, and so its inputs of information, equipment and manpower must be regularized according to its requirements and

---

[11] Merkle, Judith A., *Command and Control: The Social Implication of Nuclear Defense* (General Learning Press, Morristown, N.J.). © 1971 General Learning Corporation. Reprinted by permission of Silver Burdett Company.

stripped of ambiguity, which requires in turn that the same process be carried out on the inputs to *those* inputs, and so forth."[12]

The point we must make is that computer technology has already changed, and will continue to change, the nature of society. It requires a particular kind of behavior with which we are just beginning to become familiar. The following example from Merkle pushes us into the not very distant future. It deals with the "successful" use of a police data bank. The

> policeman stops [a] speeder (or drug suspect, or whatever); policeman detains suspect while contacting data bank; data bank, within minutes, informs policeman that suspect is wanted in another state for armed robbery; arrest is made. This speeding up and filling in of information gaps appears to be a real improvement, with no particular drawbacks. However, the continued use of such a system will actually tend to change the nature of crime itself. That is, the computer will soon eliminate the amateurs, leaving two types of crime untouched—spontaneous crime, thought of and executed on the spot, and organized crime, which to escape detection will become more tightly organized and more technically capable. Individual criminals cannot afford the services of computer technicians, but the Mafia can if it discovers that this is the path to survival. The computer has simply eliminated individual crime in favor of ever more highly organized crime. Criminals must know the location of data banks and redundant facilities as well as sophisticated techniques of sabotage and circumvention.[13]

That is fairly easy to understand. Organized crime really will become organized. But the example only sets the stage for the more important point: It is easy to substitute politics for police.

> An intensive use of such systems [political data banks] to handle urban riots would essentially change the nature of civil disobedience. First of all, it would eliminate the "amateurs." The public meeting speaker, letters-to-Congressman writers, and presidential threateners could easily be rounded up at the first signs of trouble (signs to be interpreted by the military, of course). Any person or

---

[12] Ibid., p. 16.
[13] Ibid., pp. 23–24.

organization foolish enough to publicize complaints against the established order would be eliminated from the political game. Two kinds of political potential cannot be registered before-the-fact by computers: first, genuinely spontaneous mass action . . . and second, tightly organized, technically competent, politically uncompromising . . . opposition groups, which will be the only political action groups able to withstand the onslaught of the computer. Given the right historical circumstances, this is a much finer recipe for revolutionary violence than any of the potentially inflammatory situations which the technology is programmed to pacify.[14]

BUREAUCRACY IN A MORE PERSONAL SENSE

"Did he tell you how I could ground you?"

"Just by filling out a little slip of paper saying I'm on the verge of a nervous collapse and sending it to Group. Dr. Stubbs grounds men in his squadron all the time, so why can't you?"

"And what happens to the men after Stubbs does ground them?" Doc Daneeka retorted with a sneer. "They go right back to combat status, don't they? And he finds himself right up the creek. Sure, I can ground you by filling out a slip saying you're unfit to fly. But there's a catch."

"Catch-22?"

"Sure. If I take you off combat duty, Group has to approve my action, and Group isn't going to. They'll put you back on combat status, and then where will I be? On my way to the Pacific Ocean, probably . . . all they've got in the Pacific is jungles and monsoons. I'd rot there."

"You're rotting here."

—Joseph Heller

Although it's not an extraordinarily precise way to present an argument, I would like to introduce one with a physical law: For every action, there is an equal and opposite reaction. That is the sense of what I should like to argue. While the following contains a good deal of speculation, there seems to be enough truth in it to

---

[14] Ibid., p. 24.

take it seriously. If possible, accept what is right and reject the rest: My feelings will not be hurt.

Basically, bureaucracy develops only half of an individual. It so concentrates on some personality factors that it wholly ignores others. What I shall argue is that as we become more highly skilled bureaucrats we develop urges equal and opposite to those skills. For example, as we become more developed "rationally," we may also become more anxious to be "irrational." Simply stated, bureaucracies may be driving us crazy. We may be going mad in part as a result of the organizational imperatives that have such a disproportionate effect on our lives.

It may be easiest to understand what I mean by visualizing how one learns to diagram a compound sentence in ninth-grade English. As I recall, it looked something like a straight line that was split into two lines. What I want to argue is that in the beginning an individual has some kind of wholeness, some kind of merging of qualities. At some point—indeed, we seem to have reached that point—bureaucracies overdevelop certain of these qualities, while leaving others underdeveloped. The individual with integrated skills slowly becomes an individual divided. Like our diagrammed sentence, the person is split in two. There are three areas that help illustrate the point: rationality, time, and relationships.

A basic assumption of this whole line of thought is that a healthy individual is able somehow to integrate the various factors of his or her personality. To a greater or lesser degree, the rational and the emotional would mix. One would not always be employed; nor would either be used alone. Our undivided individual would not be concerned for the future at the expense of the past or the present. Indeed, each would hold importance. Finally, he or she would not participate in relationships exclusively on the basis of roles, according to the positions held by each person. Nor would all relationships be of the encounter group type: extra-tense, personal, and, in a sense, tyrannizing. Somehow, a middle ground should be sought.

But bureaucracies develop extremes. I mean, the human cogs in the organizational machine are forced to divide their feelings, emotions, and actions into extremes. Let us begin with rationality.

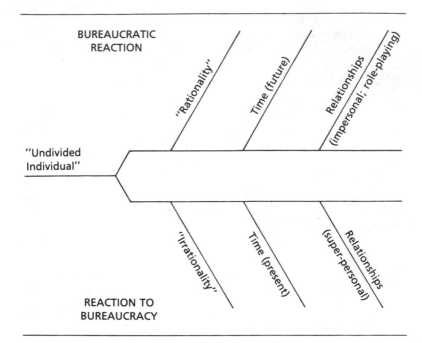

RATIONALITY

There is a certain rationality that a bureaucracy fosters. Most of its parts we understand, for in a sense the logic of bureaucracy is the logic of science. It assumes an objective reality, one that is "real" and quantifiable. The aim of the bureaucracy is to produce a count-able product at the lowest possible cost. The most for the least— just so it is objective. All questions must be technical, all problems soluble in terms of costs and benefits. To build a house or an atomic bomb cannot be judged as "good" or "bad" per se; it can be judged only in terms of organizational credits and debits.

So the bureaucracy constructs its own world and makes its own rules about what is real. For a person to get ahead in that world, that person must act according to its rules and its rationality: keep within the framework, produce and behave, stay in step to get ahead. If one believes in the outputs of bureaucracies, one is forced to admit that they function effectively. But the point is that it seems to be very difficult for a human being to be so confined for very long, difficult to leave one's emotions at the front door in exchange for wholly rational thought.[15]

The idea of a human machine in which human beings are confined to the rationality of cogs means inevitably that in some part of life "irrationality" must come out. If an individual is rational eight hours a day, we certainly should expect signs of something different when he or she is not at work.

We can begin to understand our irrationality by exploring the ideas of religion and violence in America.[16] Religion first.

There are, of course, all kinds of religions and all kinds of worshipers and "faithful." From polite Episcopalians to Jesus Freaks (read *Children of God*), people take their religion with differing degrees of intensity. It seems that we Americans have a rather singular expression of conviction: We are the land of the Revivalists. Always have been—from one fire-breathing, hell-talking preacher to the next, and almost gladly we vent our emotions at a good revival. A good Sunday revival seems as good for the pent-up, rational person as a good Saturday night drunk. Maybe the best of worlds would be to have both.

A minister named Albert Barnes once said: "The religion of forms is the stereotyped wisdom or folly of the past, and does not adapt itself to the free movements, the enlarged views, the varying plans of this age."[17] The age in which he spoke was 1844, and his idea was to return to the pure conditions of primitive Christianity, to get back to the basics. In a land where social movement is in unique combination with the confinement of work, people naturally looked for a release. They turned to God with a vengeance—or, if

---

[15] The use of the words *rational* and *emotional* is, I am afraid, a bit sloppy. While I am using them as most people do, it is important to remember that relating to the world "rationally" is simply one kind of emotional stance. To put it differently, rationality is at its root only another emotion.

[16] For an example of how dysfunctional bureaucratic organizations are in France, see Michael Crozier, *The Bureaucratic Phenomenon* (Chicago: University of Chicago Press, 1967).

[17] Richard Hofstadter, *Anti-Intellectualism in American Life* (New York: Vintage Books, 1963), p. 137.

not with a vengeance, at least with an emotional intensity that would help ease the rest of the week. Redneck religion for the confined. A perfectly rational response to a "rational" life.

Moreover, it turned out to be good business. Billy Graham, Oral Roberts, and T. L. Osborn are in the noble tradition of evangelists in America. From the days of tent revivals to contemporary TV, revivalists are not only saving souls but making a little money too. For example, by the 1880s, Dwight L. Moody was into the God business the way Andrew Carnegie was into steel and P. T. Barnum into circuses.[18] It was big business and hard sale. Moody had "expenses" for his meetings: $32,000 for Boston, $30,000 for New York, $140,000 for London. Once there, he would give his pitch: "Who'll take Christ now? That's all you need. With Christ you have eternal life and everything else you need. Without Him, you must perish. He offers Himself to you. Who'll take Him?"[19]

The point I am trying to make is *not* that all religion is insane, or that every evangelist should be institutionalized. All I am suggesting is that we are attuned to a particular kind of religious experience. We have a kind of therapy, a societally approved place in which to be emotional, to be "irrational." The bureaucrat and the evangelist may be the two sides of our selves.

The other and obvious reaction to rationality, at least obvious in our experience, is violence. It takes no keen insight or imagination to argue that violence in America is not a new phenomenon. There is no need to list examples from the Old West, or from television's version of the Old West. The ongoing violence in the South, where it was always open season on blacks, included burnings, beatings, rapes, and hangings: white men in white robes, being irrational, relieving their frustrations in an American tradition.

There is also the violence of the lonely: the seemingly senseless killings in almost every community, done by a person alone, and now so commonplace as not to "make" the national news.

We have the ongoing violence of war. It does not matter too much where the war is, or who is fighting; we Americans get a dose of violence if we decide either to watch the news or read the paper.

---

[18] Ibid., p. 110.
[19] Ibid., p. 111.

We have, over the years, watched everything from Vietnam to the British invading the Falklands (remember that?).

(There is a beside-the-point which should be added here. There is the kind of violence which we do not see, but which is real. There are the poor people who freeze to death because of bad energy policies; there are hungry people who do not eat because of rules to protect the government from "cheaters;" there are children who need special education but cannot get it because they live in a school district which does not provide it. There is real violence done which never gets on the news. But, that is beside the bureaucratic point that is being suggested.)

War may well be too obvious an example. As we know, there is acceptable and unacceptable violence. "Innocent" violence is all right. Acts that are obvious reactions to the confinement of normal existence, such as the return of panty raids or eating goldfish, are permissible. What is not acceptable is violence against the "rational" system. It is all right to relieve oneself of the tedium of the day—even irrationally—just so long as one is willing to return to that tedium. But when violence begins to mean something, when it becomes a weapon instead of a release, an important political act instead of just a childish prank, then it becomes dangerous.

So we are allowed meaningless (save to those we harm) violence in order that we may be good bureaucrats during the day. It is one way in which we can be emotional, have a little fun, feel unconfined. Our violence is as normal a reaction as it is "irrational." While it would be foolish to claim that bureaucratic rationality is responsible for all violence, it would be equally foolish never to make that connection.

TIME

> *It was Ezra Stiles who in the 1700s came to believe that the "multitudes were seriously, soberly, and solemnly out of their wits."*

A bureaucracy creates a fairly definitive view of time. As a large, ongoing organization, it points to the future, it plans on contingencies; it is problem-solving. It lives not in the Now but in the

Will-be. There is no real end in sight for a bureaucracy. The compulsion to produce, the ideology of production, means that the organization will continue to look ahead until there are no more raw materials to consume. In other words, bureaucracies live in the future until there is no more life to destroy.

This fits well with our Christian heritage. It goes well with the idea that if we work hard now, if we continue to deny ourselves in the present, then we will go to heaven. Heaven is the ultimate bonus, the best fringe benefit. So we live in the future. Let me try to explain it in a different way.

My example is really a comparison between the French view of time and the American view. Imagine a truck traveling along a road. On the back of the truck, facing the road just traveled, sits the Frenchman. His ability to see clearly from there is like a perception of time. The past is most clear, the present is whizzing by so fast that it is a blur, while the future, the road before him, is simply unknown.

Now the American sits in the cab, facing front. The future, for that American, is most clear. The present is a blur, while the past is behind him, completely unknown. Our vision is best when we anticipate. We live there, not here. For example, we go to high school in order to get into college; to college in order to get a job; get a job in order to have a family; and have a family so that our children can have those things we never had. We have an endless future, as does a bureaucracy. That is what we are taught; yet we know the reaction to that vision of time has been almost "irrational."

One way to do time was tried several years ago: There was an effort to abolish both the past and the future. The emphasis was on the now. Ah, remember the hippies? Time became the present. Plans were middle-class hang-ups. The past was dead, and future had not happened, so why not light up, lighten up, and live in the here and now.

There are still some hippies around. It is best to be nice to them, and treat them as an endangered species. While a lot of their ideas were interesting, and much of what they said was right, certain key questions like: Who's going to cook dinner? never got answered.

There are other ways of thinking about time in addition to past and future. There is good time, and bad time, fast and slow,

wasted and important, anxious and endless. Bureaucratic time, besides being the future, is not generally good time, nor is it fast, nor
is it important. It is routine time.

Einstein hypothesized, and others proved, that time—even
clock time—is not uniform. Clock time changes as the clock gets
away from the earth's gravity and increases its speed. In a sense,
bureaucracies do something like that to our psychological sense of
time, and the something they do is not particularly beneficial.

Currently, a remarkable invention has entered organizational
life. The invention is the minute. The point of the minute is this:
A good bureaucratic manager should be able to deal with any
employee in one minute. The book—a how to do it little manual—
is called *The One Minute Manager*. The book is awfully successful.
The book is just awful.

In the book there are instructions about what the attitude of
a manager should be, and such good advice as how to give praise
or a reprimand in a minute. Praise: As a manager, you should
describe what good thing was done; how, as a manager, you feel
positive about it; how the company will prosper. Then, a little pause
for all the warm feelings to be absorbed, then encouragement for
the employee to continue the good work. Finally, a little paternal
(or maternal) pat on the shoulder, or a handshake, and away you
go to the executive restroom or executive dining room or wherever.

The idea is to get it done in one minute. That seems to be the
projected attention span of employees. One minute.

At least two things come to mind. First, it makes perfect sense.
In an ideal bureaucratic structure, where roles are strictly defined,
praise or blame can readily be given and understood in a minute.
No real problem when one role player interacts with another role
player. Second, this truly terribly speeded up vision of the world
may be coming into it's own.

There are now books titled *The One-Minute Mother* and *The
One-Minute Father*. (Do you think they conceived their child after
one-minute intercourse?) Faster yet, there is also a book titled *The
:59-Second Employee*. The book explains how to keep ahead of
the one-minute manager.

If you take the right drugs, I suspect you can see where this is
all going—in an instant.

But back to the main point. Bureaucracy condemns us to the

future, while we react by claiming the present. Neither the richness of the past nor the lessons of tradition are in much evidence in such an arrangement. To reclaim ourselves from the demands of a hectic, meaningless now or a never-to-be-reached future, we might consider understanding the past. Learning about the culture that produced us and the varieties of styles that are so different from our own.

RELATIONSHIPS

> *"Well say, buddy, is this the way these little meetings usually go?"*
>
> *"Usually go?"*
>
> *"Is this the* usual *pro-cedure for these Group Therapy shindigs? Bunch of chickens at a peckin' party? . . . [A peckin' party is when] the flock gets sight of a spot of blood on some chicken and they all go to* peckin' *at it, see, till they rip the chicken to shreds, blood and bones and feathers. But usually a couple of the* flock *gets spotted in the fracas, then it's their turn. And a few more gets spots and gets pecked to death, and more and more. Oh, a peckin' party can wipe out the whole flock in a matter of a few hours, buddy, I seen it. A mighty awesome sight. The only way to prevent it—with chickens—is to clip blinders on them. So's they can't see."*
>
> —*Ken Kesey*

There are many who argue that a bureaucracy is, basically, little more than the sum of its roles that are "linked psychologically."[20] In other words, one can understand an organization simply by studying the roles of those in that organization. What is important for us is to try to get to the real meaning of such a view—the costs of role playing to those within the organization. In a sense, the heart of the question revolves around the problem of defining the individual.

Let me state the problem in a personal way. It is possible that a person could relate to me in terms of the roles he or she ascribes to me. I could be seen as playing the role of family member, tennis

---

[20] For example, see Daniel Katz and Robert Kahn, *The Social Psychology of Organizations* (New York: John Wiley & Sons, 1966).

player, teacher, and television watcher. Those would be my roles. The sum of them would be me. If I were to die suddenly, couldn't there be another person who would fill my roles? A tennis player, a part of the family of Barbara and whoever was living with us at the time, a teacher of classes, a watcher of television. In bestowing roles, society can both give identity and take it away. By relating to roles instead of to people, we are continually in danger of being no one knowing nobody.

The sociologist Ralf Dahrendorf describes the tension in the following way: "[An individual's] roles are conferred on him, and he is shaped by them; but when he dies, the impersonal force of society takes his roles away from him and confers them on somebody else in new combinations . . . man has turned . . . from the individual into the member, from a free and autonomous creature into the sum of his alien characters."[21]

Roles depersonalize. They provide an easy means whereby people can ignore other people; they are an excellent device through which an individual can hide from the facts of his or her job. In consciously playing a role, one is doing exactly what the bureaucracy demands. One acts no longer as a human being, but instead as a functioning, rule-following, member in good standing of an impersonal organization.

In part, role playing means that we are replaceable, interchangeable. To be a good vice-president is to be a good vice-president. A secretary here and a secretary there are simply the same parts in different machines. It is critical for an individual to play a prescribed role correctly so that the bureaucracy can guarantee its own survival, no matter what happens to any particular person.

Here is the place where you should expect an example: the name of a person who exemplifies a top bureaucratic personality. Years ago, the example was Robert McNamara, who went from car executive to war executive to World Bank executive. Later the example was Eliot Richardson. He floated from one bureaucracy to another, functioning as a diplomat or a department head, replacing or being replaced.

---

[21] Ralf Dahrendorf, *Essays in the Theory of Society* (Stanford, Calif.: Stanford University Press, 1968), p. 75.

This year, I suppose the award goes to George Schultz. He can direct the budget, he can preside over the world's biggest construction company, or he can be the secretary of state. Why not?

In the realm of example, of course, they are all the same person. From here, they all look alike. Or, to put it a little differently: In a large class, all you students look the same.

There seems to be a real desire among many to play more than a role—a longing to relate in more personal ways—a reaction to the system. So we go to extremes, we go to the superpersonal, we go to encounter groups. Lonely role-playing people pay their money to be tyrannized by a group of lonely role-playing people. One wonders if in an artificial environment, instant intimacy will solve any long-range problems. There is little doubt but that encounters are beneficial, but very possibly they provide only temporary relief.

Some organizations set up encounter sessions once a week for a whole office. Can you imagine the incredible emotional relief in that one hour, after emotions have been stored up for thirty-nine hours? But organizations are wise to do it. People are able to react to the inhumanity of their roles in an equally foolish way, by overcompensating and being inhumanly personal. The beauty of it is that it all takes place in an institutional setting. It is all harmless to the organization. People yell and scream and cry and kiss and then go back to work, emotionally spent, able to endure until the next session.

Now that's depressing. We know the "truth" of how our surroundings affect us: The warning is that we can always be right but miss certain truths.

To act on the intellectual framework we know is accurate may be both wrong *and* destructive.

In our part of the twentieth century, we have inherited a series of problems which are as familiar as the air we breath. We have been cut off from those around us and from ourselves. Bureaucracy is simply one way we can see how this works.

The term which is generally used in this kind of discussion is *alienation*, but it is used so much and in so many different ways. The idea that I want to talk about is that of being separated from your environment.

The separation is in part due to the roles we are forced to play, and in part due to specialization of tasks. Let me offer an example of the latter, and how our specialization leads to ignorance which in turn leads to a separation from others and the very world you live in.

Let's say you are a biologist working in a lab. You are interested in some kind of genetic engineering. You work with very sophisticated machinery, and you are doing work which you later realize evokes a powerful reaction from many citizen groups.

You may think that this next part is going to be about the social responsibility of scientists. It is not; it is about how, as a biologist, you are probably ignorant about the scientific instruments you use. In other words, you do not understand the thinking behind the tools of your trade. In many important ways, you are separated from people who are in the same business. You can only see what the instruments show, but the fact is you do not know the bias of the instrument. You are only "seeing" the structure of another person's mind.

The concern, then, is a very fundamental separation from the world. To be unable to speak the same language as those around you is to be set apart from the world. As we know, that kind of separation—from roles to technical ignorance—is common. It is common and getting more common. The more sophisticated and specialized we become, the more separated we are.

One of the struggles is to realize that much of our lives is not spent like that, and that there is a real world of family and friends, loves and hates. In this world, we need to suspend some of the "correct" ways we have been taught to look at the world and respond to it, and should begin to rethink what is really happening. We have to consider what may be possible.

What I want to suggest is that much of your identity—who you are in the world—is contained and cemented in close relationships. In a tangible way, other people carry around a great deal of who you are. I believe it's true that a person's death diminishes absolutely all those people who have surrounded that person.

How we treat the people around us—and how they treat us—forms an arena of unlimited opportunities for acts of integrity. It is the primary location of good and evil. From it, we *should* be *able* to generalize and enter into the broader world of actions and politics.

What we get is at the same time something fragile and dramatic. It certainly won't guarantee wealth or fame or even happiness. Those all seem to be the wrong words and really belong to different scales of measurement.

What intrusions may do is turn the world upside down and allow each of us—in interesting combinations—to become creators.

Beats being a bureaucrat.

AN AFTER WORD

To take this chapter seriously is to begin to understand the world in a different, depressing way. To see large organizations as lifestyles that convey a very definite ideology is to limit the use of certain kinds of analyses.

For example, much of the economic interpretation of society— an analysis that depends heavily upon the class conflicts inherent in capitalist, but not communist, societies—makes little sense. There is no doubt that wealth is concentrated in our society, that there are the rich and the poor, and that there are "managers" and "workers." But the whole dynamic of organized society—the impersonality and role playing and ever-increasing institutional growth— affects everyone.

What I am arguing is that the ideology of organizations will not change, whether they be in communist or capitalist countries, in America or England, in Russia or Japan.[22] The bureaucrat recognizes the bureaucrat, inter-office or inter-nationstate. Regrettably, class analyses are too optimistic. To eliminate the "ruling class," the upper class, would be in effect to trade one set of highly placed bureaucrats for another. To make a class analysis in a bureaucratic world leaves too many essential problems well hidden.

Essentially, it seems obvious that in an organizational society, potentially everyone might get hurt. People at the bottom—the poor, the minorities—are forced to deal with powerless organiza-

---

[22] For the classic statement of bureaucracy, see Hans Gerth and C. Wright Mills, *From Max Weber* (New York: Oxford University Press, 1958). There are, of course, alternatives. For some examples you might begin with some of the selections in Terrence Cook and Patrick Morgan, eds., *Participatory Democracy* (San Francisco: Canfield Press, 1971).

tional employees who represent an impersonal set of rules. For those in the organization the pay may be higher, but so perhaps are the costs. Organizations do more than buy people's time; they represent an impressive way of purchasing an individual's individuality.

The world is safe for bureaucracy only when everyone is a bureaucrat.

There is an eternal tug in America between the bigness of bureaucracies and the individualism of the little engine that could. A clear example of this is IBM and Apple: Computer Wars.

Apple computers started, literally, in a garage. "Computer types," with almost no money and a lot of ideas invented the Apple home computer. Boy, did they get rich. They also developed into a big organization.

IBM was already big and had an enormous amount of money. They decided to compete with Apple for the home computer market. They developed a personal computer, put it in the marketplace, and took away half of Apple's business. Not only that, the IBM became the standard by which home computers were measured.

Apple, to compete, marketed a Lisa. Too expensive. Apple was in trouble.

Meanwhile, one of the original Apple people returned to an old concept. He gathered a few of the brightest "computer types" and took them back to the garage—so to speak. Put differently, he tried to infuse the old pioneer spirit into a small group of people working in a large organization. He took the best and the brightest and let them work.

When asked about what the market research indicated, he said that Apple had done no market research. After all, his reasoning went, did Alexander Graham Bell do market research before he invented the telephone?

The point is not that the Macintosh is successful. (As I write this, it seems to be successful.) The point is that something gets lost in big organizations and the conservative market research which guides new production. What I am trying to get at is that there is a real tension between individualism and corporate life.

Interestingly, on the inside of every new Macintosh Computer are signatures of the forty-seven people who worked on its invention.

It would be a real relief if I could honestly write that all we had to do was to destroy all bureaucracies and all large complex organizations in order to solve our problems. Of course, I can't. That our organizational structure is helping to drive us mad is, I hope, now more obvious. We are surely becoming divided, and are in the process destroying ourselves. The less together we are, the more potentially successful we become. But we can split ourselves just so much.

The problem of how much organization we need is complex. We seem to be social as well as political animals. There are things we can do in groups—things that are beneficial both physically and psychologically—that we cannot do alone. So we must find new modes of organization and different ways of perceiving each other.

As long as we are simply unimportant, replaceable parts in an impersonal social machine, the best we can hope for is that some day we will go sane and become irreplaceable.

Focus Three

The theory of modern bureaucratic organization holds that ideally the work for all positions in an organization be fully described, standardized, and fit together hierarchically into an efficiently operating whole. In this theory, employees should behave strictly according to the rules of the organization for the positions they occupy. Personal variation from standard operating procedures threatens to disrupt the smooth functioning of the overall operation because everyone else is prepared by the rules to expect only a fixed kind of behavior. Thus, according to the ideal, employees are supposed to be cogs or easily replaceable functionaries in a well designed social machine able to accomplish its overall tasks in the most efficient possible manner.

Few modern organizations fully approximate the ideal. Nevertheless, they strive to do so and to motivate and train their employees appropriately. Bureaucratic organizations have been a success insofar as they have monopolized the economic and political arenas of the United States (eighty-

five percent of us are directly involved in the organizational
apparatus and are susceptible to an organizational
ideology). Bureaucracies are here to stay for us as workers
and citizens, at least in the near future. Our involvement
with them creates distinctive habits of mind and behavior
which we should understand.

The key to this chapter's argument is the assumption that
a purely bureaucratic way of life is a human possibility in
the twentieth century. The modern organizational ideal
promotes conduct carefully disciplined according to the
bureaucratic rules; that is, its own version of rationality.
The ideal also calls for impersonality and interchangeability.
The purpose of the ideal is not improvement of the human
soul. Instead the kind of human behavior encouraged by
modern organizations is a by-product of their goal of
measurable productivity: the number of automobiles,
diplomas, welfare checks, or B1 bombers. Nonetheless,
what we do and how we do it affects our hearts and minds
by cultivating the habits by which we get along with each
other in the world. As we follow a bureaucratic way of life
at work and in the polity, we also internally become
bureaucrats—to some extent.

The chapter imagines the horror of being nothing more as
a human being than the by-product of the modern
organizational ideal. It presumes no other formative
influence for human character development than
bureaucratic rules and role relations—no family training; no
religious, ethical, and humanistic practice or example; no
attempt at thinking for oneself about how to understand
what human existence means. The argument pretends that
twentieth century people could start living as though
bureaucratic roles are the only contact they have with other
human beings, with their children, spouses, friends, and
acquaintances.

Viewed from the perspective of moral, intellectual, and
psychological development, the bureaucratic ideal is
frighteningly disappointing. Of course, common sense tells
us that the modern organizational habits are not meant to

be the only guidance for life, only instruments for accomplishing certain tasks. Yet, as we increasingly bureaucratize political and economic life, we change arenas in which somewhat more wholesome ideals were able to inspire us occasionally and bolster the training received at home, church, school, and neighborhoods with confirmations that the soul counts to the wider world also. In a totally bureaucratized social universe soulcraft would be irrelevant; even the essence of human life might become interchangeable.

4

POLITICS AS
TACKY:

OR, WHAT DO I DO ON
MY DAY OFF?

I'*m usually at the desk by eight o'clock, half an hour before work
starts. Getting set for the day, writing programs, assigning different
jobs to different people. When they come in we take a head count.
You see who's late and who's not. You check around and make sure
they start at eight thirty. . . . You make sure when they go for breaks
they take fifteen minutes, not twenty. You check for lunch hours,
making sure they take forty-five minutes and not an hour. . . . All
you're doing is checking on the people. This goes on all day.*

The job is boring. It's a real repetitious thing. . . .

*A man should be treated as a human, not as a million-dollar piece of
machinery. People aren't treated as good as an IBM machine is. . . .*

—Studs Terkel

"*Early in life she had developed the ability to make a customer
wish he'd thrown up on himself rather than disturb her.*"

—William Least Heat Moon

*The prean is a sea monster with the body of a crab and the
head of a certified public accountant.*

—*Woody Allen*

YUCK

So, in a book about politics, we have finally reduced ourselves to
looking at "dirty pictures." We are forced to face what many people
just won't discuss in "polite" society—we have come to the time
to talk about economics. We have reached a topic that somehow
appeals to the very lowest and least noble instincts in most of us.
Probably the only thing worse than talking about the effect of
economics on ourselves and our society is not talking about it.

Because I do not like the subject/practice of economics does
not mean I believe it is unimportant—or that being poor is fun—
or that cutthroat competition is a lamb in wolf's clothing. I am not
saying that.

In part, what is at stake is a matter of vision: if one's vision is
no more noble than higher wages or lower prices, then that person
may be in some psychological trouble. To put economics at the
center of any important argument reduces you to a world of dollars—and, I think, casts real doubts on your sense.[1]

But this is not to say economics is not important.

It is a real and live outrage that there are some *so* rich and
many *so* poor. It is an outrage that there are whole groups of people
who take their identity from their financial inheritance, dividend
checks, or saving bonds, while others starve because they were not
"smart" enough to be born rich or of the "right" color.

But that is just the obvious bad; there is much worse.

We hide real issues with false ones; we hide moral problems
with material ones. We reduce everything to our pocketbook, then
we shoot from the hip. We have the capacity to convert every
potential political discussion into the vocabulary of currency, and

---

[1] As a courtesy to the reader, I have taken out most of the puns in this chapter, but
the material does lend itself to low humor.

then cannot figure out why our souls are so poor. We play their games.

Just how many things does one person or one family need? Why do we keep looking out for our financial interests when more often than not they will not solve our real problems? There is no guarantee that being rich will help us be ourselves, or that by gathering money we will avoid being destroyed by that very process.

The urge to acquire, more exactly the proportion and magnitude of that urge, is a sign of something cancerous in our ideology. There can never be enough things—there will never be enough "thing-security." When we put the problem of economics at the center of the universe, we guarantee that our problems will not be solved.

Here we are in college so that we can earn more money than a high-school graduate. I think it appropriate for some honest institution of "higher" education to change its motto from a noble Latin phrase to the American truism: Learn to Earn.

When it gets right down to it, people seem willing to do almost anything for a salary. Being bureaucrats with split work/leisure lives is the destiny for many of us. In an important sense our vision is limited to what is called the root of all evil—we cannot get past our very own economic interest.

Money is the visual sign of the elect, of the elite, and of some of the very worst behavior we can imagine.

It operates on the quicksand of false equality, or in the gray boredom of Soviet Marxism.

There is a classic American definition of politics—who gets what, when, and how—that is a half-step away from economic considerations. We know that the rich get richer, but is that really what politics is/should be about? What about action and behavior and public space?

In the end I'm not entirely satisfied that economics is a topic, but rather an amazingly useful symptom to study. That, in essence, is the way it will be dealt with here. In the following pages, we will look at the world, at industry as religion, and at work and leisure. What is important to remember is that many of our everyday, run-of-the-mill, common sense concepts and myths are remarkably value-laden and exact much from us. Ideas of economics certainly fall into that category.

EATING THE HAND THAT FEEDS US

> *For at least another hundred years we must pretend to ourselves and to everyone that fair is foul and foul is fair; for foul is useful and fair is not. Avarice and usury and precaution must be our gods for a little longer still. For only they can lead us out of the economic necessity into daylight.*

> —John Maynard Keynes

In a couple of chapters we will go through materialism in America. It will be tied to freedom, but with a minimum of imagination it should not be too difficult to see how the discussion would fit just as easily here. Our incredible pseudocapitalism works best when we are all out for ourselves, just producing and consuming as fast as we can. Later, we will see that one of the things we consume is our self. Here, we can start with the obvious: Because of the way we do economics, one of the stakes of our times seems to be the earth itself.

No need for scare tactics: It is simply a fact that we are going about killing the world in very effective ways. Even in economic terms—the economics of numbers and the curious kinds of facts produced by numbers—we are doing a super job of being stupid.

Put in a very simple form, we have had huge successes using technical skills to increase productivity. Nature, seen by many as a friend, has come to be understood as something to conquer. Nature is a resource, a fantastic hunting ground where living things can be converted to spendable cash. Literally the whole world becomes one big technical problem of production. To understand that as shortsighted is to miss the point rather badly.

There is simply some stuff that is irreplaceable. And (guess what?) we're using it up. As winters get cold, we remember that fossil fuels keep getting used up, and there is no reason to believe we will find an adequate replacement. The amount we burn is staggering enough, but the way it is distributed is even more amazing.[2]

The richest nations, according to the United Nations, have 31 percent of the people in the world, and those nations use 87 percent of the fuel currently consumed. If the basic question that concerns you is equality, what about this: "If the 'poor' suddenly used as much fuel as the 'rich,' world fuel consumption would treble right away."[3]

But the question, of course, is not equality. The question is how to stop consuming irreplaceable resources. There are two quick, "practical" responses. The first is the extension of the logic: Let's use it all up as fast as we can. Wonderful. What we get with this is a long pipe threatening the natural ecological balance of Alaska. With the pipeline, we can rest comfortably knowing that another generation of oil companies will make lots of money, that another generation can at least marginally forget about the problem, and at some point part of Alaska will be ruined.

The other "practical" response is nuclear power. While it is unclear that we have yet to dominate the world, it is clear that there are limits beyond which our friendly earth will not be pushed. Maybe one can get a bit of perspective from a former presidential science advisor. He said, about radioactive wastes: "One has a queasy feeling about something that has to stay underground and be pretty well sealed off for 25,000 years before it is harmless."[4]

One solution, of course, is to shoot all that stuff into space so we can pollute the heavens themselves.

The basic point, one so elementary, is that our industry is now in the process of systematically using those materials upon which it is based. Eating, if you will, the hand that feeds it.

If eating is the metaphor, then digestion is a real problem. There is little use to go into the details of pollution. To be as "free as the air you breathe" is now only a sick joke. As part of our summer weather reports, we are told if it is safe to go outside, not because of the heat, exactly, but because of the digestion problems of our

---

[2] E. M. Schumacher, *Small Is Beautiful*, p. 23.

[3] Ibid., p. 24.

[4] Ibid., p. 18.

industry. In Alaska, now that there are so many pollution-producing cars, there is an opposite problem: When it gets too cold, the exhaust freezes and it is unsafe to go outside.

All these things are true: No single person has a cruel enough imagination to dream them up.

In truth, I haven't the heart (or stomach) for the details of the argument: the children or old folks or trees or whales that just don't have a chance given the physical facts of our productive society. Most of you know the tensions that exist between those who want ecological purity and those who want employment.

It is, if we pretend sanity for just a moment, a monument to off-the-point arguments. What kind of society is it that gives us a choice of jobs that will kill us or ecological purity that will starve us? I have read that drowning in a few inches of water is, ultimately, the same as drowning in the deepest part of the ocean.

Generally, discussions of economics, especially "political" discussions, are centered around injustice. There are too few making too much and too many getting too little. Those arguments are correct. Further, unequal distribution of economic resources leads directly to an unequal distribution of power. We all know that, too, is true. But, lurking just beyond these important facts is a whole set of myths that (regrettably) we seem to share. Wanting to be rich is as strong a desire as wanting to stay rich. We are killing ourselves, equally in some ways, unequally in others. Some of us sniff pollution from our Mercedes; others, from public transportation. Some of us kill our bodies with expensive medication; others, by eating food manufactured for animals.

It is both right and wrong to argue that we are—in a true collective effort—killing ourselves. To stop there would be wrong. We are all vulnerable to our industrial/capitalist/consumptive excesses; that's true. But there is no good excuse for people to starve or have no medical care, or no dignity. That the rich are exposed to bad air, water, and food has nothing to do with the injustice of the distribution of wealth.

Instead of going through the statistics that prove wealth and equality have no obvious relationship in our country, it makes more sense to begin to play with economics, and to see it in different ways.

INDUSTRY AS RELIGION

Thus spoke the Devil to me once: "God too has his hell: That is his love of man."

And most recently I heard him say this: "God is dead. . . ."

—*Friedrich Nietzsche*

Let's back up and repeat some of the things we know. We are myth-based creatures. Our myths form the way we see, order, and understand our facts and existence. It can be set up like this: We respond emotionally to a wide range of things. We respond, in part, to what is comfortable. We are capable of creating myths in order to *fill* our feelings. There is another half of this whole.

There are social myths—constructions of reality—that help shape and supply us with myths. When there is a connection between a self-sense and a social construction of reality, it is possible to get an extraordinarily powerful myth: a religion.

At the turn of the century, our industry was pretty "uneconomical" according to almost any standard—animal, vegetable, or mineral. There were amazingly bloody labor disputes, a great many of which can only be understood as human torture; and a man named Frederick Winslow Taylor set out to right wrongs.[5] In a very serious way, Taylor wanted to make a social revolution by bringing rationality and bureaucracy (*that* kind of science) to industry.

He was outraged by inefficiency, and decided that each worker should be as machinelike as possible. He believed in—and worked out—a system to measure each movement with a stop watch so no motion would be wasted. The calculation was that output would be greater, wages would be higher, people would be forced to get along better, and a peaceful revolution could be a by-product of industrial reordering.

It was (and still is) an interesting idea. We need not dwell on some obvious points (for example, his whole scheme is built on the

---

[5] See his *Principles of Scientific Management*. The following was suggested, in part, by the work of Chuck Gleason.

twin notions that everyone is primarily motivated by economic considerations and that there really *is* one-best-way to do a job), as they are frequently dealt with. Instead, we must understand that Taylor tapped a set of basic values in us, and put them together in a brilliant (and probably wrong and destructive) way.

In a real sense, Taylor's set of assumptions led to a dynamic that might best be understood if we use the categories of religion. Think about it:

Sin =	Loafing
Reward =	Higher wages
Ritual =	Very elaborate, involving stopwatches and a whole bureaucracy of specialists performing exotic acts of neatness and cleanliness
Symbolism =	A well-ordered, right-running machine
An Ethic =	Corporate, "cooperative" capitalism
A Messiah/Leader =	Frederick Winslow Taylor, his very own self
Revelation =	It is replaced by prediction. The mystery is sucked from the magical, and we get something less spectacular but something we can count on.
Apocalypse =	In earlier history, there were angry and vengeful gods, plagues, storms, and famine. Now we get class warfare, terrible economic depressions, or the Bomb.
A Perfect Society =	Certainty. Everyone cooperates, does the task he or she is best suited for, and gets just compensation. This, in our liberal society that causes splits in our lives, means that people can go home and be happy.
"Church" =	We need a Sunday School, and we get it in the form of the University. In school we are taught to deal well with

structure. It is easy to argue that much of the meaning of the University, for most of us, is the Structure of the University. As we learn to operate in this bureaucratic setting (spring training for a bureaucratic life), as we subconsciously learn the underlying sense of the reality we are placed in, we are being shaped and molded to understand and operate in an after-university life. Grades, graduate/law/medical school: In the end we hum its hymn, whistle its tune.

Faith Itself =

Traditionally, a real belief is what would stir the gods. To stop believing was to stop the effectiveness of those gods. Now, there is an extraordinarily critical difference: We can stop believing and *this* industrial god keeps on producing.

History =

There is no doubt that we are worshipers. We go to school and learn. We become practitioners, and we strive to fulfill particular kinds of godlike urges from our past. We have come full-circle from the Deists. We become small reflections of the Big God: rational, predictable, productive, well ordered, right-working machines. We come close to filling the dreams; the personal becomes the impersonal; the I becomes the IT.

I give human traits to machines and machine traits to humans.
And it is productive and it is therefore good.
And we all say:

   Amen.

Let me try to get at some of the same material in regular paragraph form. Familiarity is sometimes useful. It seems to me that if we are to take economics seriously we must understand how each of us is involved and affected. In the case of economics, as with all "soft" sciences, it is necessary to look at the assumptions upon which exotic theory grows. Poisoned soil, after all, yields poisoned fruit.

We have seen, and we certainly know, that we don't do a very good job of making food, employment, power—and the accompanying dignity—available to enough people. Further, we are killing the earth and ourselves and leaving the prospect of misery for the next generation.

Another way to get at the problem is to see that the way those events are carried out are, in part, reflections of our mind. Yes, we are sickened by the way we organize and produce and consume and destroy. But we somehow see it as an external thing. The truth is that all those things *organize our minds*. The myths—even the partially playful Religion of Industry—do much to tell us how to see, what to look at, where to act.

There is, to my knowledge, no proof that we were meant to be wholly "rational." It is an invention that is interesting, and sometimes useful, but no one can seriously make the argument that traits of rationality are anything close to a full listing of human traits.

The models of economics, the powerful myths of economics, rest firmly on the notions that we are (or at least should be) rational "actors." The myths and their material products are powerful. They are powerful enough to organize our heads, make us ignore our hearts, and generally encourage us to be a fairly uninteresting lot.

Part of this economics lesson is about its products. I am not arguing that we should embrace poverty, starvation, or illness. Much of the material products of our economics is impressive. But the lesson has to do with our mind-set. It is one, I believe, that is faulty at its very core.

Before getting to hard times and easy times, I would like to get fully involved with "things," to get a better sense of whether more is really enough.

THING-NESS IS NOT ENOUGH-NESS

One of the overwhelming facts about people in the United States is the enormous number of things they have. While it is said and often repeated that things will not make you happy, and while we *know* a poverty of things is not all that fun, the fact is that things—material objects—fill the world we live in.

Jokes are made about our *gross* national product, and there are a number of very good criticisms about what appears to be obsessive consumption; but what seems important right now is to see the dynamic and what is beyond it.

In principle, as each of us is able to own about the same stuff—the same cars, clothes, washing machines, and on and on—we are really becoming more equal. We can all, more or less, look about the same. The *real* difference between Levi's jeans and Sasson jeans is marginal, and it is impossible to tell if a person paid cash for his or her Camaro, or is making monthly payments.

The point is that most of us, most of the time, fit into the same range of dress and action. It would follow that we are becoming more egalitarian.

I do not believe we are.

Once we are in the material-mainstream, the mere having and keeping up is simply not enough. In terms of material things, most products can be had by anyone with enough money. If you do not have the money, you can generally get a bank loan. There is no reasonable limit on the number of TVs Sony can manufacture or cars General Motors can produce.

But our liberal/capitalistic society turns on competition. It is ingrained in our national ideological character (along with other things), and if competition for material goods leads nowhere, then we need to compete for something else.

Something else?

Enter *status*. Enter status goods.

A college education can be our first example. There was a time, in the not so distant past, when only some people went to college. It was not absolutely necessary for an individual to have an education in order to get a reasonably good job, to possibly get rich, to be respected, to live an honorable life in his or her community.

We know that has changed radically. Now a college education seems necessary for just about everyone. So, again in principle, we have become more egalitarian.

But wait. That is just wrong. The fact is that there are colleges, and there are good colleges, and then even better colleges, and the best colleges, and finally the elite ones. There are two truths: The first is that a person can get a good education at any college. No doubt about that. The second truth is more intense—it has to do with status and money in the bank. To get a degree at an elite college means more status and more money. It is not a mistake that competition to get into those schools is so great.

It is the survival of the richest (or those who can take care of the tuition). Or, it is survival of the highest college board scores. It is competition for status. For social position.

Because so much is available to so many the competition will center on those things that are rare and will stay rare. It will be a race for the equivalent of gold when paper money seems worthless. Let me show you.

First there is the elite school. Then there is the job. Ah, but not any job; you will naturally want a job in management that will give you a shot at the top leadership. There are many workers, some managers, but *few* leaders. Leadership is what you want.

You will want the "right" neighborhood. Again limited, again exclusive. An address can set you apart, even if your fancy coat may not.

You will find that even vacations are cut into classes. A summer by the ocean is nice; a beachfront house is much better. After all, there is just so much beachfront. Clearly even IBM cannot produce a limitless amount of beachfront property. And the reality is this: You are either on the beach or not. Close doesn't count.

So, as you sit (or lie or stand) reading this—as you prepare yourself for the marketplace of things—remember that things are no longer enough. Know that the competition for status, and for inequality, is now fully functioning. Know that keeping up materially is actually falling behind in some ways.

Know that even in material things, more is no longer enough.

HARDLY WORKING

When I was in high school, a friend and I invented a person named Dub Hotchkiss. Dub was not too bright. When my friend and I met, one of us would say: "Hi Dub. Working hard?" The other would always answer: "Hardly working."

My secret thought is that if I still lived in Oklahoma, I would continue to have that conversation with my friend.

The point is not that when I was growing up I thought dumb jokes were funny, the point is that in those days we could joke about jobs. Although there were periodic recessions, there were also a lot of jobs. My friend and I simply assumed that we would be employed. It influenced us in ways which we were never aware of. It was as normal to expect to be employed after we graduated as it was to assume that there would always be very big, very powerful cars which would go fast and would consume huge amounts of cheap gasoline.

Now, of course, the phrase *hardly working* has an edge to it. Right now, you might be working as hard as you can and be doing very well. It is altogether possible that you will graduate, and be unemployed.

This section, if you haven't already guessed, is not going to be full of fun and games. But, before we get any more involved with it, there is a fact which we should not forget. There have been periods of unemployment before. That is not news. What I want to remind you of is that there are whole groups of people who are at the bottom of our economic system who never have periods of employment. If you are a white, middle-class college student and angry that you do not have a job waiting for you, what if you were black or brown and not in college?

The plain truth is that whites periodically experience what minorities come to think of as a fact of life. It is an ugly fact that in our up-and-down economic system, some groups are always down.

Currently, there seems to be enough "down" to go around. Our economic system is changing. The industries which we thought of as basic—like steel—are now not so basic. Basic, in the new economic reality, turns out to be a kind of computer language. We now deal in services (lawyers, dentists who practice in malls, a psychologist for our every need) and in high technology.

As college students, that change is a free-floating anxiety, ready to attack at any minute. Personally, it means that you have to cut your hair, look neat, and make good grades. It means being a business major; or maybe go into engineering or computers. It means that you have to know exactly what is expected of you—and then do exactly that.

The arts, the humanities, liberal arts, literature . . . all gone. They have no payoff. We are told that the bottom line for such studies is written in red ink. In a job market with few jobs, many people, and an unclear future, fear overcomes education and students are willing to trade the opportunity to get smarter for the chance to become a technician. For shame.

GOVERNMENT

The awful reality behind all of this is that we are caught between our collective myth of individualism, the obvious strength of the national government, and the inability of anyone to *really* know what to do.

The first thing to go is our myth of individualism. Rugged individualism does not look very impressive on your resume. The sworn enemy of bureaucracy is individualism—and entrepreneurial capitalism. The dream of starting your own business, and becoming successful, is an ongoing one for us. The number of new small businesses is almost equalled by the number of small business failures.

Not only that, when the economy is bad the first businesses to go are the small ones. As individuals, we have just about no power over our economic lives. We are no longer the little engine that could—none of us is much of an engine; in today's economic world we do not have our own tracks. Hair is styled and clothes are tailored in an effort to get onto the bureaucratic track.

Our government, of course, has much to do with this. Since the beginning of the United States, the government has made economic policy. We have never had an economic system free from governmental regulation. Our capitalism has always been one which was tinkered with by the government.

At first, the government just tinkered. As the country grew, and as industry grew, the government grew. The tinkering became much more than that. By the end of World War II, the government and big business were interdependent. From regulatory agencies, to government contracts, to tax policies, to court decisions, to money supply, to trade policies, and so on and so forth, governments at all levels influence the economy.

Too frequently, when we want to talk about politics, we talk about economics.

In a way, it should all work out pretty easily. Politicians, who always have reelection in mind, clearly want the economy to be good. All they have to do is pass those bills which will provide jobs, money for the citizens, and the like. But, the joke is this: Nobody really knows how the economy works.

Goodness knows that there are many sophisticated economic models which predict what will happen given a series of actions. They are all wonderful ideas. They are all right, even though they are mutually exclusive. The one thing they all have in common is this fatal flaw: They believe we—the economic citizens—are rational economic actors and actresses.

Well, we are; but, we are a lot more than that. We are also not rational in a variety of wonderful ways. Good for us.

Of course, that makes life tough for those in politics who want to do the right things to make the economy work. There is just no telling what that might be.

It is even worse for the rest of us. Here we are with no control; there is the government with all kinds of power; there is the economy which is almost always out of control. Free-floating anxiety for sure. In a world without answers, the economy is right at home.

How depressing.

ON HARD TIMES

What's your first reaction when the phone rings in the morning and it's a job call?

"*Oh, crap.*"

—*Studs Terkel*

*An evening of violence and brutality on the television screen
is deemed a mortality play because the culprits are punished
in the last moments of the last act. But Satan dominates
the play ... When the devil is denied, he manifests himself
nonetheless. ...*

—Kenneth Keniston

Work and leisure, two everyday economic topics, are almost too
close to us to figure out. They are givens—facts of life. They are
so common and commonplace that we really don't or maybe even
can't, think very clearly about them.

After all, we know that there is work-time and play-time: You
do one and enjoy the other, and that is just the way it is, so why
worry about it. What I want to argue is that somehow work and
leisure are important—things that we should make an effort to
understand.

Following the logic of the topic, the order will be work now,
and leisure next.

I thought it would be interesting to see how a textbook defined
work. Interesting to see what the scholars had to say. I quote: Work
is a "form of activity that has social approval and satisfies a real
need of the individual to be more active. To produce, to create, to
gain respect, to acquire prestige, and incidentally, to earn money
... the paycheck must mean different things to different people."[6]

So that is what work is in serious language. One of the truly
fantastic things about textbooks is that they often hide, deflect, or
obscure meaning. Sometimes they just lie—and teach us a great
deal by what they systematically miss. We still have our problem:
What does work mean to a person? In a most serious way, maybe
it means this: To many people, most of the time, a job is a job is
a job.

Work is what you do eight hours a day to get money to buy
things. If you do not work, society will shun you. You will not be
able to participate, you will not be able to do or make or buy. Let's
face it: Work is one way society has to keep you off the streets.

---

[6] Milton Blum, *Industrial Psychology: Its Theoretical and Social Foundations* (New
York: Harper & Row, 1968).

Cheaper than jail and very effective.

The tempo is no longer ours. It is not of people, but it is made by people. Ours is an environment genuinely not human. We serve the rhythm of mechanical movement. Labor might have been noble, for it was our own relationship with ourselves—but what we get instead is work, and the brutal logic of the time clock.

In our crazy, complex, capitalist, consuming setting—in our work and leisure life—the individual comes unglued.

Think about it. There is no clear relationship between a job and a finished product. That just no longer exists. One person does one small thing: We are a nation of experts, full of sound and fury, separately signifying nothing.[7] Certainly we know that raw materials are transformed—dead trees or high school graduates are turned into the finished products of paper or consumers. What is magical is that no person involved in that organized work process ever seems either involved or responsible.

We get separated from our very own work. And we get separated from people around us. And we get separated from our own imaginations.

So here we are. Work fills time and space; it displaces our self-worth for money; it divides us from others for material reward; it speeds us up in order to satisfy the logic of machinery.

That is hard work. Enough. Enough. It's time to relax, take a break, get into leisure.

ON EASY TIMES

> *"He did nothing in particular and did it very well."*
>
> W. S. Gilbert

The other day, after a graduate seminar, we were talking about

---

[7] The incredible part is that in the beginning science was exciting and helpful and—sadly—restricted. Listen to this mid-nineteenth-century story: "The Royal Institute, which existed in England to further the progress of science and its application to industry, was forced, when it became a fashionable place to visit and wished to preserve its exclusivity, to brick up its back door to keep out the mechanics who stole into the gallery." In Harry Braverman, *Labor and Monopoly Capital: The Degradation of Work in the Twentieth Century* (New York: Monthly Review Press, 1974), p. 134.

the differences between the modest incomes of graduate students and the much larger incomes of the very wealthy. One student was quiet for a while, and then told this story.

He had met and talked with a person of about his age, and later was invited to this person's home. He accepted the invitation and went. What he found was surprising: The new acquaintance and his wife lived in a huge house filled with very expensive things. Neither worked. Both were bored. Life was gray.

They were both very involved with therapy.

The student, a little uncomfortable and with nothing to say, did not stay long. As he told us the story he just shrugged and said: "They blew it."

In a real sense, that may be a key issue to leisure: "We blew it."

What do we do when we are free from work? One thing, of course, is that we fill our social and economic obligations. We spend money to fill time, to fulfill our ego, to try and fool our frustrations. We spend and consume, spend and are consumed.

Then we're broke—spent, if you will—and we go back to the highly structured situation of work. So we repeat ourselves.

It is more involved than that. We watch television, see a movie, get drunk, chase men or women. Essentially, just escape. Get our minds off things, off school or work or whatever. Dull ourselves. Become mindless and meaningless in our "off" hours. Leisure, to be sure.

What the hell good is it, is leisure, if it does not somehow relate to work? We work so we can escape it, but our escape is all too often uninterestingly blah. Our work and leisure should be extensions of each other. To put it differently, without meaningful labor we cannot expect meaningful leisure. To isolate the two leads directly to all kinds of alienation.

We should feel cheated. We need work and play in order to feel good about ourselves, in order to feel needed. Easy times, it seems, aren't necessarily easy in the long run, and not necessarily a blessing if you use time poorly.

To talk about economics, to get right down to it, we might want to begin with saving our lives—socially and spiritually. A reasonable economic question would be: How do we make the world safe for itself and for its people? A reasonable way to begin to answer is to do what we can to ignore corporate capitalist/socialist/Marxist economics. While it is clear that these systems do not go out of their way to abuse common sense, it certainly *seems* that way. Some kinds of capitalism can be good and some kinds of Marxism bad, and it works just as easily the other way around. To get into the details is not worth our time just now.

In an essay entitled "Buddhist Economics," E. F. Schumacher writes that work should fill these three functions: "to give a man a chance to utilize and develop his faculties; to enable him to overcome his ego-centeredness by joining with other people in a common task; and to bring forth the goods and services for a becoming existence."[8]

More gets built into that kind of work. It makes sense to continue to use Schumacher's words.

> Wisdom demands a new orientation of science and technology towards the organic, the gentle, the non-violent, the elegant and beautiful. . . . We must look for a revolution in technology to give us inventions and machines which reverse the destructive trends now threatening us all.
>
> . . . We need methods and equipment which are
> —cheap enough so that they are accessible to virtually everyone;
> —suitable for small-scale application; and
> —compatible with man's need for creativity.[9]

It is not difficult to see what is left out of these calculations. No talk of manager elites and of the masses. They simply have no place when economics becomes a serious affair for individuals. Nor is there the false calculation that large size is more "economical" than small, or the desire to try to quantify the concepts of gentleness, elegance, and beauty.

The way we choose to operate our material relationships, our economics, is a basic question of how we live our lives and how we do our politics. The important value questions we ask for ourselves should be asked of our economics.

---

8 Schumacher, *Small Is Beautiful,* p. 51
9 Ibid., pp. 31–32.

If we try tying labor with leisure, producing in a nondestructive way, making work compatible with creativity, making goods and services accessible in a more equitable way—if we decide on these kinds of values, we can only expect a world radically different (and probably much more wonderful) than we have now.

It seems safe to assume that there will be no one best way to answer the new set of questions, no one set of people, no single class or council or committee or board of directors that will give us folks the word. The way we choose to organize and to create should take its directions from our self, our physical surroundings, and our social setting. As each gets mixed in different amounts for different reasons, and as we relearn the uses of our imaginations, our economic dealings and our politics and our lives will line up in ways to make all of those things more interesting.

I can think of no way to make the notion clear and understandable. When there are no single answers, but only sets of multiple answers, one is forced to sacrifice the clarity of dogma.

Let me try it this way: Imagine that instead of General Motors, America had a number of independent, small, beautiful, organic peaceful places making different kinds of transportation vehicles. Instead of General Motors, America would be full of Specific Motors.

Focus Four

As a warmup for applying rightfittingness to American politics and in order to deal with a set of concerns intermingled with politics, this chapter puts economics, work, and leisure into the political perspective of the book.

Life requires an income; the usual source is work. Most of you will spend a significant portion of your waking hours at a job. Government decisions regularly influence work and the economy in general. Work and working conditions should make sense. How does a person decide what is best economically for himself or herself and the world of other people?

This chapter offers the following advice. First, economics is not the heart of politics because political freedom is more important than economic freedom. One can put economics into that perspective by remembering that neither capitalism nor socialism guarantees political freedom. Either may foster it even though we usually associate socialism with the Soviet Union's totalitarianism and strict political control of economic life, thus, overlooking the numerous captialist economies which also are politically repressive. Second, think what you would really like to do for work and what you might be good at before determining how much that work is worth in money. Don't be foolish about economics; money is helpful. Still, don't allow dollar signs to dictate your life's work. Simple counsel against greedy materialism.

Third, try to find and do the work you want. Follow your nose thoughtfully and prudently. Determine whether your work, as previously imagined, now actually does make intrinsic sense; that is, whether what you are spending so much time doing is worthwhile in the world regardless of its monetary value. Then check whether you are doing sufficiently well in dollar terms to live with dignity.

The chapter assumes that most Americans will prefer work that adds something of genuine value to the world, a sense of power over their jobs, and small-scale economic organization rather than large. Nevertheless, large organizations are here to stay for the foreseeable future; we need talented people in them, who are thinking about rightfittingness. The logic of the argument of this chapter is that if everyone tried hard to find rightfitting work, then the present organizational conditions of work would improve. Individual attempts at economic rightfittingness would add to more humane work envvironments since rightfittingness is connected to deep moral roots and carefully considered ideas about what is best for the individual and the world. Once work became more engaging, leisure too would be more satisfying since the urge to escape boring work into mindless leisure would diminish.

The following excerpt from a recently published fantasy suggests that the grindstone to which one puts the nose can be fair as well as practical. The point of including it is to encourage the dreaming required for trying economic experiments based on a sense of rightfittingness instead of accepting all present work arrangements as inexorably fixed.

No less ingenious than the physical quarters of *The Sun* [a newspaper] was its social and economic organization. Perhaps owing to Isaac's hard days washing pots, the Penns had always believed in a high minimum wage. Their editorial columns persistently inveighed against the idea of welfare for the ablebodied, and government social programs that were little more than elaborate patronage schemes. For this, they were repeatedly condemned in liberal circles. On the other hand, they were just as persistent in advocating what was considered to be a sky-high minimum wage. (They believed that hard and good work deserved its reward, and responded to arguments from conservatives that such a wage would create unemployment and dampen entrepreneurial drive, with the counterargument that the latter could be sustained and would flourish with the concomitant business-tax reductions made possible by greater income equality and a smaller welfare burden.)

The Penns were not a hundredth as rich as the Binkys [owners of the competing paper], and, whereas the Binkys had accumulated their wealth by grinding people into the ground, the Penns had done nothing of the sort. First, everyone on *The Sun,* from a kitchen helper who had been there for an hour, to Harry Penn himself, received exactly the same wage and benefit package—*exactly.* And it was a good one, too, good enough to make any job on the paper a great prize. Every *Sun* employee enjoyed equal privileges in regard to pension, health care, access to the athletic facilities in the basement, and admission to the cafe and restaurant. Anyone could take advantage of the generous educational benefits, and throw in music lessons on the side. And yet, there was every reason to work hard and advance within the organization.

The Sun was patterned after a whaling enterprise. After all expenses were paid out and everyone had his living, the profits were divided according to an elaborate system of shares. No one other than an employee of the paper was entitled to shares, and they were neither inheritable nor transferable. Each employee received five shares upon joining. Thereafter, for every advance he made he received another five, and one share for each year he had worked. There were twenty levels of advancement, and there was seniority. For example, after his first year, a kitchen helper would normally own six shares. After several years on the staff, Hardesty Maratta (who had come in on level eight) had worked his way to level twelve. Thus, with his five original shares, sixty for his work level, and five for the years he had put in, he would have had seventy shares. But he actually had eighty, because he had won two merit awards of five shares apiece. Harry Penn had been with the paper (starting at age ten as a copy boy) for eighty-five years. He was, naturally, at level twenty. He had five original shares, and, when he was younger and could win awards (for which the editor-in-chief and the publisher were not eligible), he had won ten of them. This left him with 240 shares, quite a lot more than his kitchen helper's six, but not that many more than Hardesty's eighty. Were the kitchen helper to stay (as indeed he probably would, for the wages and benefits alone) for ten years, advance two levels to kitchen supervisor, and win an award for his salad, his lentil soup, or, let us say, pulling a baby from the path of Craig Binky's speeding limousine, he would have a total of thirty shares.

This system tickled not only ambition, but productivity as well. Since the number of shares was not fixed, and since whatever profit accrued each year was finite (the notion of infinite profit haunted only Craig Binky, who hired economists and sorcerers to see if it was possible), it was to everyone's advantage to work hard—not only to produce a higher profit, but to hold down the number of jobs and, thus, the number of shares. *The Sun's* employees wanted to serve it as best they could, not only because doing so was in their interests, but because *The Sun* was fair—and they could feel this in the same way that they could feel beauty in a landscape. How delightful, too, to know that not only could they feel it, but it could be demonstrated by several systems of logic, and by the way people looked when they came in, morning and evening.

And *The Sun's* remarkably equitable and effective social system originated not in the barrel of a gun, nor in any cruelty, nor in the French Communes, nor with revolutionary violence, nor in the imagination of a reader in the library of the British Museum, but in the nineteenth-century American whaling ship.[10]

The most enduring American dream of rightfittingness about work has been the goal of owning a business. This aspiration had a full measure of reality in the 1800s when 80 percent of the labor force worked for themselves, usually as farmers. By the 1950s, the statistics where reversed, 80 percent of the labor force worked for someone else.[11] Although many Americans, including a number of you, will attempt the entrepreneurial dream, the statistics suggest that alternatives to the traditional theme also will be increasingly apparent. The excerpt quoted points in a direction which has been followed by some since the 1960s—not self-employment but joint employee-owner profit-sharing. The second to last paragraph of the passage states in its own way the point of this chapter—rightfittingness can be applied to economics. *"The Sun·was fair"* and its work force felt it to be so; "several systems of logic and the way people looked when they came in, morning and evening," demonstrated their satisfaction. Their corner of the economic world was organized in a way that encouraged their best selves.

Dream, hope, try hard for your own rightfittingness about work; be smart about trying. The townsmen of the 1800s were politically independent in part because 80 percent of them took sole responsibility for their own economic affairs. One twentieth century equivalent for encouraging an independent spirit is sustained effort to find and maintain rightfitting work.

---

[10] Mark Helprin, *Winter's Tale* (New York: Pocket Books, 1984), pages 391–393.

[11] C. Wright Mills, *White Collar* (New York: Oxford University Press, 1956), page 63.

5

POLITICS AS FRAUD:

LIBERALISM AND VOTING IN AMERICA

While studying liberalism, I came across the following quote which does much to sum up the problem: "The way this business is run," said the lady, "we would have failed long ago if we did not make so much money."

[People] have to make themselves predictable, otherwise the machines get angry and kill them.

—Gregory Bateson

Murray Edelman tells the story of the election-day interview of a Little Old Lady in England.

"Who are you going to vote for?" she was asked.
"Oh, I never vote," she said. "It encourages them so."

I am a good friend of a fellow whose family never tells jokes. All they say are the punch lines of jokes they told years before. Sometimes one of them will offer a new punch line, and generally the rest of the family will be able to construct an appropriate story around it. In many ways, that is how Americans are about voting. The punch line is always "vote"; only the story changes to make the punch line seem appropriate.

It would be unreasonable to begin with the idea that voting in America is a positive virtue and then to continue our study from there. Indeed, given the biases of society—of Madisonian people, in an objective world, organized bureaucratically—we cannot understand voting out of its context. It would seem reasonable to argue that, considering the way we have set up voting in America, voting is only a trivial distraction to keep the masses happy, to keep them occupied, to keep them powerless.

But that is getting ahead of ourselves. Before we get to the view of voting that makes it seem worse than irrelevant, there are certain historical and social science things we should know. We should know what our ideology has to do with government and our attitudes toward it. We should know how political scientists, and the general mythology of society, view voting. Finally, we must begin to develop a different way of questioning what voting is all about.

LIBERALISM

The United States is a self-consciously liberal country. All our scholars agree, and surely our common sense tells us, that for a long time we citizens of America have held (pretty much) the same view of the world. We believe the same general truths, have the same general kind of ideology; in sum, we are all liberals in a liberal state.[1]

It is important to make clear that when I use the term "liberal," I mean something more by it than that "Democrats" are somehow "liberal" and "Republicans" are somehow "conservative." Beneath the common liberal/conservative language of our newspapers lie the

---

[1] The following discussion of liberalism is based on Louis Hartz, *The Liberal Tradition in America* (New York: Harcourt, Brace & World, 1955).

classic liberal and conservative political theories. It would be wrong to say that liberal tradition is the only one in America, that it is the only ideology. We are now in the process of rediscovering the Puritans and the Populists, the Southern bourbon aristocracy and the Wobblies, the Native Americans, the blacks, and the Chicanos. But, as we shall see, it would be equally wrong to argue that America is anything other than a liberal state—in the classic sense—or that the vast majority of her citizens are not liberals.[2]

> *He nodded heavily and called for another scotch & soda. "It's a goddamn shame," he muttered. "But what can you really expect? You lie down with pigs and they"ll call you a swine every time. . . ."*
>
> —*Kurt Vonnegut, Jr.*

> *As for politics, I think Art Buchwald said it all last month. . . . "I always wanted to get into politics, but I was never light enough to make the team."*
>
> —*Hunter Thompson*

A LOCK(E) ON US

Liberalism, at least in its American manifestation, is in large part the intellectual formulation of the Englishman John Locke.[3] The writers of the American Constitution had read Locke, and his influence on them is obvious. At the time Locke wrote, the medieval world was ending. The guilds and the fiefs and the manors of western Europe were crumbling, and the nation-states were being built. This change led to a tension in Locke's liberalism, and ultimately to a tension in American liberalism.

There are several ways in which one can view what people were like in a mythical state of nature. Maybe people were noble savages, maybe just savages. John Locke believed that if left alone,

---

[2] Indeed, one of the first—and most important—problems for any minority is to avoid being co-opted by the liberal ideology.

[3] It is very instructive to read John Locke, *The Second Treatise of Government* (Indianapolis: Bobbs-Merrill, 1952).

most people, most of the time, would get along all right. There would be harmony, but not total peace. This was not to say that government was unnecessary. In fact, Locke wrote that government was important, especially as a counterweight to the tyranny of the Church, the guilds, and the manors of medieval times. Locke thought that the state should have control over all of them. But Locke was more complex than that. He also believed that, potentially, government could do evil.

So, in his liberal state, government was to act only as a referee, as a judge for the people. This would allow the people to do just about what they wanted to do (privately), while being assured that their property—something tied closely to their lives and happiness—would be protected. But it also did one other thing. It divided the public and the private; the crease that divided the one from the other was to become a huge split, with the important half of the split being the private.

> *There is not much difference in basic temperament between a good tight end and a successful politician. They both go down in the pit and do whatever has to be done—then come up smiling, and occasionally licking blood off their teeth.*
>
> —*Hunter Thompson*

We Americans both added to and misunderstood Lockean liberalism. Certainly our heritage seems to include the idea that a citizen should be afforded rights. We assume life and liberty and the pursuit of happiness/property. We also think we are guaranteed any religion, a fast trial, and the right to assemble. All these seem to be for the good.

But what we do not assume, what we do not seem to have, is the space in which to act like citizens. While we are given rights, we are not given the responsibility for acting on those rights.

This, in many important ways, is a major flaw in our liberalism. The citizen is granted rights but is given no place to exercise them; each person has potential power, but no place to actualize it. The individual is given political tools, but no area in which he or she may act politically.[4] Surely we have tried to turn things on their heads.

Part of the problem is due to the fact that the American experience was not the European one. Locke was well aware that institutions unchecked by government could be repressive. That was the lesson of feudalism. But America had never experienced feudalism, had never known the tyranny of the private realms. So, only half of Locke was accepted. We liberals assume that government might be evil, that it might be repressive. What we forget is that government was to be set up to protect us. Because of our fear of government, we set it up to protect us from itself. Further, we have a belief in a "private realm" that we think is best left unregulated.

> *"Politics is property," said Murry Kempton, a delegate from New York . . . and never was a new science comprehended better by a young delegate. [The President] was the first preceptor of the key that politics-is-property so you never give something away for nothing. Convention politics is therefore not the art of the possible so much as the art of what is possible when you are dealing with property holders. A delegate's vote is his holding—he will give it up without return no more than a man will sign over his house entire to a worthy cause.*
>
> —*Norman Mailer*

In essence, we have managed to make liberalism a double curse. We are continually getting raped by the private. We get polluted and paved and built around and torn down in the name of free enterprise. On the other hand, we fear government in part because we have no control over it. Both realms are uncontrolled by the people. We will not control the private because of our faith; nor can we control our government because of our fear.

So we are caught between the terror of anarchy and the tyranny of the state. We become immobilized by our beliefs.

---

[4] This point is made most clearly in Hannah Arendt, *On Revolution* (New York: Viking Press, 1963).

As it turned out, [his] campaign was totally flawed from the start. It was all tip and no iceberg. . . .

The main problem with any democracy is that crowd-pleasers are generally brainless swine who can go out on a stage & whup their supporters into an orgiastic frenzy—then go back to the office & sell every one of the poor bastards down the tube for a nickel apiece.

—*Hunter Thompson*

Locke wrote that the state was formed by a contract between the people and the government. Each had a duty, each had much responsibility. Locke carefully explained that when the government failed to carry out its responsibilities, then it was the duty of each citizen to break the contract.

That is a serious thought: to break the contract. Regrettably, it is a thought with which we all must come to terms. When we do, when we think about breaking the contract, we find a problem. A real one. We find that our liberalism gives us no hint of an alternative, no idea of anything different. We seem stuck, afraid of more government or of less government, of more freedom or of less freedom. We are waxed statues that melt under the pressure of trying to create.

We seem to be unable to think of change; so we hang our heads and hold our noses, and go to the polls periodically to vote. Once every two years or four years or more, we fool ourselves into thinking we are saving freedom, protecting democracy, by pulling a lever of a machine. We are so proud, so self-righteous.

But as we vote, we never think that voting does nothing but condemn us to the status quo. To vote is the ultimate act of futility; it is to pretend change while prolonging stability. Our only act of citizenship, our only public act, turns out to be a private farce. As we vote, we simply endorse our own immobility.

The two real political parties in America are the Winners *and the* Losers. *The people do not acknowledge this. They claim membership in two imaginary parties, the* Republicans *and the* Democrats, *instead . . . losers can join imaginary parties. Losers can vote.*

—*Kurt Vonnegut, Jr.*

Wrong you say? Imagination you say? What about Salvador Dali? Salvador Dali is a hero of mine. A man of genius and imagination who has been an artistic creator in our century. He is now an old man and lives in a castle. Nearby, in a neighboring castle, lives his wife, who was a Russian princess. They are growing old together, in a very stylized way. When Dali has a picture, or some such thing to show his wife, he sends her a message to that effect.

In return, Dali receives a formal, written invitation for tea the next day at his wife's castle. He goes and, one imagines, they enjoy themselves. It seems to be a very workable and satisfactory arrangement.

The point is that as liberal Americans, we understand *neither* part of Dali. He outflanks us on *both* sides. Not only is he more creative than we; he is also more formal, stylized, "conservative" than we. He sees the beauty of the artistic frontier as well as the richness of social form. I am not arguing we should do both, or either for that matter. What seems so striking is that we can't do much of one or the other; even our imagination cuts us off from feeling why Dali can live and do both.

We are dead-center liberals, missing the best of both worlds.

THE VOTING FETISH

To begin to truly understand voting in America, we must put the whole discussion in context. We have got to know just how it fits into our view of the world. It may be best to discuss it by "pretending." Pretend that we are constructing a state. This state is to be inhabited by evil people; the population is to be motivated by self-interest. The world view is to be scientific. That is to say, reality and value are to be attributed only to those things that are physical and material, to those things that are countable and quantifiable. Finally, the population is to organize itself bureaucratically.

As good political scientists, as good creators, we would have to deal with a very fundamental problem: How do we keep citizens within the system? How can we give them an illusion of power so as to keep them content? How can we distract them from important questions—and possibly from answers—while making trivial behavior seem important? The answer is deceptively simple: Make voting a meaningless gesture (both to the individual and to the society), but also make voting a myth of important proportions.

Discussions of voting, and the questions asked about it, almost always miss the point. To look at how voting is discussed is an exercise in understanding how questions can predetermine answers. To understand the voting fetish, we must familiarize ourselves not only with the common questions and answers but also begin to ask questions not ordinarily asked.

The idea of voting is important in America, very important. The public schools pump our heads full of the importance of elections, the TV networks spend millions on election coverage, and we social scientists study and restudy elections and electors and the electorate. Even bars are closed on election day to ensure that we become heady from voting and not drunk from liquor. Before one election has begun, people are making plans for the following one. There seems little doubt that elections—and voting—are the biggest games in town; but do they really mean anything? To put it differently, what does it mean to vote? How does it count?[5]

Political scientists have worked hard studying elections. In part, elections are perfect to study if one believes in objective reality. Voting is an objective fact. A vote is something real, something that can be counted, computed, and "played with" in a variety of ways. Further, about the time one batch of votes is used up, there is another election and another batch. So we know a great deal about voting and we are told much about elections. For example, the distinguished political scientist Austin Ranney writes:

> . . . political scientists study the behavior of individual voters in order to understand the behavior of electorates, for their object is to comprehend the forces affecting the outcome of elections, which, as we shall see, are the principal democratic devices for holding government responsible to the people.[6]

---

[5] The argument has even made that the importance of the process lies in its folly. For instance, Herbert McClosky has written, "It is not clear . . . that either the parties or voters want the conventions reformed. Like the circus to which they are sometimes compared, they are among the greatest shows on the earth." The *New York Times Magazine,* August 4, 1968.

[6] Austin Ranney, *Governing* (New York: Holt, Rinehart & Winston, 1971), p. 141.

It is all there—the myth of voting, that is. Let us examine the findings of those who study voting and elections, and see if we can understand the myth more clearly. More importantly, we could understand what they don't ask.

There have been few studies on the psychological differences between police and criminals and the reason is not difficult to discover. The studies based on the usual psychological tests fail to detect a significant difference.

If civilization has made modern man a natural schizophrenic (since he does not know at the very center of his deliberations whether to trust his machines or the imperfect impressions still afforded him by his distorted senses and the more or less tortured messages passed along by polluted water, over-fertilized ground, and poisonously irritating air), the average man is a suicide in relation to his schizophrenia. He will suppress his impulses and die eventually of cancer, overt madness, nicotine poisoning, heart attack, or the complications of a chest cold. It is that minorty—cop and crook—which seeks issue for violence . . .

—*Norman Mailer*

Indeed, the list of schizophrenic symptoms reads like a cultural inventory of postindustrial society.

—*Larry Spence*

The argument about voting often centers around the idea of democracy. In a simple-minded way, we are taught that to vote is democratic and that those who vote will have a say in determining policy. Political scientists are interested in who votes, in part to see which groups choose those who govern. Who votes? The more education a person has, the more likely the individual is to vote. The higher an individual's income, the greater the chances of his or her voting. More white people than black vote, and more white-collar than blue-collar workers vote. Finally, more men than women vote. ("One woman respondent told an interviewer, 'Woman is a flower for men to look after'; another said, 'I have never voted, I never will . . . A woman's place is in the home'; and a third declared, 'Voting is for the men.' ")[7]

The suggestion has been made that the nonvoters—the black, the blue-collar, the "uneducated"—may not vote because they believe that elections make no difference.[8] Simply stated, these individuals hold that whoever—Democrat or Republican—holds power does not hold it for their benefit. On the other hand, the voter— the white, the "well-educated," the white-collar worker—may really believe that his or her vote makes a difference and that voting in national elections could change the world.[9]

To understand the nature of elections and the nature of our party system is to begin to understand that the "uneducated" black who failed to vote may well be right.

> *But you must know in your heart that every Winner knows: that one must behave heartlessly toward losers, if one hopes to survive. . . .*
>
> *All the rest was hokum.*
>
> —*Kurt Vonnegut, Jr.*

One basic criticism of elections is that they are not democratic. There is more than some truth in this contention. It is important to understand this point of view and, then to understand why it does not get us far enough.[10] To be democratic, elections should

---

[7] Ibid., p. 147. It is just such statements that point out how difficult the task of liberation will be.

[8] Ibid., p. 148.

[9] What about advertising people? Those modern moralists of Madison Avenue? ". . . many [ad] agencies reject [selling candidates] as unethical or demeaning . . . a stand which infuriates George Lois. 'Some idiots say it's morally wrong to do political ads,' he fumes. 'They're proud of selling some goddam deodorant, but not a person who can do things for the country.' To which Jerry Della Femina, another ad agency chief who refuses political ads, replies: 'No deodorant ever bombed Cambodia.' " (*Newsweek*, April 12, 1976, p. 88. Copyright 1976 by Newsweek, Inc. All rights reserved. Reprinted by permission.)

[10] Thomas Dye and Harmon Zeigler, *The Irony of Democracy* (Belmont, Calif.: Wadsworth Publishing Co., 1970), p. 174.

fulfill the following four requirements. First, either the parties or the candidates should offer clear-cut choices to the voters. Not a choice of hair color or of speaking style, but of politics and programs. Second, the voters must be concerned with and aware of the choices. Third, voting should somehow indicate how the majority feels about the issues. Finally, when a candidate is elected, he or she should somehow be bound by his or her promises. What we know about elections indicates that none of these conditions is met, or is even in very much danger of being met.

First things first. Are these policy alternatives? The answer is no. People do not run on issues; they run to be elected. Political parties are interested in winning the greatest number of votes; so, they try to avoid taking stands that might offend or bringing up issues that seem to deviate too far from the center of things. When two parties equally intent on winning the election clash, the party that is the most vague may well triumph. Making clear the difficult issues is simply risky electoral politics. Our parties, our candidates, almost always play follow the leader; the funny part is that the leader never gets off dead center.

> *The convention had left me speechless. It was so heavily guarded, spiritually and physically, that I hadn't been able to see or hear anything that wasn't already available in an official press release. "It's Disneyland under martial law," I said.*
>
> —*Kurt Vonnegut, Jr.*

Because the major parties deliberately try not to articulate the choices, the answer to our second condition is easy: The voters cannot be aware of policy alternatives when there are none. I blush at the redundance of the statement.

If people do not vote on issues, why do they vote? Generally speaking, people join the same party their parents joined. When elections come, most people, most of the time, vote for the candidate of their party. If people vote according to party, then what do the parties do, what functions do they serve?

Robert Dahl argues that political parties are of great help to the voter because they "present to voters a very small number of alternatives out of the total number theoretically available."[11] So that is what parties do! They help us to make rational choices by limiting those choices to two. They ease our anxiety over right and wrong—or, at least over whom or what to vote for—by limiting our selection to a seemingly identical set of alternatives. Parties make it possible for us to choose between two representatives of the system—and they make the choice relatively unencumbered by numbers.

> *Ambrose Bierce once defined a President as one of two men about whom we know this: Many millions of people do not want him to be President.*
>
> —*George Will*

Is it possible somehow for voting to indicate how the majority feels about the issues? The answer, of course, is no. With two—or three—candidates hedging on the issues, and each taking weak stands on many issues, it is simply naive to believe that a vote can be translated into support for a particular policy or set of policies. Our elections are not organized so that the voter can help decide what the major policies of the country will be. When an individual is elected, all that means is that he or she gets to hold office. Because the campaign promises were vague or silly or both, and because we do not really expect such promises to be kept, policies are not the result of elections.

So maybe that poor black person is right not to vote. In 1968, 40 percent of the people who were eligible did not vote; in 1972, 44.6 percent didn't; by 1974 the percentage was up to 63.8. There just are not that many blacks in the country.

The fact is that, with all of the elections in the United States, people just do not vote very much. The average voter turnout in national elections since 1960 is about 59 percent. Let's compare: It is 75 percent in Great Britain, 88 percent in Sweden and Germany, and almost 92 percent in Belgium. If you think 59 percent is not representative. If you think 59 percent is pitiful, what do you think

---

[11] Robert Dahl, *Pluralist Democracy in the United States* (Chicago: Rand McNally & Co., 1967), p. 250.

about the fact that the turnout was 54 percent in 1976? Hardly inspiring.

Why is it so low? Well, there are rationalizations. One wonderful rationalization for the steady hundred-year decline in voting (in 1876 about 80 percent of the eligible voters voted) is that there was so much fraud then. The best example is from West Virginia. In 1888, West Virginia recorded 159,440 votes. Not at all bad for 147,408 eligible voters. Now that is really taking voting seriously: a turnout of 108 percent.

We need not go all the way back to 1888 to find real fraud. In 1983 there was a trial in Oklahoma about the voting practices in the 1982 elections. It seems that there is a long history of illegal practices in Oklahoma. The attorney general of the state said: "When I first ran for politics, someone asked me if I knew what a political taxidermist was. They said it was someone who stuffed ballots."

The case of fraud was made. Witnesses said that votes were for sale for $5 or a bottle of liquor. Many of the thirty-six people who testified said they had been paid for their votes. But, guilty was not so bad. One candidate and his wife pleaded no contest to charges of voting fraud. They were placed on probation for one year. Why? Why just probation for tampering with the backbone of democracy?

The answer, in part, is history. This is the explanation of the assistant district attorney: ". . . it's kind of difficult to put someone in the pokey for this since it has been going on for so long."

There was an old saying on election day: Vote early and vote often. While there was certainly some truth to that, it cannot explain our decline in voting.

There are other reasons why we do not vote. In one "accounting" of voting in a typical textbook, the author gives the Cost and Benefits of voting.[12] There is something sadly normal in getting a CPA vision of a supposed political act. Anyway, the "costs":

1. Having to register is time consuming.

---

[12] James Q. Wilson, *American Government* (Lexington, Mass.: D. C. Heath, 1980), pp. 195–196.

2. Learning about candidates may be difficult.

3. Voting takes time.

4. Getting to the polling place on your own is trouble.

5. Waiting in line to vote is a drag.

And maybe a point six: "Remember, federal elections are in November, when it is often cold and rainy."

Well, all is not lost. There are two reasons to vote, two "benefits": the sense of satisfaction that comes from doing your duty, and the one chance in a million your vote will make a difference. (That is a benefit?)

There are, to me, several very notable things that need to be mentioned. In the thirty-nine-page "Elections and Campaigning" chapter of this Standard Book, the author made the choice to simply drop this "fact" on us: Voting is our duty. The chapter is full of information about campaigning, campaign staffs, money, and the like. But the key to the whole process—what it means or does not mean to vote—is barely mentioned.

In Chapter 2, there was a discussion of the two levels of communication. The first level is what was actually said and done; the second level is the context which is central to the meaning of the action. Voting is the first level of communication, while the reasons to vote are the second level. What is lacking is an intelligent discussion about the reasons. Because the reasons are assumed, we are caught with the feeling that voting is foolish (at best), but must assume that our feeling is wrong.

Consider the costs and benefits we just went through. Certainly the costs are very small *if* we think of voting as an important act. We know, for instance, that many people have to go through at least that much (plus pay money) just to play golf or tennis. We might want to consider the proposition that something is wrong when voting is less important to people than either tennis or golf.

According to the two benefits of voting, it is not hard to see why people do not vote. To argue that a person might have to vote in a million elections in order to have one vote count sounds like very bad odds to me. To proclaim that voting is our duty has a way of tugging at our emotions.

What would be nice, as well as helpful, would be an explanation of why it is our duty. (A hint about studying a new subject: You can learn a great deal if you question those things that *seem* self-evident. *Self-evident* is all too often the code word for underlying bias.)

As a semi-serious aside, maybe voting is good because a person is able to label himself or herself. We know there are voting blocs—which mean something to how candidates conduct themselves. Maybe those blocs do more than that.

Periodically, whole new groups of people are discovered. Gary Hart discovered yuppies (young upwardly mobile professionals). While it is accurate to say they were not really discovered by Hart, he certainly popularized them by politicizing them. The election (and it was only a primary) gave a sense of group identity to those among us who: eat croissants and kiwi fruit, wear Nike running shoes with their business suit (female or male), just love their Saab (Volvo or BMW), can't do without their Cuisinart, own at least one Nautilus exercise machine, and "do" quality time with their infants by trying to get them to learn French verbs with flash cards.

Now, there are apparently many Americans who are yuppies, and they felt isolated until the election. Happily, they are finally an identifiable voting bloc, and presumably lonely no more.

There is another fact that seems important. The chapter following the one on elections in this Standard Textbook is about interest groups. As you might recall, interest groups were introduced in the first chapter. What we found was that—according to this normal book—Americans joined groups at a comparatively high rate because of what the author characterized as a "stronger sense of civic duty."

Why do you suppose we exercise our "civic duty" by joining private organizations instead of voting? Voting, in principle, should be a supremely political action. It seems our Standard Textbook has taken politics and, with ease, has stood it on its head. Turned it upside down. It is *1984*. It is doublespeak.

Public action is not civic duty.

Civic duty is to be done in private.

Public is private.

Now I know that sounds a little harsh. Certainly it will occur to you that the author does not really mean what I am claiming he means. Maybe he does not; the fact is, if he does not mean that, we can only guess what he really means. (Myth-maker, myth-maker, make me a myth.) Aside from that, the text itself is instructive.

What this Standard Book shows, in part, is what I am trying to show in larger part. By taking the same material that we normally read and putting that material in a context that pays more attention to all the facts, we can see the standard biases much more clearly. Public is private. Civic duty is silence.

That makes it easier to understand the fraud of voting.

In the future the definition of an exciting election may change. Instead of being excited about who might win, we might be excited to see if anyone votes.

> *Two thoughts about voting. H. L. Mencken advised: "Let us hold our noses and do our duty." Gene McCarthy, on being a good democrat: "I'm voting for Humphrey, and I think you should suffer with me."*
>
> —*Gary Wills*

Surely voting must do something, help someone. Oddly enough, it is not entirely clear just who does gain from elections. The voter may gain psychic satisfaction in knowing that he or she has "protected democracy" or whatever other symbol that citizen was serving. Someone gets elected; so certainly that someone is helped. In honesty, I believe the best we can do, the most we can say, is that voting contributes to the system. It symbolically hooks people to the process, at little or no risk to that process. Systems seek stability, and for us voting has uniquely served the status quo.

There are too many ways to make the ties between ourselves and our myths and our voting. One way to do it is to review some fairly recent history.

DUTY/PRIVILEGE

Before discussing more current events, I want to be as clear as I can about the mixture of each of us, of voting, and of the government.

It is not at all unusual for an individual to think of the vote as a privilege. After all, it is a way of being grateful for not living in a repressive society. It is, to put it differently, a way to express our gratitude for living in a free society.

The burden of the argument of the chapter has been that the government deserves gratitude and respect only to the extent that it makes popular sovereignty genuinely real. If voting is a shame; if voting has gotten to be nothing more than a symbolic act symbolizing nothing; if it is agreed that the government is out of control, then it is equally our duty not to vote. It becomes our duty (according to the contract which binds us) to go beyond voting in order to get the government back on track.

The government never simply gave us the vote, and it is not our simple obligation to just keep on voting. We have an obligation to ourselves as citizens to make certain that we each have a political voice. When that is no longer the case, it is our obligation to take back what was taken away.

DAYTIME TV

"For make no mistake about it, if our way of life derives from America's 'givenness,' Nixon is what will be given us."

—Gary Wills

Some summers ago—the summer of such good TV—we changed presidents; horses in mid-stream, or some such trite phrase. It was interesting and oddly traumatic and regrettably necessary. Regretably because we might learn things we don't want to know, for in the end, Richard Nixon is one of us. Think about it: He was the one who Made It.

That summer, people would ask questions of each other about Watergate, and impeachment, and the weather, and normal things. It finally made sense to me to try and work out some kind of Watergate Answer. After all, I taught at a Big State University and was being paid to do that. More than that, this is my country and it was important for me to know what the hell was going on.

I composed an answer to the question: What do you say when someone asks you about Watergate? Depending on my mood, the kind of day it had been, with whom I was talking, how long we had to talk, and the like, I would do all or part of the following in whatever manner seemed appropriate.

It seemed that I always got to this point: We all had a common stake in what was going on. The stake was a strange one, as almost all the *real* effect of Watergate was *mood*. Somehow, Watergate is a reflection of ourselves as a funny-shaped Sixty-Year-Old-Man. To see that more clearly is to go through levels of American myths; through levels of thoughts in our own heads until we get to the parent myths. It is, in part, to catch a glimpse of how political myths work in ourselves.

> *Cameras and recording machines not only transcribe experience but alter its quality, giving to much of modern life the character of an enormous echo chamber, or a hall of mirrors.*
>
> —Christopher Lasch

There were all kinds of preresignation explanations we all heard, maybe said, possibly even believed. For example:

Conservatives: To save the country, we must save the presidency. We cannot afford to mess around with our hallowed national institutions. If the irresponsible (crummy) liberal Eastern Establishment Press would just stop all of its idle chatter and destructive work, everything would be fine, et cetera, et cetera, BLAH, BLAH, BLAH.

American Civil Liberty Union Liberals: America is really an all right place; there are just some bad people. So, the Constitution and the courts and the country will be vindicated when the legal system gets finished. We all know that no matter how painfully and slowly it works, the letter of the law always gets the wrongdoer. [Macho, in legal language and Latin phrases.]

Radical: It would be "wrong" to impeach him. Keep him. Neuter Nixon. Let things gently fall apart. Let the corruption and rot show through so that space will be opened up for radicals. Then something constructive could go on. [My nose always keeps running, I think I'll cut it off to spite my face.]

Essentially, the first range of response is as much style as anything. While we can learn something about the person who answers in one of these ways, that fairly narrow range of newspaper-type reasoning won't get us as far as we need to go.

Another way to go about it is to talk about what the "best" impeachment case might be, and what the "best" legal case might be. Those wise people among us would say, and rightly so, that if it had ever come to trial—*The United States of America* v. *Richard M. Nixon*—the charges would be decided on "political" considerations.

For example, a very good legal case might have been made against Nixon because of his bombing of Cambodia. It was, after all, secret, unauthorized by Congress, and illegal. Fairly impressive causes for a legal case. Evidence? Sure. There were memos, military people who knew, the members of the press who saw it, and on and on. But to bring charges would be politically risky. Why?

Why? In part because of the games of our elected officials. There is, as a case in point, a congressional committee that is supposed to watch the military. To bring charges over Cambodia is to make those on the committee look like fools, or worse. If they admit they knew about the bombings, they acted illegally; if they didn't know, they weren't doing their jobs. Either way, it was pretty clear Nixon would escape this outrage.

There could have been charges stemming from the Milk Fund mess. It was only a fair case and, anyway, almost everyone took milk money. Even Congressman Rodino took $100, and there are remarkably few cows in his part of Brooklyn.

So, it was sensible to believe that the issue would be Watergate—not because it was the worst crime, the most damaging or destructive, but because no one else had done exactly the same thing. It is a kind of fun analysis to make, but, like the first set of answers, it ignores most of the interesting and important theoretical points.

DUMMIES AND CARD GAMES

If part of the purpose of our learning about politics is to see the ties that bind myths and actions and our lives, then we should study the relationship of Richard Nixon to the way our heads work. We can talk about Nixon as the ideal American: The Horatio Alger Hero of Our Times.

There are a couple of questions to keep in mind: Is there a

Richard Nixon, and, if so, do we want to see his face if we look into a mirror?

There are a couple of keys to remember: Playing the game, and proving and reproving yourself are part of our liberal upbringing. Gary Wills, in his fine book *Nixon Agonistes,* tells of young Dick as a footballer at Whittier College. There were almost no funds for the football team, and there were few players. Nixon was both small and clumsy, but determined even then. For three seasons he and one other man were literally tackling dummies for the first team to practice on.

Nixon finally lettered his senior year.

The important thing is that we have some empathy, if not respect, for that continuing effort—that trying so hard to succeed. There is an American myth that, in part, assures us that if you try hard enough, you *deserve* to win . . . and you will.

> . . . *he is a workaholic . . . he reportedly does not suffer criticism, dissent, or defeat gracefully, he has a . . . short fuse that burns down quickly. . . . What is troubling is these traits combined with his evident humorlessness.*
>
> *I refer not just or even primarily to the fact that eyewitnesses report that Carter launching a joke is no laughing matter. Rather, I refer to . . . Carter's severe case of the politician's occupational disease, an unsleeping . . . in a sense unsmiling concentration on self.*
>
> —George Will

An obvious question is: What does the world look like in the myth? The world, for the Richard Nixon in us, is one of a series of starting lines—or of card games—in which you are continually made to prove yourself. The world is seen as countless opportunities to start and restart. High school, college, jobs, sports—the American vision of competition. Every so often you line up and race to beat your mates.

Politically, the metaphor is closer to a card game than a race. We get the New Deal and the Fair Deal. Somehow, we find ourselves in this amazing game of You Bet Your Life; every once in a while we throw in our cards, which are reshuffled and dealt. We continually try to win "pots."

Of course this particular myth lacks substantial evidence in reality. In lots of senses, the rich stay rich or get richer, and the rest of us are always playing for penny-ante pots. But that's what is so fascinating about Nixon: He kept trying. He earned his letter and became president. So, he becomes a kind of perfect/ideal model. He is the modern Horatio Alger.

Who is Horatio Alger? What was this dimestore-novel novelist into?

For Alger, there was a sacredness in the running; in showing that, by effort, you *deserve* to win. The important part was on rising, on showing how hard work can mold character. Listen to the book titles: *Making His Way, Helping Himself, Struggling Upward, Bound to Rise.* The poisonous thing wasn't that Alger's heroes aimed at wealth or success; the hero didn't aim at those things.

The tricky part is that the hero aimed not at success, but at succeeding.

Wills writes that this person becomes "a martyr to duty." The self-made man or woman is the true American monster. If you *make something* outside of yourself—build a chair, write a paper, grow a garden—that *thing* comes from the self, but is apart from the self.

But the *self* maker, the self improver, is never finished; cannot stand alone; isn't apart from or severed from the self. The person must always tinker, improve, adjust, start over. There is always the fear your product—your self—will be out of date, or it will rot from non-use.

You always have to go back and begin again.

You have to have the heat of decisions—of crises in Nixon language—to know yourself. The whole stress, in '71, was not to be a good president but to be reelected. The sickness of always competing and of never completing your project—of never really having a self—was eating away at Nixon.

There may not be a Richard Nixon. If there is, and he looks into a mirror, there may be blank spaces; an incompleteness of self that is understood as moral failure.

When you vote for the Presidential-Candidate-of-Your-Choice, I think Nixon's presidency is a good model: one with no vision, or goal, or aims that are really understandable. Because he was up to his neck in his need to keep succeeding; because he was such a self-improver, Watergate wasn't really immoral. Tricky maybe, but everyone was at the starting line—and the aim was to finish first, and to start again.

> *The plug-uglies behind the White House crime wave were not a bit like those Mohicans who crept through dry forests without rustling a leaf. From the burglars who couldn't burgle to the biggest enchilada of them all, they floundered, like insects in yogurt.*
>
> —George Will

It is enormously destructive to think that Nixon really is our model, not because he made it, but because he is a vacuum.

It is in that sense that we really do have *Self*-government. We are not monsters, nor are we political. But, we're all about the same; all private and always tinkering with out products—which is our very own self.

So, Students of Voting, there is/was Richard Nixon receiving an amazing electoral mandate. Vote and save democracy. Indeed.

The most grotesque part of Watergate is that we somehow forgot that America is its people; its shared, collective past; its noble deeds and good examples, as well as the bad and rotten. We know for a fact *it is not* the institution of the presidency, nor any institution I can think of.

There is no defense for Watergate; maybe a lesson or two for us, but certainly no defense.

It is a moral stain.

THE STAIN (Cont.)

> *"I don't allow my feelings to get hurt. If I had feelings, I probably wouldn't have survived"*
>
> —Richard Nixon

There should be a political category titled: Can't Get Enough Of. It is an important category because it tells us a great deal about ourselves. The two entries into this category, for these times, are Richard Nixon and the whole Kennedy family.

In 1984, Richard Nixon reentered our homes. There he was, on television (he got $500,000 plus a percentage) answering tough questions. For example, he said he would not apologize for breaking the law. After all, he said he had resigned from the presidency. Nixon said, had he handled the break-in at Watergate, he would have done a more efficient job. When asked if he loved his wife, he said it was a private matter.

He indicated that there was a real relationship between Pat (his wife) reading *All the President's Men* (a book about Watergate) and Pat's heart attack. Richard Nixon was himself, only older. I have tried to figure out why people are still curious about him.

Academics are interested in Nixon because he sometimes sounds like an academic, especially when he discusses foreign affairs. More inclusively, I think that often he is so openly our own worst self. There is a fascination about what might happen to the bad, very American seed if he or she makes good and is then ruined. We look to Richard Nixon to see.

The Kennedys satisfy another part of ourselves. In fact, they are so popular because they help us with two things. First, of course, we get a kind of long running soap-opera about life in the fast lane. At that level, we have gotten three generations of fast lane: from the patriarch's affairs to the grandchildren's drugs.

In all of that, there have been huge successes (there is certain status in having a president in the family) which are nothing if not fast lane. We Americans like to look, and to dream.

> *"Eighty percent of air pollution comes not from chimneys and auto exhaust pipes but from plants and trees."*
>
> —Ronald Reagan

Second, and not fun at all, the Kennedys have fast-lane troubles. Automobile accidents, drug deaths, frontal lobotomies, divorces, being soft on fascism, and so on. We are able, at some level, to see that they are human. In fact, we can even judge that some of them (even with all that money and all those connections) aren't even as good as we are.

Given all that, it is safe to say that the Kennedys are with us to stay. They get top billing in America's Can't Get Enough Of mid-Twentieth Century list.

THE END?

While it is always helpful to have Nixon as a bad example, it is important to remember that he was not the first—nor will he be the last—to show us rotten things.

The next elected president after Nixon was the self-proclaimed Religious Carter. Self-righteous, morally upstanding, and as interested in being reelected as Nixon was. In his effort to be renominated, Carter used federal money in the "right" places to ensure votes; he refused to open his decisions to public debate; he was ever ready to use the Iranian crisis to his political advantage.

It is certainly fair to call that politics as usual. To contend that it is not unusual would be correct. It would be truthful to say that others have done the same thing.

All this is so, but to say that Carter's actions are normal is not to say that they are either good or right or, in the long run, helpful to anyone but the president.

For years and years Richard Nixon had a terrible reputation. He was seen as ruthlessly ambitious and not altogether moral. Jimmy Carter was different: We did not know he was equally ruthlessly ambitious and not altogether moral until he became president.

> . . . Carter . . . a politician of exceptionally elastic convictions,
> a Jell-O man who fills many molds but doesn't keep any shape.
>
> —George Will

RELAX

> "You are a very bad man," Dorothy said.
>
> "No," replied the Wizard, "I'm a very good man. I'm just a
> very bad wizard."
>
> —The Wizard of Oz

Ronald Reagan, who is president as I write this, seems relaxed. Whether that is true or not will be taken up later. Relaxed or not, Reagan showed us something about the presidency.

It is possible, we now know, to be president without the kind of great tension showed by Nixon and Carter. Reagan vacations, and naps, and nothing much seems different. His staff says awful things, and many do things which are outside of morality (and sometimes the law); bad things happen in foreign affairs (the deaths in Lebanon); bad things happen domestically (the worst recession since the 1930s) and not much happens.

Even when Reagan is upset, he sounds kind of laid back. You can tell when he is furious, but that doesn't last very long. Unlike Carter he neither dwells on nor even knows details; unlike Nixon, the corruption around him does not seem to hurt his popularity. And, even relaxed, he was able to pass a lot of legislation the first two years he was in office.

The second two years he has been less successful with Congress; but, he has done all right. He is only the second person to be reelected since Dwight Eisenhower was in 1956. The other person was Richard Nixon, and his second term in office was short.

There is a genuine question about Reagan. Is he really as re-laxed as he seems? Maybe so. Maybe everything is under control. Maybe not. The following is from *Make-Believe: The Story of Nancy and Ronald Reagan* by Laurence Leamer. He writes: "What was so extraordinary was Ronnie's apparent psychic distance from the burden of the presidency. He sat in cabinet meetings doodling. Unless held to a rigid agenda, he would start telling Hollywood stories or talk about football . . . 'He has a habit now,' his brother, Neil said. 'You might be talking to him, and it's like he's picking his fingernails, but he's not. And you know then he's talking to himself.'

'If people knew about him living in his own reality, they wouldn't believe it,' said one White House aide. 'There are only ten to fifteen people who know the extent, and until they leave and begin talking, no one will believe it.' "

Maybe it isn't true. Just relax.

NEXT

I have no idea who will be president when you read this. We have just suffered through the primaries, and the person who was supposed to win, in fact, did win. The winner, at some point, talked about the primaries as a marathon. Well, that was probably accurate.

But, think about *watching* a marathon. It is kind of interesting to look at a mob of people begin the race and try to pick out the likely winner. It is also kind of interesting to see exhausted people struggle over the finish line. They are pooped, many have lost most of their running form, and after the winner only the runners care about the order in which they finish. I mean, how many of us really care how the runners decide to go up a medium sized hill ten miles into the race?

That is, in large part, what we got from the primaries. They started out pretty good, with an unknown taking the lead. Ah, Gary Hart's big moment. But then, Walter Mondale discovered Hart's true age and former name and different signatures, and attacked those vital issues. But then Mondale was accused of old-time politics and having to answer to special interests. Big-time labor leaders came to his defense, as if to prove the point. Then, Jesse Jackson, the most exciting speaker of them all, did nothing for his rainbow coalition by alienating Jews and supporting Muslim leader Louis Farrakhan, who alienated just about everybody else.

What we got were a lot of little hills, and a winner who started with the most money, the most endorsements, and the best chance to win.

Nancy Reagan, at a political rally, was talking to her husband on an amplified telephone hookup. She said she wished he could be there to "see all these beautiful white people."

It was a marathon, all right. A lot of people, talking about new ideas, and rainbows, and bold leadership while we watched. A lot of people figuring out how to run over a lot of little hills as if we cared. A lot of people who, over the months, sustained injuries.

The most common injury of this particular primary was this: the candidates kept shooting themselves in the foot.

The winner gets to campaign against Ronald Reagan. Up to now, Reagan is ahead (way ahead) in the polls. One suspects that it will get closer as the campaign drags on: but who knows? Even a lot closer won't be very close at all.

The center of the Reagan campaign is this question: Are you better off now than you were four years ago? It is wonderfully instructive to see the two ways the question can be answered.

There is the objective side. For example, unemployment in 1984 is what it was in 1980. Or, during the Reagan years, the gross national product rose an average of 2.4 percent a year. During the Carter years, the GNP rose an average of 3.2 percent per year. While it is true that inflation has slowed, so too have real earnings. It can easily be argued that most people at the low end of the economy have less purchasing power than they had in 1980.

So, if the question is: Are we better off economically; then, the objective answer may well be: no. But, we know that objectivity is not all that important in this case.

> "Very simply, [the neutron bomb] is the dreamed-of death ray weapon of science fiction. Now, some express horror at this, charging immorality. That is sheer unadulterated nonsense. Indeed the neutron bomb represents a moral improvement in the horror of modern war."
>
> —Ronald Reagan

Robert Eisner, an economics professor, offers the following fable. A very unhappy peasant came to his priest. He complained that he and his wife and their six kids lived in a one-room hut and it was awful.

The priest said: "Tonight, move in the chickens." The peasant did, and came back the next day even more unhappy. The priest said: "Tonight, move in the cows." The peasant did, and came back the next day miserable. The priest said: "Tonight, move in the pigs."

The next morning the peasant came back in his worst state ever. He pleaded for help. The priest said: "Tonight, move all the animals out."

The peasant moved all the animals out. He came back the next day and thanked the priest. "Thank you," the peasant said, "Thank you for your help. Now we are better off then we were."

There are two important points. One is that Reagan asks us

to compare today with four years ago. What we really do is compare ourselves with two years ago. What we remember is when unemployment was 10.6% (1982); what we forget is that Reagan was president then, not Carter. Indeed, the majority of hard economic times came during the Great Recession of the Reagan years. What is interesting is that we forget it.

Like the peasant, during the last four years, the chickens, cows, and pigs all moved in and then moved out. It *feels* like we are better off. It *feels* like we should be grateful. That is one reason why Reagan asks the questions.

The second point is that Reagan seems to soothe us. The *impression* is that we are better off. Who is to say that if, indeed, we feel better off that we aren't better off? One of the things Ronald Reagan is asking is this: Wouldn't you rather have me than Jimmy Carter as president? Well, he liked the answer so much the first time he thought he'd ask it again.

For the next ten weeks, the Republicans and the Democrats will be out there trying to get power. They will be spending money, kissing babies, and making speeches, promises, and deals. People will read about the elections, and hear about them, and watch them on television. And all the while, a majority of people will not want to vote; and, if this is a typical election, almost a majority won't.

Common sense suggests that they know something important about what our elections have become.

BETWEEN THEN AND NOW

> *"It is my obligation to show you the truth, even if it doesn't mean anything to you. The curse of the educator."*
>
> —Paul Nichevo

Given the very slow magic of producing a book, I have the opportunity to add this section on the recent presidential election. There were remarkably few noteworthy happenings/events/moments given the attention and money spent during the last few years.

Certainly the most important thing to happen is cause for great mixed emotions. That a woman was nominated to the national ticket is only for the good. That we have now acknowledged more than fifty percent of the adult population is equal in ability to the other adults seems sensible. The "mixed" part is the embarrassment we should feel for having taken this long to admit the obvious. Next, it is time we admit the same obvious thing about minorities.

Of course, as a candidate, Ferraro was not perfect. We learned three things: 1) The vice-presidential candidate doesn't matter too much in terms of getting votes; 2) She had more money than the "rich" Vice-President Bush; and 3) Her husband said he told a bank he was worth $17 million when he was *only* worth about $3 million. All of that is a way to say that we didn't learn much of political interest.

Probably the most interesting part of the elections were the two presidential debates. They stand as a monument to disappointment. We the people saw one thing: ambition. We saw very little of the possible good-heartedness of the men, or even if either of them had much faith in their fellow citizens. We got a remarkable amount of facts (some accurate, some dead wrong), we got some foolish disagreements, we got a glimpse of policy choices, and we got a great deal of boring.

Walter Mondale won the first debate. He had help from Ronald Reagan, who was lost in a sea of statistics; hopeless in a effort to appear knowledgeable about what had happened during his three years of being president. When Reagan quoted his 1980 line, "There you go again," Mondale just ate him alive. Our poor president looked surprised and unhappy that someone would do that to a nice person like himself.

Ronald Reagan won the second debate. He had help from Walter Mondale, who looked tired and grumpy, and who sounded whiney. Reagan won the debate by saying he would not use the "age issue" against Mondale, and wouldn't point out Mondale's youth and inexperience. The audience laughed hard, and that was—in reality—the end of the line for the Democrats.

The election, as they say, was a laugher.

"There is wisdom in madness and strong probability of truth in all accusations, for people are complete, and everyone is capable of everything.

—*Joseph Heller*

The second debate was about foreign policy. We heard about Star Wars, and trading secrets, and nuclear war. We also heard our president ramble on about a beautiful sunset he saw in California. A commentator wrote that it could be best understood as smoking dope at Big Sur. That was how the great debate on foreign policy ended. . . . as the sun set slowly in the West.

Now that the election is over, the political scientists can get to work. Because Reagan won by such a large margin, there is speculation that the nation will become Republican. There will be a shift from the left-middle to the middle-right. That the Democrats of the Depression are gone, and the post-1960s' Republicans are in.

The only thing which stops everyone from accepting that theory is that the Democrats won a majority in the House of Representatives, and made strong showings in state and local elections.

The statistics show trends. The trends are different. What statistics do not show—cannot show—is the arrival of some very popular and ambitious person who will run for president and win big. What we know is that a day or so after the last election was over people were beginning to plot to win the next election.

Maybe someone should write a book: *The World as a Continuous Presidential Election.*

VOTING AND POLITICS

Up to here, two distinct arguments have been made. First, that our liberalism keeps us from an active involvement in politics. Second, that discussions on voting only show us that voting in America does not live up to the "requirements" of democracy. We have implied more than that. Certainly it seems possible to understand voting as fulfilling a stabilizing, symbolic function, as a method of keeping people from making important decisions and away from power. Few people ask what voting means if, in a bureaucratic society, most leaders are interchangeable anyway. But even that may not be the most important point.

If this is a book about politics, then it is necessary to ask at least one more question about voting in America. It is important to ask a very obvious question which is almost never asked: Is voting in America a political action?

> *... the duty frequently assigned to a vice-presidential*
> *candidate, that of behaving like a pyromaniac in a world of*
> *straw men.*
>
> —*George Will*

We have already discussed politics. To act politically, one must honestly work toward an eventual outcome. That means—more or less—that one must help frame the issues; one must work for those issues; and, finally, one must help carry out the results of those issues. Ideally, this is done openly and with others. The argument, stated most simply, is that we make something legitimate, make something moral, by actively participating in it. By being political, we give meaning to what goes on. It is not a simple process of acquiescing; it is action.

In order to understand politics, we must understand what it means to take action. We can get at this by discussing the differences between behavior and action. Behavior is the normal, the routine, those things that are carefully closed by boundaries. To behave is to do the predictable, to do what has always been done. Pets behave; children "should" behave. In oddly similar ways, rats behave for scientists as voters behave for the system.

> *President Robbins was so well adjusted to his environment that*
> *sometimes you could not tell which was the environment and*
> *which was President Robbins.*
>
> —*Randall Jarrell*

To take action is to cut across traditional boundaries. It is to invent new methods, create new means, make new connections. It is to consciously help define who you are by what you do. It is an individual's way of relating to the whole, but in his or her own unique, special way. You are what you do, if you act. You are what you are told to be, if you behave.

In order to act, one must have space. There must be political space provided by the state. Space metaphysically and actually. Space in which citizens may come together for creative political action, not simply for normal behavior. The greater the space available, the greater the opportunity for each citizen to act. But people must want and fight for and finally protect their political space. It is as much a human property as a property provided by the state. In other words, one of the reasons we have no political space is that it might endanger the system; another is that we are not actively working to get that space.

Briefly, a person must have space in order to act creatively, in order to engage publicly in politics. But just what does that really mean?

For the purposes of our discussion, it simply means this: Voting as we practice it is not a political act. We know that we have no real say about whom we vote for. All the candidates look the same. It is like being given a choice between identical twins in a beauty contest. We surely cannot feel creative, nor can we feel we are defining ourselves by what we do. There is no sense of participation.

The way voting has been set up, it is neither politics nor action. It is not even public. It is simply a fact that having three minutes alone in a three-foot-by-three-foot space once every few years neither furthers democracy nor enhances freedom. It is almost all those things that we were taught it was not.

> *It is precisely this division of the individual into actor and onlooker, and its extension within the social mind, to which we owe the birth of the hero. . . . This is the division that is insanity. This is the division that is the hero. As there can be no hero without an audience, there can be no insanity without an audience.*[13]
>
> —*Trigant Burrow*

In many places, voting has come to mean behavior in the most confining sense. It is only a method of endorsing those who will keep doing the same old thing, in the same old way, according to

[13] Cited in Larry D. Spence, *The Politics of Social Knowledge* (University Park, Pa.: Pennsylvania State University Press, 1978). The preceding quotes were taken from: Norman Mailer, *Miami and the Seige of Chicago* (New York: Signet Books, 1969); Hunter Thompson, *Fear and Loathing on the Campaign Trail '72* (New York: Popular Library, 1973); George Will, *The Pursuit of Happiness and Other Sobering Thoughts* (New York: Harper, 1978); Kurt Vonnegut, Jr., "In a Manner That Must Shame God Himself," *Harper's* magazine, 1973. The Randall Jarrell quote comes from Hannah Arendt, *Men in Dark Times* (New York: Harvest, 1968).

the same old rules, under the same old system. It is the meaningless raised to important societal myth.

Voting keeps you where you are. It is not action, it is not politics; it is merely reaction, simply endorsement. The rulers keep ruling, the people keep voting. The franchise has widened: Eighteen-year-olds now vote. We have spread the Novocaine; everyone gets deadened. The numbness of voting merely envelops more of us.

At the end of a creative political act, people should vote; but as it is now carried out, voting is a terrible fraud.

It is best we heed these words of Nietzsche: "I say unto you: a man must have chaos yet within him to be able to give birth to a dancing star."

Focus Five

The main point of this chapter is that, while Americans consider voting in elections their major political activity, voting makes more and better sense as a part rather than the whole of political action. Compared to the elements of political action argued for in Chapter 1—morally based stands on issues, responsibility for carrying out joint decisions, public arenas in which to take stands and join with others to carry them out—mere voting as done today is private, passive, and not very democratic. According to this chapter, the primary effect of voting today is to provide citizens the psychic satisfaction of having done their duty and to protect the political process from too much activity by the citizens.

Since one of the purposes of this book is to analyze the myths that discourage direct exercise of political power by citizens, the argument attacks voting as a deception. When Americans believe that all political activity beyond voting and working in electoral campaigns should be left to the professionals, they have forgotten the central part of their political heritage as citizens. Insofar as voting encourages citizens to believe they have done all that they are permitted in politics —with the occasional exception of becoming candidates themselves—it makes them quiescent about direct exercise of power. Hence voting is a fraud we perpetuate upon ourselves.

Some perspective. In the 1800s voting was only a part—and not the most important part—of citizenship. The early American townsmen legislated and executed local laws themselves *as well as* voting for representatives to state and national political offices. At the grass roots level, these citizens needed no other qualifications than membership in the town in order to exercise political power. Among them, they constituted an active power base upon which all higher levels of government were built. The people actively were the source of government. Their own sense of joint efficacy encouraged them to imagine how politics ought to work at the higher levels and, if threatened by a higher level of government, these grass root actors' life-long experience with common endeavors had prepared them for effective protection of their rights. Thus, the grass roots political institutions offered both experience with creating and using political power and a safeguard against tyranny.

Thus, voting for representatives was not the entirety of their political activity. Instead, voting was an efficient means for finalizing decisions after all the engaging work of debate and deliberation about issues had been done and for selecting representatives who were familiar with those final decisions. When elections to higher office occurred, the town meeting provided an institutional framework within which to arrive at an effective joint voice for instructing and calling to account their representatives. In addition, the qualifications of representatives often were known to the townsmen from years of experience together in local public arenas. Entrusting others with political power still was a risky business but at least the experience upon which wise decisions could be made was present. The operation of early American political institutions, especially the grass roots arenas of the town meetings, was not perfect. One salient defect was their provinciality. Nonetheless, as a benchmark for seeing that voting is only a part of what we might be doing as citizens, these earlier institutions are something we need to recall. To do so is to focus on a traditional American notion of political rightfittingness.

6

POLITICS AS LONELINESS AND PRESSURE
(OR, WHAT HOLDS AMERICA TOGETHER?)

How else do things work always unless by imitation bred of the passion to be liked? All the processes of society are based on it, all individual development. For some reason, it was something that we seemed to have a conspiracy to ignore or not to mention, even while most single-mindedly engaged in it. There was some sort of conspiracy of belief that people—children, adults, everyone—grew by an acquisition of unconnected habits, of isolated bits of knowledge, like choosing things off a counter: "Yes, I'll have that one," or "No, I don't want that one!" But in fact people develop for good or for bad by swallowing whole other people, atmospheres, events, places—develop by admiration. Often enough unconsciously, of course. We are the company we keep.

—Doris Lessing

> *One of the guarantees of freedom in a planned society will be the maintenance of the individual capacity for adjustment.*
>
> —Karl Mannheim

> *The theory of infinite human plasticity . . . errs by confusing the ability of man to adapt successfully to these pressures: it confuses the ability to survive with the ability to flourish. . . . Psychosis is after all a form of adaptation. . . .*
>
> —Kenneth Keniston

We are all here. All together in the same country, products of more or less the same culture. We are mass-produced Americans. The nation in which we live is seemingly vital. Like a huge machine or a giant hungry animal, it continues to produce and grow, grow and produce.

But what does that really mean? What does it mean to be a part of America, to be American? More specifically, what holds the machine together? Why doesn't it fall apart? Why does it cohere; what is the glue that holds us as parts of the system, and in turn holds the system together?

To begin to answer these questions—even to get wrong answers—there are several steps we must take. The punch line of this chapter will be the suggestion that, just possibly, the system is held together at our expense. That by sacrificing some of our rights and powers, the system continues to run. To get to that point, however, it is first necessary to understand more about what a system is and is not, and what that has to do with politics and people.

SYSTEMS

The easiest way to outline what a system is is simply to list some of its most salient features. Social science tells us that a system has a boundary; that it has some kind of communications network; that it may be natural or voluntary, legitimate or illegitimate, efficient or effective or both or neither, functional or dysfunctional, accessible or inaccessible, open or closed. Also, it would appear that the bias of most systems is to want to survive and, in most cases, to grow.[1]

If you consider these traits, sweeping and vague as they are, the conclusion is obvious: We know for sure that we have a "system" in America. To be more exact, we know that segments of our society can be accurately understood in terms that describe a system. It seems equally obvious that what we call the political system cannot be separated from most social and economic goings-on. Social scientists tell us that a political system must have methods of formulating issues, deliberating them, resolving them, and finally finding solutions for them. What they do not tell us is that most issues are political ones and that many are "resolved" in less than open, political ways.

In other words, the system may work well on its own terms. It may stay together, function normally and smoothly, yet never really be a "political" system. The high school as an institution is a political system in which the students are rarely given a political voice. The important questions are decided by the "experts" within the system: the teachers, the principal, even the school board. Students are simply an "input" into the system. At the end of a few years, the students leave school, thereby becoming "outputs" of the system. In systemic terms, nothing has changed basically. The only thing that has really been affected is the student, who has been exposed to what it means to be a "citizen" of the system. It will not come as a big surprise to learn that college is not very different. There *appears* to be more freedom, and maybe there actually is. There should be, because by the time a person has spent thirteen years in public schools, his or her imagination should be sufficiently limited so that he or she can be trusted with a small increment of freedom. In systemic terms, a functional output is one that will continue to support the system. It is clear that our educational system, in spite of signs encouraging to some, continues to produce functional outputs.

While the school system enables us to understand more about systems in general, it does not help enough. One of the critical

---

[1] The classic statement of systems analysis is to be found in David Easton, *The Political System* (New York; Alfred A. Knopf, 1953).

deficiencies of systems analysis is that it is blind to either change or values; it cannot really tell us about ourselves and can tell us only a very little about our surroundings. A systems analysis seems to assume that whatever is functional is good and that whatever is dysfunctional is bad; but to know that is to remain completely uninformed about either good or bad. It is simply to know what makes a system stable, to know what might affect the status quo. We must know more than that. What we are most interested in is what the system means to us; how, essentially, the system holds itself together, with us in it.

One way to begin to understand what our system does is by studying what it does not do. More accurately, we can begin by discovering what is not included in the system.

From James Madison, writing in *Federalist* No. 10, we learned that ours was a rational system, one that was set up to run almost in spite of people. Power was separated, balanced, federated, and, some believe, pluralized. But what about the relationship among politics and the people and the state? To get at those questions, we may begin by asking these:

1. Do we have any idea of what it means to have a political community?

2. Do we have any idea of political obligation?

COMMUNITY

> ... *suburbanites who philosophize over their back fence with complete sincerity about their "dog-eat-dog-world," and what-is-it-all-for, and you-can't-take-it-with-you, and success-doesn't-make-you-happy-it-just-gives-you-ulcers-and-a-heart-condition would be enraged should their children pay serious attention to such a viewpoint.* ...

> *We seek a private house, a private means of transportation, a private garden, a private laundry, self-service stores, and do-it-yourself skills of every kind.*

> —*Philip Slater*

It is possible to relate to some of the concepts of a "political system" simply because we are surrounded by its words. "Community" is different. The idea of a system and the idea of a community are very different. Different in almost every way, from the way each is set up to the way it feels to live in one.[2] Let us begin with how each is created.

There are several theories about how governments, or political entities, are created. For example, there are those who believe that God chooses someone to rule: Hence, a divine right provides legitimacy to the leader, to kings and queens, and such. Our tradition is not divine right. In a society infatuated with law, it is no mistake that we believe that governments are founded by contracts, by people banding together and agreeing to the conditions under which the state will function.

For our purposes, there are at least two ways in which this contract can be drawn up. The first way is for all of the people individually to give their support to one source, for each person to make his or her own pledge and to have his or her private compact. This kind of contract leads to a "political system" as we know it. There is no community, for everyone is alone; no politics, for each has his or her own private interests; no power other than that of the state, for everyone is isolated. As we shall see, this is the contract of individualism.

The second kind of contract binds each to the other. Each citizen becomes responsible for every other. The bonds among people are personal ones, visible ones. Identity comes from membership in and participation in the actions of the community. Decisions are reached communally and openly and, hopefully, for the good of those concerned. Power resides in the group, in the many. In theory, power is held by all, in common.

Ours is a political system, not a political community; ours is a society created by 230 million single contracts, pledging support

---

[2] For an analysis of the differences between community and what we now have in America, see Robert Nisbet, *Community and Power* (New York: Oxford University Press, 1962). Another approach to the problem can be found in Perry Miller's brilliant book on the Puritans, *Errand into the Wilderness* (New York: Harper & Row, 1958).

to an impersonal system. As we shall see, the illusion is individualism, the reality political isolation; the hope is equality, the truth much different.

In place of community in America, we have interests. Of course, interests may be greater than any single individual, but interests are not communities. Our interests are private. Further, our interests are either social or economic, and in America these are generally the same.

We serve our interests because we are on the make, not because there is a better vision of the world. The calculus is precise: We are driven into the public realm only to the extent that we must protect our private interests. Our business is predominantly private, very often selfish, and has the long-run effect of leaving us isolated. By substituting the idea of interest politics for political community, we have put business in the place of brotherhood. Of course, we have good friends, and some of us even have an idea of what a nice neighborhood is, but these are difficult to achieve. If they exist, they exist in spite of, surely not because of, our system. These things speak more to the urges of people than to the dynamics of the process.

Interest politics is a popular subject (and rightfully so) in books about American politics. We are well acquainted with the arguments that private interest groups—pressure groups—often exercise a great deal of influence on national, state, and local policy.[3] We also know that the most effective of these groups are generally well organized, wealthy, and white. What I would like to argue is that the system is set up to reward these groups, while teaching that each of us is an individual, each with a contract with the state, each equal in power—or powerlessness. The reality of most private interests and of politics based on them is privatization.

Privatization is not a bad thing, if one does not care about those major decisions that affect one's life.

There is an advanced form of individualism—individualism's logical psychological ending—that is important to discuss. While it is not really political, the dynamic is too real to ignore.

---

[3] For a fine treatment of interest-group politics, see Grant McConnell, *Private Power and American Democracy* (New York: Alfred A. Knopf, 1966). A further discussion of interest groups is found in this book, Chapter 9.

INDIVIDUALISM AND ILLNESS: THE PERSON BESIDE THE POOL

"What do you want?"
"Me!"
"When do you want it?"
"Now."

—*Proposed chant for a single-person demonstration, held alone.*

To be honest about it, I am not always happy when the language of psychology is randomly used in everyday instances. The words seem to make normal, unpleasant things appear sick. Nor am I much of a fan of the exclusive use of psychological explanations for social and political problems. It was with some reluctance, then, that I decided to do a mild form of "analysis" in a political science book.

The logic seemed compelling enough. If what has been argued so far is accurate, and we are forced into ourselves more and more, then it follows that our *self* has become extraordinarily important. There is good reason to be interested in what is known by psychologists as narcissism.

The seventies were called the Me Decade in part to distinguish them—in a dramatic/cute way—from the more socially active sixties. What I want to work out here is how that "me" gets exaggerated, and how that very exaggeration becomes destructive. More exactly, it is time to see how individualism (which is as American as a publisher of dirty magazines being born again) becomes something else.

Let me remind you of the Greek myth of Narcissus. Narcissus was a remarkably handsome young man, the son of the river god Cephsus. He was not only handsome but also regrettably vain about it. There were many young women who loved him; one, Echo, even had her voice fade away calling him. But, being vain, Narcissus had nothing to do with them.

The other gods, not at all pleased, decided to punish him.

One day, Narcissus came to a very calm pool of clear water. He stopped, looked into the pool, and at once fell in love . . . fell in love with his own reflection. The love was so strong that he could not break his gaze: He could not leave. At last he died, staring into the pool.

In many ways, self-love has become an accepted form of life in America. When the psychiatric community understood that extreme forms of self-love were sick, it seemed to make sense to talk about a narcissistic personality. What Christopher Lasch has argued so well—to use the title of his book—is that we now are a culture of narcissism.[4] Much of what follows is taken from his book.

Today, people seem to be looking for some kind of personal well-being; for good health and security. It is more and more difficult to find. That search represents a real switch: Where the rugged individual always saw America as a land of opportunity, a place that could be changed to suit his or her tastes and desires, the narcissist is different. He or she now "depends on others to validate his self-esteem . . . for the narcissist, the world is a mirror."[5]

But an insecure person looking into a mirror may have problems. We will return to that theme later, after we see some social forces at work.

One problem is bureaucracy. As we saw, bureaucracies take what should be collective grievances and make them appear, and feel, like personal problems. When something becomes a personal problem, one acceptable way of dealing with it is to go to a therapist.

Please do not misread what I am writing. I *am not* saying therapists or therapy is bad. I *am* saying that to assume social or political problems are personal problems, that they have their roots in an individual's personality, is wrong. And evil. Personal therapy cannot resolve societal problems, and it is an open question whether we should try to force ourselves to "adjust" to social sickness.

What could be better for our new insecure Narcissus but to be able to talk about himself or herself, exclusively, for a forty-five-minute hour, several times a week?

Of course individual therapy is not the only way a true Me Decade person can get taken care of. The whole consciousness movement helps administer to him or her. The variety of groups, and their costs, are staggering. The methods of really getting into yourself—from primal screams to not going to the bathroom—seem to have different effects on different people.

Often, though, the messages of these groups are the same.

---

[4] Christopher Lasch, *The Culture of Narcissism* (New York: Warner Books, 1979).
[5] Ibid., p. 38.

Generally people who go to these things are advised to live for the moment, to avoid too much dependence on others, and to make no major commitments in love.

All of that, on the surface, is appealing enough. It seems to be an extension of our individualism, and clearly it will help protect us in a world of evil people. But there is trouble with that advice, real trouble, and it is this: The advice itself contains the very dynamics that lead to many of the personal problems in the first place.

The cure is only an articulated and socially enforced form of the illness. Not a good deal.

With the more traditional individualism (itself the carrier of an impressive amount of sick-making problems), there was always the assumption that there would be all sorts of difficulties. That old individualism assumed that with hard work, those difficulties could somehow be conquered. This view has changed, just as the world has.

Now all we really want to do is just to survive the problems; at best we hope our own little world will simply be "reasonable." One of the words I dislike a great deal is *growth* when it is misapplied. We have come to idolize the whole notion of personal growth without admitting what we are idolizing. What growth has come to mean is mere survival. A kind of ongoing ability to cope.

While the word itself is optimistic, its meaning has become one of profound despair.

In the book *1984,* one of the powerful tools of that totalitarian government was its systematic abuse of language. That is a fairly common practice today, and my latest addition to the *1984* vocabulary is the word *growth:* To grow is to stay the same. To stay the same is to stagnate. To stagnate is to die. To grow is to die.

Let me put individualism in a different context. Before, there was some chance for a person with relatively honest virtues to make it in the world—to earn a decent amount of money and respect. But the rules seem to have changed. Society is too unpredictable. Everything is getting increasingly hostile and violent.

Lasch describes it this way: ". . . the normal conditions of everyday life come to resemble those formerly confined to the underworld, men live by their wits."[6]

---

[6] Ibid., p. 107.

The circle now closes. Living by your wits is a lonely business.
The dynamic of individualism and insecurity leads to several things.
For example, in order to get along with others, as well as to live
in an environment of large organizations, you have to fulfill certain
fairly specific requirements.

A person can easily begin to think of himself or herself as a
commodity. Sell yourself, in terms of dress, speech, manners . . .
facade. While you need affection, there will always be the theme
of manipulation in personal affairs. One commodity manipulating
another, in a well-thought-out way. Lasch calls it "the deadly game
of intimidating friends and seducing people."[7] In another place, he
talks of people practicing "the classic arts of seduction . . . hoping
to win your heart while picking your pocket."[8]

In a narcissistic culture, played in a violent atmosphere of large
organizations, the pursuit of pleasure masks the struggle for power.
Close human ties resemble psychological hand-to-hand combat.

This excessive self-involvement can be seen outside the context
of simple relationships. No longer are we interested in fame—the
admiration of achievement—as much as we worship celebrity. The
beautiful people (ah, the old Greek pool) command our attention
now. As we look back, past the Bee Gees, the Beatles, even Elvis,
we begin to understand celebrity better.

John F. Kennedy was an incredibly attractive president. Yet
when we try to remember what he accomplished, we get stuck. The
fact is the high point of his presidency was his inaugural, his "Ask
not" speech. It was wonderful: It made him a celebrity. He was
already rich and handsome; so he was an instant success.

We seem to demand that kind of celebrity now. We want our
reflection to be beautiful. The darker side of this is equally obvious:
When our objects of envy remind us of our own insignificance, we
really hate them. Stars may burn out quickly if we happen to see
a blemish, or if they say something wrong. Celebrity, and in a sense
leadership, is denied humanness.

Skills are out. Glamour is in.

Where the Greek Narcissus was secure, the new Narcissus is

---

[7] Ibid., p. 127.
[8] Ibid., p. 106.

insecure. The current Narcissus now looks at his or her reflection not so much in admiration but in an "unremitting search of flaws, signs of fatigue, decay."[9] A pound overweight, a hair out of place, a new pimple—something inferior with the commodity you make of yourself.

We live in a world of jazzercise, Nautilus, Jane Fonda's exercise, and the twenty-minute workout. You can flatten your stomach, build up your arms, reduce your thighs, or do the diet of the Stars. You can lift your face, pad your bottom, lengthen your fingernails, or put hair on the top of your head. It would be foolish of me to argue that I think that this is silly. In some cases, a lot of it is needed. I am simply suggesting that it has probably gotten out of hand; that a lot of it is done for the wrong reasons.

Self-centeredness is not a casual pursuit.

There is, of course, some irony about all this self-searching and self-consciousness. Before, people often cursed fate and tried to conquer it. Now people welcome fate, simply as a relief from their total self-involvement.

Irony, as it turns out, is not necessarily funny.

HAVE WE ANY IDEA OF POLITICAL OBLIGATION?

Back to the more readily understood political questions. Do we really have any political obligations? Does the system encourage us to be political? Some things seem clear. It appears that we have a war obligation to the state. We must also assume a tax burden. There is pressure to vote—but little pressure to understand what that means. After all, voting has come to mean that apolitical act we go through from time to time to choose a person already selected by the system to serve the purposes of that system. We seem to have a greater obligation to the system than to the body politic, to the private sphere than to the public, to the anonymous than to the known. In an important sense, the essence of our political obligation is simple: We are taught that one should not talk about income, God, or politics in polite company.

One argument is that the system may be held together by people

---

[9] Ibid., p. 166.

being political. In its most simple form, the logic is this: If privatization makes us vulnerable by way of powerlessness, then politics—openness and publicness—is the solution. But instinctively we know that a true plurality of interests would be unpredictable. We know that when presented in a public, political way, plurality looks like chaos, and chaos is dysfunctional to a willful, self-protective system. The combinations of isolation and representation, individualism and Madisonian liberalism, seem to pull us further and further away from any positive, healthy sense of the political. It pushes us toward behavior which is best understood as systemically functional.

I am not arguing that the potential for politics has never existed in America. Just the opposite. The sense that politics was a way in which the individual could interact with the many and ensure personal freedom and individualism was expressed most clearly during the 1830s by a Frenchman named Alexis de Tocqueville. Tocqueville, an Old World aristocrat, well understood the tensions between liberty and equality, between individualism and isolation, and believed that the best way to guard against the triumph of equality/isolation was through politics. In *Democracy in America* we can find an analysis of the potential problems and solutions in the then new democratic state of America.

The following passage is from the first volume of his two-volume work. It describes, in Tocqueville's terms, "Political Associations in the United States."

> In no country in the world has the principle of association been more successfully used or applied to a greater multitude of objects than in America. Besides the permanent associations which are established by law under the names of townships, cities, and counties, a vast number of others are formed and maintained by the agency of private individuals.

> The citizen of the United States is taught from infancy to rely upon his own exertions in order to resist the evils and the difficulties of life; he looks upon the social authority with an eye of mistrust and anxiety, and he claims its assistance only when he is unable to do without it. This habit may be traced even in the schools, where the children in their games are wont to submit to rules which they have themselves established, and to punish mis-

demeanors which they have themselves defined. The same spirit pervades every act of social life. If a stoppage occurs in a thoroughfare and the circulation of vehicles is hindered, the neighbors immediately form themselves into a deliberative body; and this extemporaneous assembly gives rise to an executive power which remedies the inconvenience before anybody has thought of recurring to a pre-existing authority superior to that of the persons immediately concerned. If some public pleasure is concerned, an association is formed to give more splendor and regularity to the entertainment. Societies are formed to resist evils that are exclusively of a moral nature, as to diminish the vice of intemperance. In the United States associations are established to promote the public safety, commerce, industry, morality, and religion. There is no end which the human will despairs of attaining through the combined power of individuals united into a society.

I shall have occasion hereafter to show the effects of association in civil life; I confine myself for the present to the political world. When once the right of association is recognized, the citizens may use it in different ways.

An association consists simply in the public assent which a number of individuals give to certain doctrines and in the engagement which they contract to promote in a certain manner the spread of those doctrines. The right of associating in this fashion almost merges with freedom of the press, but societies thus formed possess more authority than the press. When an opinion is represented by a society, it necessarily assumes a more exact and explicit form. It numbers its partisans and engages them in its cause; they, on the other hand, become acquainted with one another, and their zeal is increased by their number. An association unites into one channel the efforts of divergent minds and urges them vigorously towards the one end which it clearly points out.

The second degree in the exercise of the right of association is the power of meeting. When an association is allowed to establish centers of action at certain important points in the country, its activity is increased and its influence extended. Men have the opportunity of seeing one another; means of execution are combined; and opinions are maintained with a warmth and energy that written language can never attain.

Lastly, in the exercise of the right of political association there is a third degree: the partisans of an opinion may unite in electoral bodies and choose delegates to represent them in a central assembly. This is, properly speaking, the application of the representative system to a party.

Thus, in the first instance, a society is formed between individuals professing the same opinion, and the tie that keeps it together is of a purely intellectual nature. In the second case, small assemblies are formed, which represent only a fraction of the party. Lastly, in the third case, they constitute, as it were, a separate nation in the midst of the nation, a government within the government. Their delegates, like the real delegates of the majority, represent the whole collective force of their party and like them, also, have an appearance of nationality and all the moral power that results from it. It is true that they have not the right, like the others, of making the laws; but they have the power of attacking those which are in force and of drawing up beforehand those which ought to be enacted.

If, among a people who are imperfectly accustomed to the exercise of freedom, or are exposed to violent political passions, by the side of the majority which makes the laws is placed a minority which only deliberates and gets laws ready for adoption, I cannot but believe that public tranquillity would there incur very great risks. There is doubtless a wide difference between proving that one law is in itself better than another and proving that the former ought to be substituted for the latter. But the imagination of the multitude is very apt to overlook this difference, which is so apparent to the minds of thinking men. It sometimes happens that a nation is divided into two nearly equal parties, each of which affects to represent the majority. If, near the directing power, another power is established which exercises almost as much moral authority as the former, we are not to believe that it will long be content to speak without acting; or that it will always be restrained by the abstract consideration that associations are meant to direct opinions, but not to enforce them, to suggest but not to make the laws.

The more I consider the independence of the press in its principal consequences, the more am I convinced that in the modern world it is the chief and, so to speak, the constitutive element of liberty.

A nation that is determined to remain free is therefore right in demanding, at any price, the exercise of this independence. But the *unlimited* liberty of political association cannot be entirely assimilated to the liberty of the press. The one is at the same time less necessary and more dangerous than the other. A nation may confine it within certain limits without forfeiting any part of its self-directing power; and it may sometimes be obliged to do so in order to maintain its own authority.

In America the liberty of association for political purposes is unlimited. An example will show in the clearest light to what an extent this privilege is tolerated. . . .

In 1831, when the tariff dispute was raging with the greatest violence, a private citizen of Massachusetts proposed, by means of the newspapers, to all the enemies of the tariff to send delegates to Philadelphia in order to consult together upon the best means of restoring freedom of trade. This proposal circulated in a few days, by the power of the press, from Maine to New Orleans. The opponents of the tariff adopted it with enthusiasm; meetings were held in all quarters, and delegates were appointed. The majority of these delegates were well known, and some of them had earned a considerable degree of celebrity. South Carolina alone, which afterwards took up arms in the same cause, sent sixty-three delegates. On the 1st of October 1831 this assembly, which, according to the American custom, had taken the name of a Convention, met at Philadelphia; it consisted of more than two hundred members. Its debates were public, and they at once assumed a legislative character; the extent of the powers of Congress, the theories of free trade, and the different provisions of the tariff were discussed. At the end of ten days the Convention broke up, having drawn up an address to the American people in which it declared: (1) that Congress had not the right of making a tariff, and that the existing tariff was unconstitutional; (2) that the prohibition of free trade was prejudicial to the interests of any nation, and to those of the American people especially.

It must be acknowledged that the unrestrained liberty of political association has not hitherto produced in the United States the fatal results that might perhaps be expected from it elsewhere. The right of association was imported from England, and it has always existed in America; the exercise of this privilege is now incorporated with the manners and customs of the people. At the present time the liberty of association has become a necessary guarantee against the tyranny of the majority. In the United States, as soon as a party has become dominant, all public authority passes into its hands; its private supporters occupy all the offices and have all the force of the administration at their disposal. As the most distinguished members of the opposite party cannot surmount the barrier that excludes them from power, they must establish themselves outside of it and oppose the whole moral authority of the minority to the physical power that domineers over it. Thus a dangerous expedient is used to obviate a still more formidable danger.

The omnipotence of the majority appears to me to be so full of peril to the American republics that dangerous means used to bridle it seem to be more advantageous than prejudicial. And here I will express an opinion that may remind the reader of what I said when speaking of the freedom of townships. *There are no countries in which associations are more needed to prevent the despotism of faction or the arbitrary power of a prince than those which are democratically constituted.*[10] In aristocratic nations the body of the nobles and the wealthy are in themselves natural associations which check the abuses of power. In countries where such associations do not exist, if private individuals cannot create an artificial and temporary substitute for them I can see no permanent protection against the most galling tyranny; and a great people may be oppressed with impunity by a small faction or by a single individual.

The meeting of a great political convention (for there are conventions of all kinds), which may frequently become a necessary measure, is always a serious occurrence, even in America, and one that judicious patriots cannot regard without alarm. This was very perceptible in the Convention of 1831, at which all the most distinguished members strove to moderate its language and to restrain its objects within certain limits. It is probable that this Convention exercised a great influence on the minds of the mal-

---

[10] Emphasis added.

contents and prepared them for the open revolt against the commercial laws of the Union that took place in 1832.

It cannot be denied that the unrestrained liberty of association for political purposes is the privilege which a people is longest in learning how to exercise. If it does not throw the nation into anarchy, it perpetually augments the chances of that calamity. On one point, however, this perilous liberty offers a security against dangers of another kind; in countries where associations are free, secret societies are unknown. In America there are factions, but no conspiracies.

The most natural privilege of man, next to the right of acting for himself, is that of combining his exertions with those of his fellow creatures and of acting in common with them. The right of association therefore appears to me almost as inalienable in its nature as the right of personal property. No legislator can attack it without impairing the foundations of society. Nevertheless, if the liberty of association is only a source of advantage and prosperity to some nations, it may be perverted or carried to excess by others, and from an element of life may be changed into a cause of destruction. A comparison of the different methods that associations pursue in those countries in which liberty is well understood and in those where liberty degenerates into license may be useful both to governments and to parties.

Most Europeans look upon association as a weapon which is to be hastily fashioned and immediately tried in the conflict. A society is formed for discussion, but the idea of impending action prevails in the minds of all those who constitute it. It is, in fact, an army; and the time given to speech serves to reckon up the strength and to animate the courage of the host, after which they march against the enemy. To the persons who compose it, resources which lie within the bounds of law may suggest themselves as means of success, but never as the only means.

Such, however, is not the manner in which the right of association is understood in the United States. In America the citizens who form the minority associate in order, first, to show their numerical strength and so to diminish the moral power of the majority; and, secondly, to stimulate competition and thus to discover those arguments that are most fitted to act upon the majority; for they always entertain hopes of drawing over the majority to their own side, and then controlling the supreme power in its name. Political associations in the United States are therefore peaceable in their intentions and strictly legal in the means which they employ; and they assert with perfect truth that they aim at success only by lawful expedients.[11]

Tocqueville gives us a vision of what he believes should be an idea of politics, a form of association that would not only protect individuals from tyranny but actively involve them in the making of decisions. It is the poetry of our democracy: It is the image of what we have never become.

To return to one of our central questions: If we are to use Tocqueville as a model, it becomes clear that our system is not being held together by the kinds of creative political activities he describes. This is true, in part, because the ideology of the system encourages neither political community nor political obligation.

THINGS AND SYMBOLISM: WHAT DOES HOLD US TOGETHER?

"The truth isn't news, and the news isn't true."

—*Jon Winters*

To know that politics does not hold us together gets us just so far. It gives us one less thing to worry about—we can check it off our list—and it gives us something to aim for. But the point is that we still don't know what holds us together. We might get closer to an answer by trying to understand what seems to be really important, what we seem to believe, and how that affects staying together.

Maybe the system is held together by material objects. It is possible, if one is cynical enough, to argue that in this land of electric can openers and vibrating beds, possessions are far more important than politics. Houses and cars and big bikes and boats really do count. People work very hard to be able to buy and to own. In the end, we may have to conclude that "things" hold us together, tie us to the system, and ensure the status quo.

---

[11] Alexis de Tocqueville, *Democracy in America*, Vol. 1 (New York: Vintage Books, 1945), pp. 198–206.

There are other equally important products of the system. There is the violence of television sports or the gooey-ness of the ice cream from the local parlor. Somehow, these things are important. We do identify. Maybe it is ice cream that holds us together. Sweet and sticky, available and fattening: Prisoners of Ice Cream.

But the ice cream image can easily be strained and over emphasized; while true, its truth is not inclusive enough. Let's try something else. What about television.

In a discussion of what holds us together, how could we not talk a little about television? It forms the core of much—probably way too much—of what we now have in common. We have national experiences together; in an odd way. If something important happens (a national election, the shooting of a president, the Super Bowl) we can all be expected to go home and "experience" it.

Now, we know that watching something, that being an observer, and not actually being at the event puts us in an interesting position. We can only see through a mechanical eye, we can only hear from a mechanical voice, and we are at the will of technicians who aim those eyes and ears.

As a nation, we are both tied together and passive. In the old days, it took months for news to get from one part of the country to another. We would never stand for that. We want to know now, and be done with it.

But to talk about the "main events" of our national life is to miss the point of our electronic ties. It is important to remember our faithfulness. How religiously we watch our favorite soaps, our favorite prime-time fantasies, our favorite games. The truth is, in an everyday way, our schedules are held together, in part, by television programming. "General Hospital" is a specific event for millions. Doesn't that qualify for holding us together?

If ice cream has the drawback of calories, and potential pimples, then television may be more dangerous. The passive part of television probably dominates everything else. Never mind the violence, the give-away shows, and the general moronic level of much that goes on. Think about what happens when you watch television.

You have choices: You can stand, sit, or lie down. If you are serious, you will not stand. You can eat, or drink, or smoke, or none of those things. I guess you can knit, if you do not have to watch what you are doing. Put a little differently, there is nothing you can do with another human being.

The television set receives the picture and sound and transmits it to you. You are the true receiver. You look and listen. You absorb.

Nothing is left to your imagination. If you simply listen to music, your imagination is free to fantasize. If you simply listen to music, you are free to associate it with whatever is going on. If you *watch* music (MTV) then you are tied to what you receive.

Studies show that one's imagination and intelligence is effected (as in lowered) by watching too much television.

(Note: I watch television. I enjoy it. There are programs I feel strongly about. I even have a little thing that changes channels for me. I love it. Also, I do not let my children watch nearly as much as they want to. All of this is simply a way of explaining a socio-logical way in which television makes us the same.)

So, we are receivers. We are tied together not so much in the particulars of what is shown as much as in the specific way we have given up social activities for passive ones.

There is one other way to learn about the system that I want to present. By discussing words, and understanding some of our language, we can see another way in which the system is held together.

THE USE OF WORDS

> To know the reality of politics, we have to believe the myth, to believe what we are told as children.
>
> —*Norman O. Brown*

We all know that systems are dependent, in part, upon the use of a common political language. Common language carries common myths. These words, these myths, are terribly important for any system—for any set of related institutions—as they provide the most subtle, most economic method of self-maintenance. It is critical for the government to set societal rules through language, through the words it uses, in order to keep order.[12]

---

[12] Words? George Carlin gives us the clue to "Our Creator." Think about it, Carlin tells us: God had his/her choice of *any* name and took the very best one.

For a simple example, we are taught that we have a representative democracy. Those are the words used; they frame our ideas
of what is. It takes little insight to know that what we have is only
marginally related to representation and that it has even less in
common with democracy. The words only represent our official
institutional myth. They are part of the symbols that work well to
keep the system going. What I should like to argue is that much of
our symbolic glue works at our personal expense, at the expense
of the citizenry.

If we examine two more myth-laden words, perhaps that
thought will be clarified. The words *equality* and *justice* are as
familiar as they are misunderstood, as they are systematically effective. Because they are words that are so common, words that we
seem to understand implicitly, it is important to try and figure out
their implications.

As we know, the Constitution was written as if all men (to be
sure, white, Protestant, propertied men—the framers did mean men)
were equal. What that has come to mean, what we have understood
it to mean, is that no individual is entitled to more rights than
another. Each person—in the public realm—is to be treated equally
by the system of rules to which all are equally subject. It is difficult
to fault such a formulation: Equal is equal.

Justice came to mean equality of rights and equality of treatment. Moreover, justice was equated with fairness. A just or a fair
decision was one that *had no objective standard of reason or justice,
or even passion;* it merely meant a decision lacking bias. Again the
formulation is a standard, everyday definition of what we feel/know
to be true. What we must do now is to put the two words together.

By merging the myths of justice and equality, the system is able
to overlook many kinds of inequalities. In the process, the system
helps protect itself. It works in a simple enough manner: In our
alikeness, we become alone. A "fair trial" can overlook the money,
connections, color, and cultural background of the defendant. We
all become bleached white; we all look the same—each alone, each
the same, no matter what. Justice comes to mean the equality of
everyone, equal or not. When we try to band together to work out
our public problems, whether we become Panthers or militant

PTAers, we learn that equal rights and equal treatment mean simply this: equal dependence and equal subjection.

Let me put it a little differently: To put equality together with justice, yet ignore such things as politics, community, and culture, results not in interesting kinds of individualism but in mass conformity.[13]

What I have been suggesting is that the system is held together—and this may seem a paradox—by the very fact that each of us is alone. The system coheres—and coerces—because the one has no defense against the mass. Even though it can be demonstrated that some people control much more wealth than others, that some make much more wide-ranging decisions than others, the fact remains that people don't think of America or of themselves in very meaningful class terms. The point is that those who hold "real power" are well limited by the boundaries of the system. (Indeed, one wonders if it is worth the price to get it.) It is the unique, the challenging—in a word, the political—that is mistrusted. The "real power" is the power of the guardian, and the guardian is as limited in creative political terms as those he or she "watches over." The powerful and the powerless are equally susceptible.

Most of us think of ourselves as some variation of middle-class; and it is arguable that our imaginations are as limited as our self-definitions. The seeds of our powerlessness lie in the isolation of being the same. We may turn again to the writings of Alexis de Tocqueville to understand the problem he identifies as the "Tyranny of the Majority."

> A distinction must be drawn between tyranny and arbitrary power. Tyranny may be exercised by means of the law itself, and in that case it is not arbitrary; arbitrary power may be exercised for the public good, in which case it is not tyrannical. Tyranny usually employs arbitrary means, but if necessary it can do without them. . . .
>
> In general, the American functionaries are far more independent within the sphere that is prescribed to them than the French civil

---

[13] In a sense, this is the logical extension of the public-private problem of liberalism that was discussed earlier in connection with bureaucracies. The point here is that private advantage is often overlooked in public alikeness.

officers. Sometimes, even, they are allowed by the popular authority to exceed those bounds; and as they are protected by the opinion and backed by the power of the majority, they dare do things that even a European, accustomed as he is to arbitrary power, is astonished at. By this means habits are formed in the heart of a free country which may some day prove fatal to its liberties.

It is in the examination of the exercise of thought in the United States that we clearly perceive how far the power of the majority surpasses all the powers with which we are acquainted in Europe. Thought is an invisible and subtle power that mocks all the efforts of tyranny. At the present time the most absolute monarchs in Europe cannot prevent certain opinions hostile to their authority from circulating in secret through their dominions and even in their courts. It is not so in America; as long as the majority is still undecided, discussion is carried on; but as soon as its decision is irrevocably pronounced, everyone is silent, and the friends as well as the opponents of the measure unite in assenting to its propriety. The reason for this is perfectly clear: no monarch is so absolute as to combine all the powers of society in his own hands and to conquer all opposition, as a majority is able to do, which has the right both of making and of executing the laws.

The authority of a king is physical and controls the actions of men without subduing their will. But the majority possesses a power that is physical and moral at the same time, which acts upon the will as much as upon the actions and represses not only all contest, but all controversy.

I know of no country in which there is so little independence of mind and real freedom of discussion as in America.[14] In any constitutional state in Europe every sort of religious and political theory may be freely preached and disseminated; for there is no country in Europe so subdued by any single authority as not to protect the man who raises his voice in the cause of truth from the consequences of his livelihood. If he is unfortunate enough to live under an absolute government, the people are often on his side; if he inhabits a free country, he can, if necessary, find a shelter behind the throne. The aristocratic part of society supports

---

[14] Emphasis added.

him in some countries, and the democracy in others. But in a
nation where democratic institutions exist, organized like those
of the United States, there is but one authority, one element of
strength and success, with nothing beyond it.

In America the majority raises formidable barriers around the
liberty of opinion; within these barriers an author may write what
he pleases, but woe to him if he goes beyond them. Not that he
is in danger of an auto-da-fé, but he is exposed to continued
obloquy and persecution. His political career is closed forever,
since he has offended the only authority that is able to open it.
Every sort of compensation, even that of celebrity, is refused to
him. Before making public his opinions he thought he had sym-
pathizers; now it seems to him that he has none any more since
he has revealed himself to everyone; then those who blame him
criticize loudly and those who think as he does keep quiet and
move away without courage. He yields at length, overcome by
the daily effort which he has to make, and subsides into silence,
as if he felt remorse for having spoken the truth.

Fetters and headsmen were the coarse instruments that tyranny
formerly employed; but the civilization of our age has perfected
despotism itself, though it seemed to have nothing to learn. Monarchs had, so to speak, materialized oppression; the democratic
republics of the present day have rendered it as entirely an affair
of the mind as the will which it is intended to coerce. Under the
absolute sway of one man the body was attacked in order to
subdue the soul; but the soul escaped the blows which were directed against it and rose proudly superior. Such is not the course
adopted by tyranny in democratic republics; there the body is left
free, and the soul is enslaved. The master no longer says: 'You
shall think as I do or you shall die'; but he says: 'You are free to
think differently from me and to retain your life, your property,
and all that you possess, but you are henceforth a stranger among
your people. You may retain your civil rights, but they will be
useless to you, for you will never be chosen by your fellow citizens
if you solicit their votes; and they will affect to scorn you if you
ask for their esteem. You will remain among men, but you will
be deprived of the rights of mankind. Your fellow creatures will
shun you like an impure being; and even those who believe in
your innocence will abandon you, lest they should be shunned in

their turn. Go in peace! I have given you your life, but it is an existence worse than death.'[15]

UNIFORMITY AND INDIVIDUALISM: THE POLITICS OF OUR VERY OWN TYRANNY

Imagine a mass of cancerous tissue, the cells of which enjoyed consciousness. Would they not be full of self-congratulatory sentiments at their independence, their more advanced level of development, their rapid rate of growth? Would they not sneer at their more primitive cousins who were bound into a static and unfree existence, with limited aspirations, subject to heavy group constraint, and obviously "going nowhere"? Would they not rejoice in their control over their own destiny, and cheer the conversion of more and more normal cells as convincing proof of the validity of their own way of life? Would they not, in fact, feel increasingly triumphant right up to the moment the organism on which they fed expired?

—*Philip Slater*

To understand how the system is held together, it may help to think of a huge machine. The machine, when healthy, seems almost organic. Looking inside the machine, one could see the hundreds of thousands of political associations Tocqueville described in the first excerpt in this chapter. While there could be no single "rational" plan of action for that kind of system, neither could there be an ongoing tyranny of the individual by the many.

Now imagine the same machine sick. Indeed, imagine those political associations gone, the insides of the system rotted. The system is then dependent not upon the politics of the citizens but upon the strength of the state, the oppressiveness of the cover of the machine. As the inside weakens, the outside gets strong. As the population becomes isolated, the force of the state goes unchallenged. As we become less interested in joint action, in politics, we become more susceptible to oppression.

The tyranny of the majority, the terrible conformity and con-

---

[15] Tocqueville, *Democracy in America*, Vol. 1, pp. 269–272.

finement of which Tocqueville warns, is as important as it is obvious. Each of us is, at one and the same time, both the tyrannized and the majority. Our instincts drive us into private life, while the majority determines our choices in that life. It may be instructive to anticipate that discussion here.

When I was growing up, there were four of us in the family. The usual assortment: a mother, father, older sister and myself. One day my sister (I think she was maybe fourteen or fifteen) brought home the fifth member of the family. We took in They Say.

You know They Say. "Why do you *have* to do that?" "Well, They Say," or "Is it really important that you do that?" "Well, They Say," or, "How do you *know* that?" "Well, They Say."

Put differently, we can name—can actually see—the pressure of the faceless majority that comes right into our homes. That majority can walk right in and be a faceless power and force in how we think and act. The tyranny of the majority is as real as They Say, and carries the weight of all those around us.

What is so magical is that everyone seems at the mercy of They Say. Equally true, it always seems that everyone *else* is a member of They. It comes to this: The power of being part of the They does us no good, while being at the mercy of the They all too often hurts.

There is a way in which the They is more national than ever. Before, They were fairly local and, at best regional. Of course generations took on a particular look, but the details were handled from high school to high school. Now, They are on national television and all Americans can see how they each should look and should act. They Say, and millions listen.

I'd have probably been happier had They Say stayed away.

As individuals, we like to believe that there is a series of choices—important ones—we will have the opportunity to make. We fret not only over the make of the automobile we are going to buy but also over its color. In weaker, less guarded moments, we realize that these decisions are not really critical ones; indeed, they are not even important. These insights rarely mean that we will stop worrying over such matters of consumption. To review the preceding chapter on voting is to begin to understand that doing things alone does not necessarily lead to individualism, and that doing things in association does not automatically eliminate it.

Symbolically, voting is American democracy at its height, the apex of political participation: the common person, spending a few minutes every two or four years, alone in a small booth, choosing between two individuals who were selected by people he or she does not know, to make decisions that individual should be able to participate in. Behavior is our substitute for action; psychic satisfaction, our substitute for power.

Our concerns are those of the majority, those the system prescribes for us. When we make a choice and then take an action, we generally do it alone. Our choice is the same others make; our behavior, the same as theirs too—but somehow we convince ourselves that it is unique and that we are individuals. Philip Slater describes the phenomenon thus:

> When a value is as strongly held as is individualism in America the illnesses it produces tend to be treated by increasing the dosage, in the same way an alcoholic treats a hangover or a drug addict . . . withdrawal symptoms. . . . The desire to be somehow special inaugurates an even more competitive quest for progressively more rare and expensive symbols—a quest that is ultimately futile since it is individualism itself that produces uniformity. This is poorly understood by Americans who tend to confuse uniformity with "conformity," in the sense of compliance with or submission to group demands. Many societies exert far more pressure on the individual to mold himself to fit a particularized segment of a total group pattern, but there is variation among those circumscribed roles. Our society gives far more leeway to the individual to pursue his own ends, but, since *it* defines what is worthy and desirable, everyone tends, independently but monotonously, to pursue the same things in the same way. The first pattern combines cooperation, conformity, and variety; the second, competition, individualism, and uniformity.[16]

One must agree that there is irony in the great traffic jams that occur when hundreds of thousands of vacationers all leave for home early in order to "beat the traffic."

---

[16] Philip E. Slater, *The Pursuit of Loneliness* (Boston: Beacon Press, 1971), pp. 7, 8–9.

Maybe the system is held together—and continues to function in lock-step precision—because of the symbolic value we give to what we ironically call individualism.

The more peaceful a community has become, the more cowardly the citizens become; the less accustomed they are to standing pain, the more will worldly punishments suffice as deterrents, the faster will religious threats become superfluous. . . . In highly civilized peoples, finally, even punishments should become highly superfluous deterrents; the mere fear of shame, the trembling of vanity, is so continually effective that immoral actions are left undone. The refinement of morality increases together with the refinement of fear. Today the fear of disagreeable feelings in other people is almost the strongest of our own disagreeable feelings. One would like ever so much to live in such a way as to do nothing except what causes others agreeable *feelings, and even to take pleasure in nothing more that does not also fulfill this condition.*

—Friedrich Nietzsche

Focus Six

There is a great irony in the main point of this chapter. The mainstream American emphasis on individuality results in uniformity. Given our myths and the structure of our institutions, the more each of us tries to be his or her own distinct person, the more each of us behaves like everyone else. The core of the irony is that seeing each person's distinctiveness is difficult within the institutions available for showing something about ourselves to each other. We are unique individuals—each of us unlike anyone who has ever lived, lives at the present, or will live in the future—but we don't do a very good job of providing opportunities for revealing that about ourselves. Hence, our genuine individuality remains hidden while we strive arduously to make it known in terms which seldom are successful.

For example, if I strive to get grades higher than anyone else, or to get a better job or to make more money than all others, I almost always will be overshadowed by someone else's achievement. The ground of comparison of being the one best at a certain endeavor means that only one person will be at the top on any specific criterion. There can be at any moment only one richest person. So, if we assume that we all are unique, and that the mainstream criteria of distinction are fewer than the population, then most of us will never be able to demonstrate our individuality.

Fortunately, most of our competition in the United States does not create disorder. The simplest reason is that we agree that striving for distinction on grounds such as grades and money is so inevitable, essential, and helpful for human beings that partial success is preferable to changing the grounds of competition. Hence, we accept by and large the prevailing ladders of success. And, when we accept the criteria for competition, we establish the basic dynamic for uniformity. Everyone goes to school; everyone tries to make money, for example. Everyone agrees that individuality is measured by the standards for those activities. The nation is held together by the desire to engage in those activities in an orderly way.

A delightful and telling example of uniformity is used toward the end of the chapter. It argues glibly that the reason for traffic jams on warm summer Friday afternoons is the rush of individualists who have independently and voluntarily decided to leave town early for the weekend—in order to beat the traffic! One important assumption in the book is that the ability to laugh at ourselves about uniformity is preparatory to perspective on our myth of and institutions for individuality. We believe that everyone actually is unique but also unable to give worldly reality to his or her distinctiveness. One reason for continually raising the example of the town meeting is that it is the kind of forum within which both individuality and common purpose are possible. The citizens bring unique perspectives to political issues. During debate and deliberation, they strive to make their viewpoints known to each other while also working toward agreement on proposals each can support willingly. When this method of opinion formation and exchange is operating well, individuality becomes real because it is seen and acknowledged as the legitimate viewpoint and unique biography brought to the arena by each citizen.

In addition, the community is held together actively when common agreements are reached. Competition is encouraged on the grounds of being best at your own viewpoint while simultaneously being best at finding ways to enable everyone to agree on joint action. Politically, the lone individual is powerless, but when good at being his or her best self *together* with others, that person creates power together with them. The irony of individuality is resolved, and not at the expense of the uniqueness of each citizen insofar as he or she can genuinely agree to the collective decision. The promise of politics is that the rightfittingness of one person can prosper together with those of other people when they take moral stands on public issues and act responsibly with others in public forums.

7

POLITICS AND FREEDOM

Albert Camus writes of the myth of Sisyphus.

Sisyphus was a Greek god who was condemned to the earth to push a giant rock to the top of a mountain. Once at the top, the rock would roll back to the valley of its own weight, and Sisyphus would walk down and again begin pushing the rock up. The fate of Sisyphus is the ceaseless rolling of the rock up the mountain.

Camus argues that Sisyphus experiences a kind of silent joy. "His fate belongs to him. His rock is his thing." He experiences joy— but not simply when the rock is at the top, when his task is "completed." Camus writes:

"I leave Sisyphus at the foot of the mountain! One always finds one's burden again. But Sisyphus teaches the higher fidelity that negates the gods and raises rocks. He too concludes that all is well. This universe henceforth without a master seems to him neither sterile nor futile. Each atom of that stone, each mineral flake of that night-filled mountain, in itself forms a world. The struggle itself toward the heights is enough to fill a man's heart.

"One must imagine Sisyphus happy."

If everyone has the right to express his will . . . what does this right mean if their will is merely an echo of the chorus around them?

—*John Schaar*

ON FREEDOM

It is a tricky thing to be free, and awfully hard. One would guess that there are a lot of people who want to be free—but surprisingly, there are many who do not. We know that there are many people who think that they are free, and that there are very few people who really are.

In this chapter, we can only begin to understand why there is so much confusion about being free. There will be a short essay, and some explanation, and a few excerpts from literature to help show us how hard it is to arrive at a meaning of freedom. As a topic, it is pretentious. I admit that. But it seems so sloppily defined, so misunderstood, yet so often assumed an important part of life, that it seems reasonable to spend some time thinking about it.

Out of all of our literature, out of all of American letters, it seems natural to begin with Henry David Thoreau. Maybe he wrote about freedom. Maybe we all want to go to Walden Pond to commune with nature, with the ghost of Thoreau. Or to the mountains or to the ocean or to an island to just be away. To just be free. To do whatever we need to do, alone. Do it by ourselves, to ourselves, and for ourselves.

But is that being free, or is it simply being separated from others, experiencing anomie or being alienated? Thoreau might be a part of the American Dream, but is he truly part of the legacy of freedom?

Get away. Now that is a good idea. We Americans are impatient types. There has always been a West, and somehow freedom was always there. So, with covered wagons, or iron horses, or some exotic van or bus or camper or God-knows-what, we all move West to get free and get rich. Americans move and move and move.

Those in the East move West. We go from the South to the North. From small and middle sized towns to big ones; from big ones to bedroom communities. Some of us even go to villages (now electronic) or even to the country. But we all move. We are restless. We are in search of the perfect place or the perfect job or the perfect neighborhood. We are, in the end, looking for ourselves, we are looking to be free.

We run to any place, going nowhere. Nowhere people living in a Nowhere land. Is it really freedom, to move from but never to?

As we go, we waste one place after another. The pattern now seems to be well established. In our restlessness, we buy and destroy, buy and destroy. Our home is only where our investment is. As soon as the river is polluted, or the land is barren and the winds carve out a dust bowl, or all the trees are down and the land will not support even animal life, then we move on. We move West. We move free.

We consume and, in doing so, destroy; then we restlessly move to more consumption and destruction. We do this as a free people, yearning to stay free.

But if we have no freedom in our physical "homes," then are we free in our beliefs? Doesn't it seem logical that we all might believe in the same thing; in other words, that in our similar moral beliefs and actions we could find a kind of freedom?

For example, the Puritans believed that they had a covenant with God and that by working together they could build the New Jerusalem in the New World. A model community that would stand out as a beacon against the depravity they perceived in Europe's Christian community. What I would like to suggest is that, in fact, the Puritans had a kind of freedom we no longer possess. That, despite their "Puritanism," they were tied together by a vision of the world they wanted to create.

Can we define our own freedom in any kind of positive terms? Are we truly naive enough to claim that what we call freedom includes the ideas of building or creating? Do we even have any kind of binding belief that might lead us to the freedom that comes from shared visions?

Of course the questions are rhetorical. It seems impossible for us to understand freedom as truly something positive. We have a terrible time trying to distinguish between *freedom from* (running away) and *freedom to*. What we need is freedom to; what we have is freedom from. One of the most frustrating things is that something so normal as attending college in order to get a good job may not end up what it appears to be.

The fact seems to be that we work hard, that we move from place to place, looking for Walden Pond, looking to escape. We continually prove our freedom from by running away as fast as we can. We are bound by nothing, tied to no one. And we call the isolation and destruction freedom, and defend it with our very selves.

THE IDEOLOGY IN OUR LETTERS

> *He slept on the straw with the groom, and memories weighted heavily on his chest; he awakened many times. Scattered and infertile, the scenes of his life stretched out behind him, rich in magnificent images but broken in so many pieces, so poor in value, so poor in love! In the morning, as they rode away, he looked anxiously up to the windows. Perhaps he could catch another glimpse of Julie. A few days ago he had looked just as anxiously up to the windows of the bishop's palace to see if Agnes might not appear. She had not shown herself, and neither did Julie. His whole life had been like that, it seemed to him. Saying farewell, escaping, being forgotten; finding himself alone again, with empty hands and a frozen heart.*
>
> —Hermann Hesse

There are, as indicated above, different ways to think about freedom. In the rest of the chapter, I will discuss, in turn, freedom and how it has been interpreted in American letters, freedom and economics, freedom and psychology, and freedom and politics.

To begin with Thoreau is to begin with the classic statement on being free by being alone. He makes one case all too well: What we must do is to get away; discover ourselves by being alone; find freedom by experiencing nature. Thoreau was a poet, a spokesman for that urge in us that tells us to ignore society and relearn primary associations, and to learn to commune with nature.

By sketching in Thoreau's experience at Walden and understanding some of it in his own words, the point of our common past can best be made. He was born in 1817 and did what the bright men in those days did: He went to Harvard College. For a time, after he graduated, he wrote, opened a private school, and was friendly with people like Ralph Waldo Emerson. He made a little trouble (he was fired as a school teacher for refusing to administer discipline) and had problems deciding on a vocation, but he was generally regarded as a promising scholar. On July 4, 1845, Thoreau went to live at Walden Pond. There he kept a journal.[1]

"The real attractions," Thoreau writes of Walden, "were: its complete retirement, being about two miles from the village, half a mile from the nearest neighbor, and separated from the highway by a broad field." So he is set. In the wilderness, but by a town. Indeed, only a field away from a highway. But by himself. For what?

"To enjoy these advantages I was ready to carry it on; like Atlas, to take the world on my shoulders—I never heard what compensation he received for that—and do all those things, which had no other motive or excuse but that I might pay for it and be unmolested in my possession of it." That is what he wanted: to enjoy the benefits and to be unmolested. Certainly we understand that. He knew what that meant, and counseled: ". . . to my fellows, once for all, As long as possible live free and uncommitted."

To examine Thoreau's Walden thoroughly is not the object of these paragraphs. But it would be unfair not to glimpse his "day" at the pond; it would be a loss to miss his perceptions.

> Morning is when I awake and there is a dawn in me. . . . The millions are awake enough for physical labor; but only one in a million is awake enough for effective intellectual exertion, only one in a hundred millions to a poetic or divine life. To be awake is to be alive. I have never yet met a man who is quite awake.

> I went to the woods because I wished to live deliberately, to front not only the essential facts of life, and see if I could not learn what it had to teach, and not, when I came to die, discover that I had not lived. I did not wish to live what was not life. . . . I wanted to live deep and suck the marrow of life . . . to drive life into a corner, and reduce it to its lowest terms. . . .

---

[1] Henry David Thoreau, *Walden,* ed. Sherman Paul (Boston: Houghton Mifflin Company, 1960) The following quotations come from the chapter titled "Where I Lived, and What I Lived For."

Our life is frittered away by detail . . . simplicity, simplicity, simplicity! I say, let your affairs be as two or three, and not a hundred
or a thousand; instead of a million count half a dozen, and keep
your accounts on your thumb nail. . . . Simplify, simplify . . . the
nation itself, with all its so-called internal improvements, which,
by the way are all external and superficial. . . . If we do not get
out sleepers and forge rails, and devote days and nights to the
work, but go to tinkering upon our *lives* to improve *them,* who
will build railroads? And if railroads are not built, how shall we
get to heaven in season? But if we stay at home and mind our
business, who will want railroads? We do not ride on the railroad;
it rides upon us.

Of course Henry is right. What American could disagree with
that? Just to have two problems; to simplify and to be awake. But,
of course, to be only half-awake is at least to be aware that the
world has some problems. Are we Americans—or is anyone who
has decided to live in a world with anyone else—perhaps too complex simply to be simple? More importantly, at least practically,
what do we do if there are not enough ponds to go around?

In other words, Thoreau's powerful experience, and equally
powerful prose, are limited in their helpfulness. We are not much
farther along in understanding ourselves in a world full of people.
We cannot understand who we are in terms of social or cultural
interactions. We are no closer to the idea that freedom might be
contained in commitment, or that being free might include something more than ourselves.

FREEDOM AS A HIGHWAY

What remains of the ideology is the quest. The search. The Open
Road. What the pioneers helped start and Thoreau romanticized,
Walt Whitman described and D. H. Lawrence analyzed.

In a remarkable essay, D. H. Lawrence took Walt Whitman
to task for what Lawrence saw as an empty quest. What follows
is part of what Lawrence has to say about Whitman's long, rambling
American poem *Leaves of Grass.*

The Open Road. The great home of the Soul is the open road.
Not heaven, not paradise. Not "above." Not even "within." The

soul is neither "above" nor "within." It is a wayfarer down the open road.

Not by meditating. Not by fasting. Not by exploring heaven after heaven, inwardly, in the manner of the great mystics. Not by exaltation. Not by ecstasy. Not by any of these ways does the soul come into her own.

Only by taking the open road.

Not through charity. Not through sacrifice. Not even through love. Not through good works. Not through these does the soul accomplish herself.

Only through the journey down the open road.

The journey itself, down the open road. Exposed to full contact. On two slow feet. Meeting whatever comes down the open road. In company with those that drift in the same measure along the same way. Towards no goal. Always the open road.

Having no direction even.[2]

As you might have noted, I described the Lawrence essay as "remarkable." Notice that I did not say accurate. The fact is that the essay is very well written, very funny, often very insightful, and just as often, very wrong. Most people believe that the part just quoted has everything to do with Lawrence and not very much to do with Whitman.

Whitman, more than most, had a vision of the American people which celebrated the possibility of individualism in an American community. There is a real appreciation of the variety of lives which has made up who we are. The use of Lawrence is really to show, in almost parody form, what he understood to be the urge to run away which is so common among us. That he misused Walt Whitman is a shame.

There are other examples. We can read these words from Henry Miller's "The Air-Conditioned Nightmare":

---

[2] D. H. Lawrence, *Studies in Classic American Literature* (New York: Viking Press, 1966). The passage comes from the chapter titled "Whitman." Larry Spence insisted that the reality of Whitman not be ignored. I am once again indebted to his thoughtfulness.

America is made up, as we all know, of people who ran away
from such ugly situations. America is the land par excellence of
expatriates and escapists, renegades, to use a strong word. A
wonderful world we might have made of this new continent if
we had really run out on our fellow-men in Europe, Asia, and
Africa. A brave, new world it might have become, had we had
the courage to turn our back on the old, to build afresh, to erad-
icate the poisons which had accumulated through centuries of
bitter rivalry, jealousy and strife.

But the desire to keep moving, to be left alone, is just one way
to handle freedom. Deep down, it may be the one with which we
have most sympathy; it is certainly a most obvious one. It is going
to Europe to get away (for one summer); it is traveling cross-country
just to count the miles you are away from where you started. At
some point, the quest for some thing—for some meaning some
where—changes into the simple idea of leaving, of getting away,
of movement. Whitman is Thoreau on the road. It seems both
legitimate and necessary to ask if either gives adequate advice about
freedom.

We have already raised problems connected with this approach.
But we are not yet ready for an "answer." It would be premature
to present a full-scale retort or even to tentatively offer a different
approach. There are other ideas, other circumstances and ap-
proaches that must be dealt with before we get to politics and
freedom.

FREEDOM AS MATERIAL

*Instead of being primarily concerned over right and wrong,
men would learn, while fighting over these issues, that political
arithmetic could be substituted for ethics, that they could live
more peaceably by a calculus of forces than by the spirit. At
the end of the seventeenth century, the medieval synthesis,
in which all activities were gradations within a coherent
organization of existence, was broken apart. Into this new
world of reason and commerce, Virginia was prepared to
enter as early as 1624; it was stripped of its medieval notions
and was started on the road which led from teleology to
competition and expedience, where the decisive factor would*

> *be, not the example from the Apostles, but the price per pound of tobacco.*
>
> —*Perry Miller*

There is buried in us—maybe deeply, maybe close to the surface—an idea that somehow freedom is tied to material things. Certainly there are impressive advocates of such a position. The argument is that people who are free from material wants are free from oppression; they are, in fact, free to be themselves. There is little doubt that the advocates of material freedom have a point. It is neither intelligent nor sensible to argue that people are best off when they are hungry, or have no shelter, or are in poor health. That is not what I wish to defend.[3]

I want to argue that we have connected freedom and materialism in extreme ways. That we have probably long since passed the point where we could all be fed and housed and medically treated. Yet we still pursue a material goal. We pursue that goal without realizing its costs.

If the preceding sections about Thoreau and Whitman—ideas about us—are right, then we should expect to find some evidence somewhere of the pursuit of goods. There should be some evidence in our history that points to a moving towards freedom from the past. Moreover, that moving might have economic overtones.

There is evidence, and it lies right in the middle of one of our nicest, most romantic myths: the myth of the yeoman farmer.

Remember the yeoman farmer? The brave and noble pioneer who moved West to settle the land? To find roots? To be self-sufficient, to be away, to be hard-working, and to be free? Had we just been born *last* century, then we could have known the land. Then we could have communed with the stuff of our primordial past—with nature.[4]

---

[3] For a fine argument that people can be more than their material surroundings, see John Schaar, *Escape from Authority* (New York: Harper & Row, 1961). To quote: "Some part of the mystery and grandeur of human beings lies in the fact that they make paintings on the walls of miserable caves and write poetry and philosophy in the midst of hunger and filth."

[4] For a fine example of the restlessness involved in moving West, see Ken Kesey, *Sometimes a Great Notion*.

There is no doubt that the myth of the yeoman farmer stems from the facts. There *were* those who went West and felt free. There *were* some small towns where a communal spirit existed; where each person took an interest in the other; and where citizens personally got together and personally helped their neighbors. Rural America, with the Noble Farmer, is a part of our collective past worth remembering—at least in that vision.

The facts about the farmers seem much closer to our assumptions than our myths: They moved a great deal, wanted to be "free," and were interested in the land primarily for the money they could make from it. Not much romance in that. Richard Hofstadter, in *The Age of Reform,* tells us:

> The predominance in American agriculture of the isolated farmstead standing in the midst of great acreage, the frequent movements, the absence of village life, deprived the farmer and his family of the advantages of community, the chances of association and cooperation, and encouraged that rampant, suspicious, and almost suicidal individualism for which the American farmer was long noted. . . . The characteristic product of American rural society was not a yeoman or a villager but a harassed little country businessman who worked very hard, moved all too often, gambled with his land, and made his way alone.[5]

Not very noble, that vision of freedom. The vision of the small isolated farmer continually moving for profits, relating to the land primarily for the economic reward, communing with an investment while thinking about future riches. But that is the past, a part of the past buried almost as deeply as our treatment of the Indians, who really did have a home in the land.

We have not lost the idea that wealth is important, that it is "freeing." We move from our civilization—from our problems, from our cities—to the suburbs. Money or at least mortgages physically remove us from social responsibility. To be free in a tract home. But we know that enough money will also buy us power, will enable us to control. There has been a whole literature in sociology and political science telling us where power is, who pos-

---

[5] Richard Hofstadter, *The Age of Reform* (New York: Random House, 1955), p. 45.

sesses it, and why they have it. A nice example of such a book is *Who Rules America?* by G. William Domhoff.[6]

Domhoff tries to prove what many people suspect:

1. that there is an upper class;

2. that it owns a disproportionate amount of the country's wealth and receives a disproportionate amount of its yearly income;

3. that it—along with its high-level executives—controls the nation's major banks, corporations, elite universities, and largest mass media;

4. that its control extends to the executive branch of the federal government;

5. that it merely influences the Congress, most state governments, and most city governments.

That is a big job for any group of people. I suppose one could conclude that this is no mere idle rich. But there are more important implications. If power and freedom are tied together (whoever heard of powerlessness being freedom in America?), then the message is clear: Get rich. Money is power, power is freedom. We work out a perversion of this every day. Instead of being rich, we can at least appear rich. So we earn small and buy big. We give ourselves the charge of power by changing what we buy.

I am not happy to leave the analysis at that. Too many things are forgotten, too many things are assumed. We forget that people really do need food and shelter and medicine, and that we are skilled enough to provide everyone with all these things. We are, if nothing else, a productive people. We also assume that to have money is to have control, is to be free. I am unconvinced. I am simply unsure. Henry Kariel hints at the problems:

> But freedom from want and for leisure is not enough. . . . Abundant resources may themselves be produced by means utterly indifferent to the values of political freedom. In point of fact,

---

[6] See G. William Domhoff, *Who Rules America?* (Englewood Cliffs, N J : Prentice-Hall, 1967).

abundance is made possible by large-scale technology and a
sweeping division of human labor, which have already entailed
the subordination of personal interests. . . . Men must be free,
therefore, not only from the necessity of finding the means for
sustenance but also from the presumed imperatives of
technology. . . .

In short, it matters *how* material abundance and the amenities of
life are provided.[7]

What Kariel implies is that there are hidden costs to our
overabundance, real prices we must pay in order to buy our way
to freedom or power or both. Let us list some of the costs. In our
search for freedom we have lost our home. While developing the
skills of speculation, buying, and then selling for profit—in other
words, developing the skills of a "developer" who does not stay
on his or her development—we have lost touch with the land. We
have sacrificed any meaningful relationship with our surroundings
by thinking of it in terms of debits and credits. It is simply a ledger-
book relationship where wheat and grass have come to mean money
and possible independence. Maybe even freedom.

As we are beginning to find out, this kind of dynamic can go
on until we have destroyed our surroundings. There are just so
many trees to be cut, deer to be shot, lands to ruin, oceans to muck
up, and lakes to kill. We produce things by destroying other things.
The price of material freedom is paid, in part, by breathing our
own air. Taxes seem cheaper.

That, of course, is the common argument, the easy one. Part
of what I would like to suggest is that even if we had cleaned up
everything—air and water and minds—we might not be much better
off. The problems of "clean" are certainly solvable. Ralph Nader
knows that.[8] What is at stake is our freedom. Do we really have

---

[7] Henry Kariel, *The Promise of Politics* (Englewood Cliffs, N.J.: Prentice-Hall,
1966), p. 39.

[8] The whole Ralph Nader/ecology problem is in itself a problem. Nader promises
cleanliness but not really reform. If he is successful, it will merely mean that we can
live in the same system—which will have been made stronger—without the pollution.
We will soon find out that there is much money to be made from ecology and that
lawyers have found yet another way to funnel public problems through the courts.

power? Can money give us the control to make us free? As argued earlier, I think not.

There are at least two ways to get at the problem of money and power leading to freedom. The first way is to look at those at the "top"—the rich, the executives. The whole idea of dealing with this group is obvious. These are the envied, the ones who have won, the ones, we suspect, who might be free. But the point is painful for the belief. These people, as much as or more than any others, are in many ways the prisoners of bureaucracies.

They are where they are because they have best learned and acted out the money/production/freedom ethic. That is their morality, the defining limitations of their imaginations and actions. They are different only because they push bigger buttons from more comfortable offices. Given a choice between comfort or discomfort, money or poverty, big buttons or no buttons, most of us would choose comfort, money, and buttons. But that set of choices may mask the real issue of freedom: the freedom to act together, the freedom to define oneself by one's actions.

The second way to get at the problem is by looking at those who have not "made it," those who are outside the ethic. It seems clear that things other than money can lead to freedom, if money is not the principal value. Minorities that have not been allowed to participate equally in the pursuit of materialism may be more free than those at the top. The militant minority may have understood more about freedom than the executive.

All I want to suggest is something that I believe most of you already suspect: Materialism as an ideology may not lead us to freedom. Materialism, no matter how much we invest in it and attribute to it, is not the entire answer to our dreams. Further, that those we consider "economically disadvantaged" may be able to teach us valuable lessons about the costs of financial success—and the power of ideology.

FREEDOM AND PSYCHOLOGY (WITH A WORD ABOUT DOPE)

"Everything else in this world is being turned on and off—lights, television sets, refrigerators, stoves, fans, phonographs,

vacuum cleaners, and so on—so why shouldn't we want to be
turned on too?"

—Leslie Farber quoting a young student

There are times—all too frequent—when it occurs to me that freedom is a used-up, unrealistic problem. Most people do not consider
it for long enough to count; they are able to "common-sense" it
out, to come to terms with it, and then to let it go. Essentially, Who
Cares? There are other times—almost as frequent—when it occurs
to me that *that* is part of the problem. We act as if we know what
freedom is, without working on it. We accept what we are told, or
what we observe, and leave it unquestioned.

If freedom is an important concept that ought to be acted upon,
then it makes sense to try to figure out what it means. Further, if
freedom has something to do with other people, then it should be
properly studied as a topic of politics.

It is possible that we—"we" being an ill-defined group of people who are either young or "hip," or modern, or "liberal," or
simply identify with Now—have gone beyond some of the preceding
American definitions of freedom. While the Open Road may still
be attractive, materialism may not be quite so alluring. While nature
may be attractive, maybe obvious destruction has lost some of its
appeal. But while some science seems to have lost its appeal, other
science has taken its place. It is this latter science, the science of
people's behavior and people's minds, that now purports to have
insight into a new freedom.

The new scientists—the behavioral psychologists, for example—are serious people who make serious claims about our lives
and our freedom. It is only fair to take them seriously.

Behavioral scientists are capable of formidable magic. They
can train animals to run the right way or to salivate on cue; they
can teach pigeons to play Ping-Pong. These scientists are even able
to make human beings feel good or bad, angry or happy, by running
electric currents to certain parts of the brain. No sense in being
frightened or outraged or anything else, it is simply a scientific fact:
Scientists can make us feel and do certain things they want us to.
They put their faith in determinism: the belief that each act is caused

by something, or a series of somethings, and that if one can only determine the stimulus, then one can predict the response.

That, of course, is science and determinism reduced to simplest terms. But the kernel of the belief is there: that it is theoretically possible to understand every action by discovering all the things that have gone into determining the action. Given this assumption, freedom—standing by itself—is a nonsense concept. If we learn what to do, how we act and react, then the behavioral sciences are surely right. In the book quoted at the beginning of this section, *Requiem for Democracy?*, arguments for "freedom" are presented and then discussed.

For example, we are told that it is foolish to believe that people can be free in the absence of "scientific behavior control." The authors write: "We cannot deal rationally with the behavioral sciences until we realize that control *per se* is not even an issue. From the scientist's viewpoint, all human actions follow laws and patterns, just as physical events do, and are, in that sense, controlled. . . . The real question is not 'Should [people] be controlled?' but 'How should [they] be controlled?' "[9]

The words used seem so reasonable, so value-free, so . . . scientific. It is as if rationality really were the basis of the world, and that we know what that rationality is. It is as if physical events are controlled by laws and patterns that we know—and so too human actions. There is no hint of Einstein's descriptions of the relativity of perception; there is no recognition of the phenomenologist Hussurl's idea that rationality has its roots in subjective thought. What we get is "value-free reason" run amuck, a belief system in behavioral science clothes.

Back to the argument. Andrews and Karlins continue by assuring us that the scientific control of behavior is not evil ("An atomic reaction can light a city or burn it") and that it does not appear, at this time, as if an elite corps of scientists or a tyrannical government could use behavioral control technology to regulate

---

[9] Lewis M. Andrews and Marvin Karlins, *Requiem for Democracy?* (New York: Holt, Rinehart & Winston, 1971), p. 39.

human conduct. There are, of course, some potential problems seen by Andrews and Karlins that they formulate as follows:

| Effective behavior control technology | + | Alienated individuals | = | Conditions conducive to formation of a psytocracy |

To put it another way, we may be more easily controlled by the technology of the behavioral sciences if we persist in being alienated from our fellow citizens. In part, a good insight. But the avoidance of a psytocracy does not mean that we are not determined, does not mean that we are "free."

According to the behavioral scientists, "If man's sense of freedom is to be restored, it must be expressed within the framework of science."[10] It is as simple as that. Freedom is determinism. Science makes us free. Not only is it science that frees us, but it is, more particularly, the mind. The process-people (those who accept determinism but think it is complicated, those who think the key lies in the "highly elaborate information-processing organ," the brain) believe that we are determined. But determined in a special way. That way involves our thought: *". . . the quality of thought is not a given; it is a product of training and experience."*[11]

So this is where behavioral science takes us, to where we can be free, to where we can determine our own quality of thought. Some scientists assume that is freedom. The ultimate freedom. Certainly the ultimate if one accepts that freedom is bound by the rules of science. The human condition is pretty easy to understand if we just believe. The struggle to be free (they mean within boundaries, of course) is as easily managed as this:

> When conflict arises, the man with simple information-processing skills will fall back on ethical systems, serial sets of priorities, and other external criteria. His behavior is determined in the rigid, classical sense of the word. The free man, on the other hand, *has*

---

[10] Ibid., p. 103.
[11] Ibid., p. 116. Emphasis added.

been determined to resolve his conflicts by generating new ideas and concepts.[12]

We can be free if we enter the world of these scientists. We have a chance if we can stop being old-fashioned, if we just drop those old "serial sets of priorities" and "ethical systems." Indeed, many of those "external criteria" should no longer be considered if we *really* want to be free. But why be cynical? The points are fairly obvious: Everything has an ideology: nothing is value-free. The question is, why accept the ideology of science? Aren't there worlds we cannot predict, actions we cannot determine? Why should there be total emphasis on our minds, our brains, our "elaborate information-processing organ"? Is there any reason to abandon "ethics" for the ethics of a process? Is science really the highest freedom, and have we finally reached our destiny?

Have we lost serendipity?

The problems raised for freedom by the behavioral scientists are not easily answered. What we cannot do is to accept their pronouncements without understanding their biases, their beliefs. We must examine what they do not say, as well as what they do; we must try to understand what their words would mean if they constituted a valid vision of our lives; we must ask if their offer of good is accompanied by unarticulated "bads."

I do not mean to limit the people who may be defined as behavioral scientists. There are all of those human-relations-behavioral-scientists who operate in our corporations. One corporation where they are becoming increasingly visible is well known to us. It is the humanist as teacher.

POWER, SCHOOLING, AND STUDENTING

The topics of being a student, and power (or powerlessness), seem to go together naturally enough. As we went through earlier, the student finds himself or herself in an institutional bind of impressive magnitude. After all, if you think about it, it is not hard

---

[12] Ibid., p. 115. Emphasis added. Much of the following discussion is similar to that in Theodore Roszak, *The Making of a Counter Culture* (Garden City, N.Y.: Anchor Books, 1969).

to figure out that everybody seems to have more power than a student.

In a way, that is right.

But as times change, we are able to understand that there have been variations on the theme of student/teacher power, and to examine these variations can give us some perspective about power . . . and not incidentally, about ourselves.

Not very long ago, both college life and course life were restrictive in straightforward ways. The student was forced to take many subjects that were disliked or "irrelevant" or seemingly simply unnecessary. In most classes, there were set assignments, tests, papers, and "rigorous" standards.

A normal course then was like a pre-med course now.

As you know, attempts—ranging from serious to rowdy—were made to change all of that. Successful attempts. Now, in most places, there are fewer required courses, there are a multitude of experimental programs and schools; and those students who make the effort can generally find a series of very easy courses to take.

I have no stake in defending the overly rigid, pre-protest programs. In those days schools really exercised power in two ways that seemed very wrong. First, the students had, most of the time, no way in which to comment on policies in general or professors in particular. That was the most visible fact.

The less visible use of power had to do with the huge sums of money colleges and universities got in order to do highly secret work for the government. There were, rightly, many questions about how an institution could both encourage independence while seeking the truth and take money while doing morally questionable things.

Those kinds of power are easy enough to understand.

They were the issues raised by another generation.

But there is another kind of power that has grown as a response to the past. Personal feelings (affect) are now rooted deeply in the academy, and it is important to examine the relationship of this pop-psychology humanism with power. It is social science playing soft.

While it is always inaccurate to stereotype (we know it can never be precise in any single case), there is some use in stereotyping.

If done well, it is possible to get a sense and even a clear picture of what is being stereotyped. What follows *may* be an exaggeration, but in important ways it is true.

Let me describe the pop-psychology, new humanist class.

The person teaching the class is kind; that, at least, is his or her professional stance. The person is dressed casually and is very soft-spoken. If the occasion arises he or she will look deeply into your eyes, or will touch you, or both.

The course outline and assignments will also appear to be casual. Many assignments will be optional, and the real amount of work will often be small. There will generally be no exams, and often not even a paper.

Some kind of class presentation is a real possibility.

In class there will be little formal lecturing and much meandering talk. Students are urged to "get in touch with" and then "share" their feelings. People in class always seem supportive. Students are given the "space" to be creative. Periodically, someone will cry. There is—with the honesty, confessions, and all—an impressive amount of moral superiority that gets passed around.

And it often *feels* so good.

And it is often such bullshit.

Aha! The question: How are feelings, bullshit, and power related?

As this "revolution" in the academy becomes solidified, I am of the very firm belief that power relations in contentless/feel-good classes are worse (well, certainly no better) than power relations in classes with content, tests, and clear designations of authority. Let me explain.

Any student goes into any new class with a certain amount of anxiety. Like it or not, that just seems to be a fact of going to college. In a class with books to read and material to learn—a class where there are papers to do or exams to take—the student is at least in a situation where the rules are clear. The professor, in some important ways, is now out of the anxiety pattern of the student.

Books, thoughts, ideas, and papers are ideally the focus of the student. Put differently, learning has a chance to become central. It seems right to get nervous about that. It is not an easy job.

I do not want to suggest that the professor is no longer important, is no longer a threat. Certainly someone reads those things students write, and someone comments on the work and even grades it. But by then the real work is finished. The student either did or did not learn. Either the student tried to do excellent work or did not try. The person doing the grading can make mistakes—either way, in favor or not in favor of the student—but the basic work has been done.

What about the other kind of class? Where there is no content or little content, where there are few books but many feelings, where there is really no academic or intellectual focus for the natural, more healthy anxiety mentioned earlier? The fact is this: The professor is in an extraordinarily powerful position.

Students can turn only to the professor to deal with their anxiety.

The course now revolves around the professor. Anxiety, which is now free-floating, can easily be manipulated by the person in charge. To be able to manipulate is merely a "human relations" learned skill. There are no facts that can help the student, because the whole course is fuzzy. There are no books to refer to, because what books there are get treated as secondary. A research paper on your feelings seems an odd thought. Making a decision not to be nice and supportive of your classmates seems heartless . . . not to mention the amount of social pressure there is to be like everybody else.

No, you sit in a class and muck around with feelings. How many times do you go to class *hoping* that you are not the topic of the day?

The neat trick, the one that is so wicked, is that the power is hidden; power is masked in all of that affect. While growing up we are rarely taught that it is easier to manipulate feelings with a smile and a soft voice than be being stern and authoritarian. After all, our parents have a size advantage and often use it.

In college, though, a whole generation tried to trade the stern for the soft. What was traded, or course, were merely forms of power. In the process, the university lost some of its legitimacy.

Interestingly, the whole dynamic was like much of what goes on in everyday life. There is a small tax here, a hidden law there; a fun advertisement for the Army here, a logical argument for nuclear energy, huge oil profits, or junk food there. All soft and hidden. All demeaning in one way or another.

Do you recognize yourself? Has fear of the world, or the job market, or failure gotten you to the point of forsaking your education, forsaking your chance to learn about your surroundings and to learn how to be thoughtful for a chance to get a middle management job? What a bad trade you're making. Not only that, what a bad citizen you are about to become.

While some of the soft still lingers, there are many students who will have nothing to do with that particular "pop" new world. What is the new currency of the academic realm? Where have we gotten to in our demands on the university?

People now want frequent quizzes on the material that was just learned. They want study questions for exams; cut and dried, black and white answers which require no real understanding of what was discussed and no development of what the material means. The New Student wants certainty. Wants to be told and wants to then repeat it.

Being a student and being a citizen have certain things in common. Both require a sense of what is going on, an idea of what needs to be done, and enough self-respect and autonomy to do something well. And this same thing holds true for both: Either kind of authoritarianism—soft or hard—is destructive in the American context.

In school, we have progressed from a hard rap on the knuckles to a warm hug by an incompetent to a great desire on the part of students to avoid being educated. It is not hard to see that whatever good education might do, and however good education might help encourage politics and freedom, we have—on the whole—messed up.

DOPE: DRUGS AND DRINKING

"Better Things for Better Living Through Chemistry." So reads one of the prominent hippy buttons, quoting E. I. DuPont. But the slogan is not being used satirically. The wearers mean it the way DuPont means it.

—Theodore Roszak

It may be helpful if we examine a small part of our behavior-changing science, a real-life, everyday offering of our new "freedom." Like most offerings, it is a very mixed blessing. Like most, it carries with it a distinguishable idea of freedom. The example is of dope, of drugs. Of course it would be foolish to condemn scientists for the tremendous abuse of drugs. I do not mean to suggest it, and have no intention of doing so. What I would like to suggest is that, if understood in a certain way, the drug head and the scientific mind have something in common—and something to teach us.

Certainly drugs are not new. They have a distinguished history—from Indians of this continent to the great religions of the East. They have religious meaning, hold the key to certain kinds of magic, and can help cure the sick. There are those in our time—people like Aldous Huxley—who have combined science and intellect and knowledge with drugs, and have increased our shared knowledge. Drugs have broadened our worlds and have helped increase both our understanding and our perception of the things around us. Moreover, we have medical drugs—for every ill from headaches to ulcers—that will help us to live longer and with less pain. Drugs are simply not all bad, unless one likes pain. Even the stuff we call "dope" (marijuana, mescaline, and so forth) is not all bad; but we will get to that later.

Most of the following discussion is about things other than alcohol. I do not mean to suggest that alcohol is not a popular way to go. In fact, more younger people are drinking more than ever before. There are very young alcoholics, there are more drinking problems on college campuses than drug problems, there are far too many automobile deaths caused by drinking than anything else.

Alcohol is not the topic here because it rarely leads to the kinds of experiences that will be discussed. Alcohol is a depressant. Maybe it is the drug of choice, now, because it so mirrors much of what is going on: An hour or so of feeling good—with something socially acceptable—then becoming depressed and, maybe, hung-over the next day. In truth, the *reason* we drink is a real topic, but it is not the current one.

What is important for this discussion is the dope user, the individual who is seeking something and finds drugs. Part of the seeking, of the pursuit, is for freedom. It is that part that is in the tradition we have been discussing. Philip Slater writes that drugs "promise a return to pure experience, to unencumbered sensation."[13] Not only that, it is just the way the behavioral scientists would want it: through the mind. Drugs extend freedom, in that particular sense. We find our new solutions by willingly changing our minds. We determine our own response by our own artificial stimulus.

The body simply becomes a kind of machine. It becomes our "property," our "asset." We can use it; we can direct it through drugs. Freedom to be ourselves, as long as it does not harm anyone else. That is apple-pie American. But what I want to argue is that it has become self-destructive. There seem to be too many of us to have visions of Walden Pond, to think of freedom as physically escaping, to believe that science has our social answers. As the businessman farmer used the land, so the drug abuser uses himself or herself. The doper is used up, then destroyed. It is solitary and mental and "freely" done.

The politics of dope is more complex than that. In fact, many people seem to have learned something from dope. Indeed, just taking an illegal drug and finding out that one does not become some kind of mad-dog-drug-freak makes one wonder about the value of the "official" pronouncements. But there is the question of the end of the experience. If we all took dope, would we all become better people and revolutionize the world and live in love forever after? There is no reason to venture an answer to that until we ask just why we do dope, and what it means.

Isn't it possible that freedom is the issue, that freedom is the value, but that instead of freedom we get drugs? Maybe we have created a world in which we just cannot live; so we escape, or, at least, we learn to regulate ourselves according to a new pace, a different drummer. We can make ourselves speed up, slow down, go to sleep, be mellow, or wake up. Could it be possible that the union of people and science has become an unhappy one? That we are not suited—in any kind of natural way—for the "freedom" of

---

[13] Philip E. Slater, *The Pursuit of Loneliness* (Boston: Beacon Press, 1970), p. 93.

science or the society it has built? In that case, we need to rethink society and science and ourselves.

But what if, Theodore Roszak asks, we, on drugs,

> suddenly find ourselves blessed with a society of love, gentlemen, innocence, and freedom? If that were so, what should we have to say about ourselves regarding the integrity of our organism? Should we not have to admit that the behavioral technicians have been right from the start? That we are, indeed, the bundle of electrochemical circuitry they tell us we are—and not persons at all who have it in our nature to achieve enlightenment by native ingenuity and a good deal of hard growing.[14]

To seek freedom through drugs is, at once, to misunderstand freedom and to give in to the very dynamic that is causing many of the problems. Drugs—dope—can provide extraordinary experiences. They can lead one to startling flashes of insight, to moments of heightened perception. But there are at least two important points that should be made.

First the visions, the flashes, the moments must be prepared for to be fully understood. It's only another Open Road if you are not ready to look for something. Read Aldous Huxley's *The Doors of Perception* or, better yet, Carlos Castaneda's writings to begin to understand elaborate preparations, intelligent perceptions, and potential dangers.

Second, momentary insight changes nothing unless one works at what the insight means. To rely on drugs to keep you in a more or less constant state of "insight" is to be little more than what Roszak suggests: a "bundle of electrochemical circuitry." Dope can be fine. It can point you in the direction of the hard work—but little more.

What I want to argue is that freedom is a positive concept that involves people's relationships with one another. And that Thoreau, and Lawrence's Whitman, materialism, behavioralism, and drugs only help show us why we think as we do. They do not give us clues to politics, hints about how we might make freedom a part

---

[14] Roszak, *The Making of a Counter Culture* (Garden City, N.Y.: Anchor Books, 1969), p. 177.

of our world. To change our ideas of freedom is hard; to explain such a concept may be impossible. The best we can do is to explore one possibility of freedom. To stay as we are is to leave power— and powerlessness—and the possibility of real change untouched. Freedom is safely out of our reach if we continue on our current ideological path. We will remain unfree, busily involved in the politics of self-deception.

FREEDOM TO

> *He breathed deeply the moist, bitter-scented air of the park and at every step it seemed to him that he was pushing away the past as one who has reached the shore pushes away a skiff, now useless. His probing and his insight were without resignation; full of defiance and venturesome passion, he looked to the new life, which, he was resolved, would no longer be a groping or dim-sighted wandering but rather a bold, steep climb. Later and more painfully perhaps than most men, he had taken leave of the sweet twilight of youth. Now he stood, poor and belated in the broad daylight, and of that he meant never again to lose a precious hour.*
>
> *—Hermann Hesse*

The heading "Freedom To" is full of promise. Freedom to what? To the Revolution, or to The Movement? Freedom to have a fixed income, or freedom not to go to school? Freedom to grow up, or to continue as we are now—freedom to hurry from the cradle to perpetual adolescence? There is no doubt that there are many things I did not mean to suggest when I wrote the words "Freedom To." What I propose to do is to make some suggestions about a place where we might be free, and to explain the thoughts behind it. The discussion is taken, in part, from Hannah Arendt's *The Human Condition*. The book deserves much thought.

Instead of beginning with the assumptions of the behavioral sciences, with the belief that we are determined to be, it seems sensible to start again. In the final analysis, it seems impossible to "explain" human nature. Certainly the words of our surroundings do not explain us. We know that words like *life* or *mortality, love* or *home,* can never fully answer our questions about who we are.

This is not to deny that we may be in part determined, nor is this to argue that there is a God who created the heavens and the earth. It is simply to say that the problem of human nature seems unanswerable.[15]

That we have no final answers does not mean that we cannot solve at least parts of ourselves, especially those parts that have to do with being free. A possibly helpful model offered by Hannah Arendt has to do with the Greeks. In particular, it has to do with the Greek idea of what is involved in freedom.

For the Greeks, political life was important. A particular kind of politics and organization. For them, it was the *polis,* a place where people—as equals—could get together, make common decisions, and take actions. It is important to understand that the political realm was not the household, that the polis was not private. The household dealt with those things necessary for survival. The household, in Arendt's words, "was born of necessity, and necessity ruled over all activities performed in it."[16]

But the polis was the realm of freedom. It was a public realm, where individuals met as equals. In one sense, freedom meant neither to rule nor to be ruled. It ignored the kind of material and "power" differences that so characterize contemporary "politics." What freedom—and, hence, politics—formerly included was a common world of thought and action. In this commonality existed a kind of freedom that is hard for us to understand. Everyone became involved with the same object, with the same cause, with trying to figure out how to define the same thing.

It was this sharing, this tugging at the same object in order to give it meaning, that helped limit the chances of being tyrannized. When people are isolated, when they are alone, when they have no common vision, then no one can agree with anyone else. But by ignoring everyone else—all other seeing and hearing and insights—

---

[15] I think it is important to recall the earlier discussion on phenomenology. We do seem to be social, and we can understand consciousness as a form of reaching out to the world. This carries with it the importance of understanding the relationship between the individual and the world he or she lives in.

[16] Hannah Arendt, *The Human Condition* (Garden City, N.Y.: Doubleday & Co., 1958), p. 159.

each becomes dependent upon some central source to define a common world for everyone. To put it differently, without deciding on common things, we become terribly susceptible to the tyranny of conforming to the perceptions of some other force. We accept another's vision; we accept it as a chorus of strangers, unable to communicate felt differences.

In this public world, this political world, people were defined by their acting and their speaking. To act is to do the unexpected: to begin, to initiate, to lead. It is through speaking and acting that one becomes distinctive, one begins to define self. In the polis, people publicly, in sight of their peers, answered the question of who they were by taking positions and taking actions. To quote Arendt, "In acting and speaking, men show who they are, reveal actively their unique personal identities and thus make their appearance in the human world, while their physical identities appear without any activity of their own in the unique shape of the body and sound of the voice. This disclosure of 'who' in contradiction to 'what' somebody is—his qualities, gifts, talents, and shortcomings, which he may display or hide—is implicit in everything somebody says or does."[17]

In creating and revealing, an individual experiences freedom. It is far from an easy thing; there are surely costs one must pay. The future becomes uncertain, unseeable, and an individual is no longer the unique master of what he or she does. But that is the price of freedom, the price of citizens being equals, and of reality being a shared experience. Certainly the struggle of creation, of action, the possibility of understanding one's self and of helping to make important decisions in a public way are rewards in themselves. They are, indeed, the stuff of freedom.

The people who are not bigoted are the people who have no convictions at all.

---

[17] Ibid., p. 159.

Focus Seven

The subpoints of this chapter revolve around the following
theme: The way a person understands freedom affects his
or her way of life. Similarly, the way a nation understands
freedom will affect its political life. The five American
conceptions of freedom stated and criticized in the chapter
might be summed up as "freedom is doing what you want
as long as you don't hurt others." In other words, freedom
is the absence of constraints except those which prevent
injury to others.

The chapter criticisms of the variations on this theme also
might be summed up this way: most American definitions of
freedom, however attractive and widespread, are not very
political. They all boil down to doing what you want far
enough away from other people so that you don't hurt
them. Almost everything we do affects someone else directly
or indirectly. If freedom, as defined, includes avoiding harm
to others, then the best way of ensuring no harm is to live
in isolation. A hermit in a cave runs the least risk of
detrimentally affecting others. Yet, even the hermit will
have left his or her parents, perhaps saddening them.

The crux of the matter is that while we may try to
determine beforehand how our behavior will affect others,
we cannot predict reliably their response to our actions, if
we assume that they can do what they want, including
surprise us.

To see the apolitical thrust of the definitions requires
one more consideration. The essence of politics is to live
together publicly with other people. Politics strives to affect
other people in beneficial ways; politics at its best wants the
best for its citizens. Those whose definition of political
freedom revolves around the desire to minimize consultation
with others about the likely effects of action really are
striving implicitly for isolation, or kidding themselves about
human interdependence. What we do affects people in some
way almost every moment of our lives. Thus, assuming that

one can escape interdependence muddles almost all American attempts at political freedom because how we understand what we are doing shapes—to some extent—what we do.

This chapter's suggestion for a more political perspective on freedom is "Freedom To." The point is to acknowledge interdependence and to turn it into an asset by understanding freedom as what arises when we are together with other people in a way which encourages our own and their rightfittingnesses or everyone's best sense of self. Thus, the chapter suggests moving cautiously toward being together with other people instead of heading for isolation.

One last query. Wouldn't it be better, given that we have to live with other people and that they can be difficult at times, to be in charge oneself? Wouldn't it be better to be rich and powerful, hence, able to do what one wants, almost regardless of the effects on others? The answer turns, we think, on the question of the kind of company you want to keep and be for yourself. I doubt we'll ever know personally what it is like to be really rich and powerful. Certainly some wealthy and influential people are good company. But, it does seem obvious that no one is good company unless he or she tries to be so. And trying to be good company requires understanding that freedom best occurs not in isolation but in striving for a dignified way to be with others. What better encouragement and practice for keeping good company than a political ideal of direct participation in a twentieth century grass-roots public forum modeled after the eighteenth century American town meetings where community differences were argued out explicitly and freely. After deciding on the priority, the engaging and hard work of "Freedom To" begins in earnest.

8

JUSTICE:

FREE LAST MEALS
NEXT DOOR?

Trout's favorite formula was to describe a perfectly hideous society, not unlike his own, and then, toward the end, to suggest ways it could be improved. In 2BR02B he hypothecated an America in which almost all of the work was done by machines, and the only people who could get work had three or more Ph.D.'s. There was a serious overpopulation problem, too.

All serious diseases had been conquered. So death was voluntary, and the government, to encourage volunteers for death, set up a purple-roofed Ethical Suicide Parlor at every major intersection, right next door to an orange-roofed Howard Johnson's. There were pretty hostesses in the parlor, and Barca-Loungers, and Muzak, and a choice of fourteen painless ways to die. The suicide parlors were busy places, because so many people felt silly and pointless, and because it was supposed to be an unselfish, patriotic thing to do, to die. The suicides also got free meals next door.

—*Kurt Vonnegut, Jr.*

A fact: Lightning strikes the earth about eight million times each day and kills about a hundred and fifty Americans every year.

For in the land of the free, the greatest delight of every man is getting the better of the other man.

—D. H. Lawrence

THE PROBLEM OF JUSTICE

Law n'order, law 'n order. No culture without order—no order without law. Do you hear?

Is that clear?

Rules and regulations/regularity/judges and Judgments.

Trial by jury/Trial by peers. It is a trial to see you/it is a trial to hear.

Justice is process/the evidence is in. Objective. Be objective. Know the law/weigh the facts/judge from other judgments.

The Truth—is the rule—is the law—is Our Order. Let's get together/have a trial/go to Court/fight it out.

How can you see/Blindfolded.

The question is obvious: Does all this have anything to do with justice, or is it simply the ideology of our leaders, the beliefs of those in power?

The "title" of this section is "The Problem of Justice." A simple, misleading set of words. The word *problem* suggests that there is a solution. I am firmly convinced that there will be no clear solutions to the problems we discuss. The word *justice* is just as misleading. To write about it is to assume a definition of it. Not necessarily the truth in this case. This chapter will consist of thoughts in search of a definition, of ideas and phrases that try to capture an illusion. Maybe justice is simply an illusion. Maybe this section should be titled: "The Unsolvable Problem of an Illusion."

So much for accuracy. What about justice? What about law?

Most of us have a great respect for the law. At least, a respect for the *idea* of Law. We are taught to think that our system of law is only natural and normal, well and good. What we do not question is the respect. Moreover, we rarely ask about the law itself. We seldom seem to think about the basis of the law, and we think even less about justice. Let us begin by trying to understand what we might assume about the law.

I think that most of us assume that there is a kind of perfect order that exists somewhere. A world where all forms are perfect. A realm, possibly, of thought that is uncorrupted by anything material. We seem to believe that from the perfection of such a world, we might get an idea of some ultimate order, an idea of the perfect working of things. It is also from this world that we seek our definitions of justice.

The world of thought is untouched and perfect. In our heads, there might be an idea of justice. From our heads, we get our laws. From our laws, we assume we are just.

The idea that law and justice are mental, that they are an ideal, is neither new nor unique to the United States. Plato, of course, presented the argument most clearly. He thought, silly ancient that he was, that a world of perfect forms really did exist. That because we were but imperfect reflections of that world, we must spend our lives striving to think perfect thoughts, to be perfect.

His arguments were—and still are for many—compelling for the mind, for the world of the perfection of thought. We can conceive of a perfect circle; we cannot make one. Plato wrote an allegory about a cave. It is helpful to understand it.

Imagine a huge cave. In the cave sit many people facing a wall. They are chained and can neither move nor turn away from that wall. There is light coming in from behind them. There are people constantly moving between that light and those chained, and shadows are cast upon the wall. Those casting the shadows carry puppets and other objects, which make interesting and bizarre images on the wall.

The prisoners, having been exposed to nothing else, soon understand the shadows on the wall to be real. It becomes their shared life: They know and recognize the images; they converse and argue about the shadows.

What Plato argues and what we often believe is that our reality is simply a reflection. That there is a true order of things and that we must strive for this order intellectually. The Republic of Plato is nothing more than a society striving to find that order, and by doing so have that society be in accord with the justice of the universe.

There are powerful social implications in the neat arrangement of Plato's Republic. The divine order included, indeed depended on, a rigid social scheme. Plato tells us of the intelligent and the less intelligent, of the warriors and the farmers, of the bureaucrats and the merchants. There was to be a right place for everyone, and everyone was to be in his or her place.

From the world of perfect forms came the idea of perfect order. With a great deal of schooling and training, the intellectuals of the Republic were to understand better the world of perfect forms. We are asked to assume that their rule would be just, that it would lead to harmony in the society.

Find the right order; get the right law; the result would be justice.

Of course, that formulation of justice has its shortcomings. We shall involve ourselves with different views of justice later on and, in doing so, reply to the Republic. But it may be helpful to anticipate some of the obvious problems. To believe that, ideally, there is a universal definition of justice is to avoid something important. It is to avoid much of reality. To put it simply, intellectual abstraction can be a way of bypassing unpleasant forms of reality. To base a legal system on a particular form of mental process means that the enforcement of that law will be but an attempt to force unwanted reality out of existence.

To posit a perfect order, a mental realm of universally "right" ways of acting, may be to deny our essentially confused, chaotic selves. I do not intend to argue that there is no room for idealism, but I hope to avoid the mistake of making an individual a slave to his or her mind.

Let us shift the discussion a bit, make it a little more personal. What do we feel about justice? What does it seem like when we are involved in it? What are our thoughts when we think about justice? We *might* think about justice in this way: We will try to make people do what we think is best for them. To put it another way, we judge other people by imposing our standards and desires on them, and then we decide what is best for them.

This approach to justice is many-sided. It might be the basis of a system in which all people would be given food, or it could support something quite the opposite. Let us now worry about only two of the possibilities implied by this approach to justice.

The first part of the formulation would go something like this: "If we were they, this is probably what we would do." But what does it mean if justice is to judge matters that way? Doesn't this approach mean that we assume a great deal? Aren't we saying that we can be objective and, moreover, that other people will want what we want?

It strikes me that at it's heart this is a very pompous attitude. Can we know? Should others want what we want? There may well be a place in justice for the mingling of people's ideas, for a sharing of and deciding on wants. But to truly know one another takes a kind of intimacy, a kind of knowledge that one must spend a great deal of time and effort developing. Even then we rarely know for sure, and what we do know may not be the basis of justice.

The point is simply that it is both necessary and important that we have an idea of what is right and that we try to make others understand that idea. But we must also understand that to translate our ideas into the world of real people with real ideas and feelings is difficult. The problem of how this can be done is the other matter we must discuss.

The second part of the formulation ("We will try to make people do what we think is best for them") assumes that justice has something to do with judging from above. It is to impose. To regulate. To set ourselves over others, and to demand that they do what is right. But is this justice, or is it the rule of the strong parading under a different label, under a nicer name?

To sit in judgment of another may be many things, but it is not necessarily an essential element of justice.

What I should like to argue is that there are dynamics at work in our conceptions of law that may have nothing to do with justice. It seems clear that we rarely get too far from the idea of perfect images, from the enticing pictures of the mind. We link justice with ideas that are drawn from an independent, unearthly existence. We try hard to suck from justice a vital, human element. We try to make it the reflection of something we are not—perfect. Or we believe that if we can impose something on those less powerful, we are just.

With these elements at work, it is not surprising that some consider us a nation of law and order that lacks the soul of justice.

D. H. Lawrence writes: "Anger is just, and pity is just, but judgment is never just."

THE NORMAL VIEW

In earlier chapters we have described and discussed liberalism and, in appropriate cases, dismissed it as harmful or unhelpful. We must return to liberalism, for it is almost impossible to write about justice and law in America without coming to terms with its liberal framework. Liberalism represents the rules of debate for most of what we consider justice.

It seems reasonable to begin once again with the writings of John Locke, as they were very influential in the drawing up of our Constitution. Locke believed that the natural state of human beings was peaceful and reasonable enough. He thought that most people, most of the time, could be counted on to cause little or no trouble. In fact, there was almost no reason for government to exist—almost, but not quite.

According to Locke, sometimes there were disputes; some people did break the rules. Therefore, there was a need for impartial magistrates, a need for fair judges who would settle arguments and punish wrongdoers. In a sense, it was government as referee, an idea that should not sound entirely strange to us. In many ways we have simply taken this formula of Locke's and turned it into an elaborate belief system.

The rules of our debate about justice (*sic*—law) have become the rules of intricate processes and definitions of "impartial" judgments.

The liberals want to make the debate on justice easy: All we must know is how fair and impartial judicial decisions seem to be; then we can measure justice. If we can spot trends in court rulings, then we can determine whether we are becoming a more or less just nation. It is the way judgments are made, the process, that is important. Because we always debate within the framework set by these rules and assumptions, it is necessary to understand more fully what the liberals are talking about so that we can at least know what we are missing.

The liberal argument as written by a liberal: "In essence, the distinction between civilization and savagery is the willingness to settle disputes by other means than force. We say that we are governed by the rule of law, which means that we accept decisions by impartial courts rather than by force of arms. If we are going to remain civilized, we must continue to accept the decisions of our courts, whether we agree with them or not."[1]

The liberal continues by offering proof that those impartial courts are deciding cases justly. During the last twenty years, for instance, the Supreme Court has made decisions that, seemingly, widen our freedom. Since 1954 it has been illegal to have segregated school systems, bathrooms, drinking fountains, motels, or lunch counters. Further, people accused of crimes must now be told of their rights (they cannot be forced to incriminate themselves), and individuals brought to trial must be represented by an attorney. The Court has also held that wiretapping—except in certain circumstances—is illegal, and that "one person, one vote" means that every citizen's vote should count about the same.

Who could argue with these decisions? Who would challenge them? The system seems so reasonable. Laws are made, and then impartial justices decide whether they are constitutional or unconstitutional, good or bad.

In the liberal framework, given the basic premise of what people are supposed to be like and what governments should do, it is hard to fault recent decisions. It is not comfortable to advocate wiretapping, self-incrimination, or segregation. No, it is foolish to challenge a recent set of decisions. What we need to do is to understand the biases of the framework itself and to understand that we have more of a choice than that between "civilization and savagery" if we give up the rule of law.

---

[1] The quote is from Erwin Griswold, and was found in James Clayton, *The Making of Justice* (New York: Cornerstone Library, 1964), p. 7.

DOING JUSTICE

> *You can't get away from this.*
>
> *Blood-consciousness overwhelms, obliterates, annuls mind-consciousness.*
>
> *Mind-consciousness extinguishes blood-consciousness, and consumes the blood.*
>
> *We are all of us conscious in both ways. And the two ways are antagonistic in us.*
>
> *They will always remain so.*
>
> *That is our cross.*
>
> —*D. H. Lawrence*

It should be obvious that laws and trials mean something. They carry with them a way of looking at the world, a way that permits some people to control the actions of others. What has been argued is that the law, as Americans conceive of it, leaves out some important elements. Our law and "justice" seem an attempt to impose our mind over our other reality. In a sense, it means that justice is something thought, not something actively done; something imposed, not something shared.

The Bible admonishes us to "do justice, and love mercy." Part of justice, it seems to me, is to be done; it is something a person does. Justice is not necessarily created in a void and then imposed on others. Maybe it is more an action than a judgment, more an activity than an idea. In a sense, I mean to suggest that justice may include more than a proper judicial process; it may include, but go well beyond, the world of equality of procedure.

I am not saying that process and procedure are necessarily evil in and of themselves. I am suggesting that justice is much more complex than that; and although one might have a sense of security in knowing that a lot of money can buy a good attorney who will assure a "fair" hearing according to our laws, there is no reason to equate security with justice. Indeed, there is a real question about "fair" to whom and "impartial" to what. There are weaknesses in our liberal idea of justice; there are built-in biases.

First, property is protected. More precisely, private ownership is protected. That makes sense to us, but we rarely think of it in terms of justice. Sometimes private property—a lot of it—is defended as having been "earned" by a hard-working, intelligent person. We know that this means, more precisely, that the person has a marketable skill and that he or she is willing to sell. We also know that people can acquire property by having a relative die. But all this is obvious. The point is that built into our legal system is the idea that private property is sacred; yet relevant to justice may be the fact that some people go without food or clothing.

Back to John Locke. He believed that many problems in a pre-governmental society arose out of disputes over property. One reason for instituting government was to protect that property, to protect the fruits of an individual's labor. When our Constitution was written, and the public and private realms were split, it became the duty of the public to protect the property of the private. The business of government was to protect private business. Contracts bound the relationships.

The case is easily documented. It was the Supreme Court, in the Dred Scott case of 1857, that ruled that slaves were property and that property was protected by the Constitution. Indeed, in its history the Court has struck down laws that attempted to regulate the hours per week worked by children and the age at which they were permitted to begin. There was a long series of rulings during the early 1930s that held, essentially, that government could not regulate the wages or prices of industry. It was, primarily, the *principle* of the thing that mattered: the principle being that property was to be protected; the social costs seemed to be an entirely different matter.

Second, our system is built on the premise that in every case there is an innocent and a guilty party. It is an adversary method—one against the other. Neighbor versus neighbor doing battle in the court of law. One must be right, the other must be wrong; one is praised, the other blamed. In the end, one often gets a cash reward. We never consider the possibility that a problem might extend way beyond the two who are actually engaged in the proceedings.

This particularized, personalized liberal justice makes almost no attempt to incorporate the principle of collective rights, or the idea that a people might collectively be wronged. The law is blind to groups of people: Everyone looks alike; single and alone.[2]

Third, the system leaves us at the mercy of those who know the law. Our instincts for justice are exchanged for the expertise of the attorney. Lawyers are simply an elite. Their backgrounds are generally upper-middle class, their educations particular and expensive, and they possess the power to shape real events into a form unrecognized by us, but recognized by our system. They are the agents of the Process, no matter which side they take. Theirs is a profession that is almost exclusively involved in adherence to rules. We, in turn, are dependent upon them.[3]

To stay within the liberal structure of the debate is too limiting. We will forever be forced to talk about Process. Think back to the "advances" made by the Court. Most had to do with the process itself. To understand the Court as a biased, elite-oriented part of the system is to understand that *even if* the process were to become "perfect," we might still be no closer to justice than we are now.

If justice is nine people (appointed and approved for life by an elite) whose decisions generally favor what white, upper-middle-class people favor, then ours is a system of justice. There is a less complicated way of saying the same thing: American "justice" sings the song of the upper-middle class. A brief history should be helpful. According to the account given by Thomas Dye and Harmon Zeigler:

> Before the Civil War, the Supreme Court was spokesman first for the Federalists under John Marshall and later for Southern planters and slave holders under Roger Taney. . . . Following the emergence of industrial capitalism in the second half of the nineteenth century, the Supreme Court became the spokesman for the prevailing elite philosophy of social Darwinism. The Court struck down the federal income tax; prevented prosecutions of corporations under the Sherman Antitrust Act, while applying this Act against labor unions; and struck down child labor laws and laws

---

[2] This is too important to be left unexamined; so we shall return to it at the end of this chapter.

[3] For a beautiful account of this, see Alexis de Tocqueville, *Democracy in America* (New York: Vintage Books, 1945).

limiting the work week. The Court gave such a restrictive interpretation of the interstate commerce clause that it prevented federal regulation of the economy. It interpreted the "due process" clause of the Fifth and Fourteenth Amendments and the contract clause of Article II, Section 10, in such a way as to protect business enterprise from almost any form of government regulation.[4]

The time the Court was in greatest trouble was when it "failed to respond swiftly to changes in elite philosophy. . . . In a four-year period, 1933–37, the Court made the most active use of the power of judicial review over congressional legislation in its history, in a vain attempt to curtail the economic recovery programs of the New Deal. It invalidated the National Industrial Recovery Administration, nullified the Railroad Retirement Act, invalidated the National Farm Mortgage Act, and threw out the Agricultural Adjustment Act. Having denied the federal government the power to regulate manufacturing, petroleum, mining, agriculture, and labor conditions, the Court reaffirmed the notion that the states could not regulate hours and wages."[5]

During the 1960s, the Court seemed to be most interested in civil liberties. Certainly "progress" was made. But the fact seems to be this: Essentially, nothing has changed. The Court is still a group of individuals with the biases of stability and security. Even as liberals work hard to purify the process, justice in America is still only judging. Rhetoric aside, justice's proverbial "blindness" to differences, the "majesty" and "sacredness" of the law, and the "equalness" of due process, remain confining and biased concepts.

Justice is greater than any sum of judgments, generally more inclusive than two arguing individuals, and should be accessible to more people than the few who know the "secret" language. In a sense, justice is too important and too immediate an activity to be left in the hands of only a few. It is too far-reaching to be limited to laws as interpreted by a minority.

The history of the Supreme Court comprehends more than its rulings. It is the history of a people openly able to avoid justice

---

[4] Thomas Dye and Harmon Zeigler, *The Irony of Democracy* (Belmont, Calif.: Wadsworth Publishing Co., 1970), pp. 458–59.

[5] Ibid., p. 259.

under the label of law; the history of a few judging for the many; the history of the law following the times, with only a passing nod at the doing of justice. The liberalism of Locke called for the government to be a referee when the private affairs of individuals came into conflict. It did not offer many useful guidelines as to what it means to practice politics or to do justice. It is possible to understand our reliance on the Supreme Court as a justification for the individual to be uninvolved in justice. Our judicial system has inherited the weaknesses of Lockean liberalism.

As we know more about the weaknesses of liberalism, we also know more about the very human weaknesses of liberals. Let me give an example.

BRIEF-LY

I would like to introduce the example with a new category. It is the "Is nothing sacred?" category, and we can now put the Supreme Court and its justices in it. We found out that no particular president is sacred, when Richard Nixon was dissected in the newspapers, on television, and on the radio. Psychologists and handwriting experts, in addition to reporters, lawyers, and next-door neighbors, told us much more about the man than we wanted to know.

Neither the president nor the presidency is now sacred.

With the book *The Brethren* we get the story of the Supreme Court in general, the justices in particular, and the chief justice for example.

While there is an amount of injustice about briefly characterizing a long book, there are some general lessons to be learned. The short of it is this: The Supreme Court acts about the way we would imagine it would act. Some justices are brighter than others, some more careful legal scholars than others, some better athletes than their colleagues, some more interested in power than their brethren.

What the court decides on any single issue is our rule of law. The rule of law, as we learn, has to do with majority rule of the justices, and majorities may be the results of deals made, bargains struck, favors granted, and the like. Lawyers negotiate; Supreme Court justices are lawyers supreme. The argument is not that the deals, negotiations, and such are bad; the argument has to do with the mystique of the court.

Basically, the mystique tells us that those nine justices are the nine wise and fair people of our land. That they embody the good about us, and their concerns are for justice and fairness. They are impartial, nonpolitical seekers of the truth about a controversy. *The Brethren* is a book about that mystique—and how it is wrong.

In a way, the argument of the book finds its best symbol in Chief Justice Burger. Have you ever seen a picture of him? There he is, white hair and distinguished looks: The man *looks* like a chief justice. Much of the book is about how those looks mask a relatively incompetent judge. He is not all that careful or smart. He bumbles things. Put differently, the mystique of the looks really hides the works of the man.

We can understand the same lesson in more substantive ways. The mystique of the court hides the very human-ness (indeed, liberal/capitalist/lawyer human-ness) of how the court works.

They really aren't perfect?

Is nothing sacred?

But to know that biases exist—and that justices are sometimes fools—doesn't necessarily mean that we will change. Indeed, most people still think that this system is the best we can do. There is the taught fear that if we had a system of people, it would simply become a tyranny. One person's whim controlling other people's activities. Certainly an unhappy situation. Another possibility is that a system of people would turn into chaos, into anarchy. It would mean that the worst of us would be unchecked. It would mean that we could not walk the streets after dark.

But does it?

BIASES SHOWN

While it is not much of a surprise to find out that the law is biased, it is occasionally comforting to see the argument worked out. In that spirit, it is interesting to take a short look at a book by Morton Horowitz titled *The Transformation of American Law: 1780–1860.* It is an interesting book because it documents, clearly and carefully, changes in how the law has been understood and how it has functioned since the constitutional period. Let me repeat two basic arguments of the book.

First, Horowitz shows us that, as commerce and industry developed, they had clear effects on the law. As merchants and entrepreneurial groups gained political and economic power, they became closely allied with lawyers to advance their interests.

Many basic doctrines changed. The old understandings of property were done away with, and laws that seemed to hinder commerce were destroyed. As Horowitz puts it:

> Legal relations . . . were increasingly subordinated to the disproportionate economic power of individuals or corporations . . . law once thought of as protective . . . and above all, a paramount expression of the moral sense of the community, had come to be thought of as a facilitative of individual desires and as simply reflective of the existing organization of economic and political power.[6]

By 1850 this shift in the law had pretty well been completed. We were, legally, a product/market-oriented society. Not just in our earning a living, but also legally. Industry and industrialists were blessed. So were lawyers. Workers, consumers, farmers, and basically the rest of us were made to play by the industrial/legal rules.

Having the bias set up like that is really not enough. There is a second thing that happened that was necessary for enforcement of the bias. During this time—from 1780 to 1860—there was an effort to make the law seem objective: different from and above politics. An effort to change the meaning just a little, toward formalism.

Laws and legal doctrines became increasingly general in order to include more and more areas. Sometimes it seems everything we do is connected to our legal system. In addition, and in a really amazing way, there is a great increase in the number of rules surrounding the law. There was a time when legal rules—prescribed conduct—were set up to help protect moral principles. Now the

---

[6] Morton Horowitz, *The Transformation of American Law: 1780–1860* (Cambridge: Harvard University Press, 1977), p. 253.

rules *themselves* have become moral principles. The rules are the morality. Lawyers and the legal profession have become the knowers and keepers of the faith.

To just barely overstate the case, the lawyers are viewed as above politics, above citizens, above restriction. Again, Horowitz: "A scientific, objective, professional, and apolitical conception of the law . . . now comes to extend its domain and to infiltrate into the everyday categories of adjudication."[7]

What we know from the evidence is that "everyday . . . adjudication" has a specific economic bias. Put simply, what Horowitz—a Harvard Law professor—is arguing is that the fix is on. He tells us there was a fight over what the law was going to be about. More than a hundred years ago, the fight was effectively over. Now, today, the spiritual descendants of the winners are still winning, and the others are still losing.

If our law is supposed to be unbiased, I wonder what biased would look like?

A HEAD JOB

It is said that to every generation ten just people are born. No one knows who those people are.

There is more than a little reason to believe that many of the people who read this book will want to become lawyers. Some for fairly standard, greedy reasons: money and power. Others will study law because of pressure from parents, and still others in order to do "good" work. You know about "good" work: work within the system to change it . . . and who knows more about the system than lawyers? (Rhetorical questions are wonderful. While the *answers* are always clear, the *implications* of the answers are seldom considered and are often very strange.)

I want to spend some time with the do-good-lawyers-to-be among you. Anybody may read this section, as it has to do with all of us; but the people who might want to take notes are the future do-gooders. They are often blind to the fact that law cuts at

---

[7] Ibid., p. 266.

least two ways: (1) It is the agggressive carrier of our particular brand of liberalism, and (2) its first victim is the law student/lawyer. The lawyer becomes the law, the state becomes the person, the person becomes the lawyer becomes the state.

Law changes you. It does a head job.

You don't have a chance. Not only is it silly to assume *you*, as a lawyer, are going to change the system: it is especially wrong-headed to believe you will escape being changed. They'll get you. Count on it.

Law is something that is done; and, in the twentieth century, the fact seems to be that you are what you do. More than that, what you do, you're responsible for. In the end, law—that "neutral" arbiter of our society—is built on a whole set of attitudes and results in a prescription for how each of us is *supposed* to relate to the world. Law goes to our heads, and our heads have a lot to say about what we do.

In an interesting piece of research, Jacqueline Smethurst looked into this problem.[8] She studied women who went to law school. She talked to them before they studied law and then again after they were lawyers. One of the underlying questions was this: Now that women were lawyers, would they be different than their male counterparts. After all, there are a series of issues (like having children) which have traditionally been women's. Also, there has been new research indicating that there is a women's way of thinking which is more integrative and less combative than men's way of thinking.

What Smethurst found was that lawyers were lawyers. That more women became lawyers meant that there were more women lawyers. Now, it is nice that there is more equality of opportunity; but it seems foolish to think that things will change. In the law, it is ambition against ambition, brain against brain, hard work against hard work, push against shove. What difference does it make, in the long run, if either or both or neither of the pushers and shovers are men or women?

---

[8] See, Jacqueline Smethurst, *Women Becoming Lawyers: A Process with Implications for Public and Private Spheres*, (Amherst, Mass. unpublished dissertation, 1984).

Our system of law will easily assimilate people that the law school educates and are able to pass the bar.

To believe you will be different is fantasy of the highest order.

A second way to get a view of the law (get a view of ourselves) is to look at how lawyers structure and do their work. The case in point deals with some ideas that seem so common-sensical as to be almost foolish to discuss. It may well be that it is these most common-sense ideas that will give us the best mirror to see ourselves. Our mirror image, I must warn you, may not be our self-image.

The case has to do with how "radical" lawyers understand the problems of native Americans, and how they try to solve those problems. It is important not to get too far from the fact that answers are built into questions and that we have about as much to learn from the answers the lawyers give as from the questions they ask. The following comes from a dissertation written by Linda Medcalf. The details of the lawyer/Indian interactions are not fully explored here, as the *Preface* is not the place for the full lesson. But there are things that should be learned.

THE CASE: ONGOING SHAME

Almost since the time of Columbus, the native Americans have suffered cruelly at the whim of the invaders. That is simply a very terrible, shameful fact. There has been everything from early germ warfare (Lord Jeffrey Amherst gave Indians disease-infested blankets that killed them and made old Lord Jeff even more wealthy), to broken treaties and promises, to forced marches from swamps to dust bowls, to simple murder.

To understate, Liberal America has not done itself proud in its dealings with the natives of this land.

Before we started mucking around and moving and murdering the Indians, they seemed to live as they wished. Their tribes were strong communities; their relationship to the environment was one not of control but of respect; they were, mostly, peaceful people. To fast-paced, alienated, bureaucratized, controlling, standard Americans, the Indian—both in fact and myth—seemed to be more whole and together than we are.

They were, in odd combination, a good example, and because

of that, a threat.[9] We have gotten rid of almost everything but the myth.

In an effort to "make things right," there has been a move to provide tribes with aid. Regrettably, it has generally been legal aid. Well-intentioned attorneys have done their best with native Americans, made real attempts to do what they understood as necessary for a group of people who have been systematically abused.

As a group, the Indians are a little different from other minorities.

1. They own about 2 percent of the land in America, and the land is in large enough blocks so that they need not integrate into mainstream city or suburban living.

2. The land they occupy is rich in natural resources—water, timber, oil—to be used if and how they wish.

3. They have done things in accordance with our law, and the courts of the United States regularly uphold their claims.

For attorneys, they are often "difficult" to relate to but are certainly "good" clients.

The attorneys believe the problems of the Indians they represent can, in a rough way, be understood as: (1) the poverty of the individuals, (2) the lack of power—both personally and tribally, and (3) the lack of education and skills of the people. These are all problems we can relate to; after all, we sort out much of the world with those very categories. Lawyers are trained to solve these problems in very specific ways, and we know that their training doesn't stop at the Reservation Door.

The problems—poverty, power, and education—are so interrelated as to be inseparable in any real way. When a lawyer makes an attempt to solve one of the problems, he or she is also working on the other ones. The changes, the solving, go on in the context of an ongoing tribal life that the attorneys are committed to keep. Keep, and make better. Those are the words they use.

---

[9] Michael Rogin has done a first-rate job on this theme. See his *Fathers and Children: Andrew Jackson and the Subjugation of the American Indian* (New York: Vintage Books, 1976).

In an attempt to keep the form of the tribe, the lawyer makes it over into a corporation. The tribal member becomes a shareholder. Of course the corporate style—the *needs* and *aims*—of a corporation are a little different from those of a tribe. The reorganization is built, in part, on the premise that to be strong and to avoid poverty, all those natural resources on the reservations must become economic assets. They must be well managed to bring in more money.

That means, naturally enough, some different qualities in the Chief (Chairperson of the Board?) and his or her legal advisors. Instead of carrying and refining the traditions and wisdom of the tribe, the Chief now has to have the skills of a corporate manager.[10] There's more. In order for the shareholders (i.e., native Americans) to be good citizens/capitalists, they must become educated in the ways of liberal America. The America we learn in school. The one that demands that people see the world and make arguments in the form and language of a liberal/individual/competitive style we know as normal.

No more "passive" Red People. No more "submissive" aboriginal tribes. If the lawyers have their way, strong tribal leadership and a powerful tribe will be the result of a vigorous, intratribal politics based on economic self-interest.

RIGHT(S)?

Once you get to that point in the logic, it seems sensible that people need some protection. It becomes necessary and logical and seemingly normal to make certain that every person in the tribe be granted *rights*. After all, the individual has certain duties and responsibilities as well as some "freedom" from repression. Rights form a basis of much of our political thinking and it *seems* good that everyone has them. I mean, *what could possibly be wrong with rights?*

The answer, if I understand correctly, is plenty.

The concept of rights is a cultural one. Nothing universal about it. Rights as done by the lawyers for and to native Americans is

---

[10] The language being used is of my choosing.

wholly culturally based. The rights that seem so natural to us are built on the assumptions of individualism, which require certain kinds of aggressive actions. To quote: "A human being is not a bundle of legal rights; it is a much richer complex of emotions and mind and interaction with others and the environment which has very little resemblance to the bare contractual outline individual rights gives. To reduce human relationships to one of rights and responsibilities, one against the other, is to render the human relationship possibilities barren, to make of human relationships an 'irreducible minimum' before they become nothing at all."

Rights divide and liberalism/legalism conquers.

Let's go back and judge the lawyers. Judge those who have power to ask the questions, define the problems, then solve those very problems. In fact, many tribes now have more money. They are becoming (in the most mainstream way) more viable economic actors. The lawyers "did" the law and were successful at it.

The real question is: Successful at What?

Think about the triad of Economics, Education, and Power. Sound familiar? Strike a chord you've heard before? Once those things take on our definitions, and once they become the central issues, the rest simply flows. Corporations, competition, individualism, efficiency, rationality, rights.

We've *Americanized* native Americans.

And the do-gooders? The lawyers? What they do *is* the law. Of course there are well intentioned, nice, good lawyers. It just seems a crime that we are forced to live in a world that they help create and perpetuate because of the very structure of *their* thought and activity.

It seems more an indignity that we are trying to "save" the native Americans by introducing our "neutral" legal system into their lives.

Why are we forcing them to trade even the possibility of a whole life for one of pieces?

Enough is enough.

"JUSTICE" MARCHES ON: I SAW THE NEWS TODAY, OH BOY

So far, two specific arguments have been made: (1) that justice is something to be done, and (2) that our legal system helps protect and perpetuate a rather clear set of beliefs. From here to the end of this chapter, I want to explore the ways in which the law pervades and invades everything from everyday life to what we think of as politics and how we think about ourselves. We will start with everyday life, and work from there.

Last night, a Sunday night, I watched a five minute segment of a news show. The segment was titled "Week In Review" and reported on six trials which took place that week. It was a kind of America Marches On in our courts. While I was not able to absorb all of it (these pieces of America were so stunning that it took me some emotional time to understand what was really going on) I did get most of it.

Part of what I want to suggest is that most of our serious issues become matters for our courts, and when that happens they are somehow no longer our serious issues. Put differently, we lose personal touch with them as soon as they are translated into matters of law.

So, what follows are six cases which are current as I write.

1. Miami. A white police officer was found innocent of shooting a black young man in the face and killing him. The officer, not surprisingly, was happy and relieved. Some people in the black community were unhappy and showed their unhappiness by rioting. The police reported that the violence was not as great as they had expected.

2. Fall River. There are two separate trials for six men accused of raping a woman on a pool table in a barroom. The first of the trials is over, and the two men were found guilty. The two men were stunned. The woman attorney for them was not pleased. A surprising number of people in the local community were unhappy. In fact, the police arrested several people after the trial for disturbing the peace. There was no report about the woman who was raped.

3. Tulsa. A woman from a small town in Oklahoma sued her church. It seems that she had an affair with a man and people in the church found out. The members of the church said she could no longer be a church member; and not only that, but they wrote a letter to other churches and described her as a

"fornicator." She sued, claiming that the church had consciously inflicted psychological pain on her. The jury awarded her several hundred thousand dollars. A church elder said, in an interview, that he believed God's Law and not in man's law. I got the feeling that he was really saying that he did not want to pay the money.

4. Los Angeles. They are trying to select jurors for the trail of John DeLorean. He of car-making fame was arrested for making a twenty-four-million-dollar cocaine deal. The videotape they made of the transaction seems to indicate that he is guilty. He says that he is a good Christian man, loves his wife and children, and would never do such a thing.

   The prospective jurors were asked if they believed that rich people generally got off easier in trials than poor people did. It seemed to me that there was a great Catch-22 at work: If you told the truth (law works better for the rich) they wouldn't want you to be a juror because you might be prejudiced against the rich DeLorean. If you told a lie, you would not be wanted as a juror because you were a liar. Maybe the strategy is to never have a trial, just an eternal process of jury selection. Who knows?

5. Las Vegas. A public prosecutor was being brought to trial for accepting a bribe. We saw a picture of him getting out of a car. From what we saw, the bribe was not spent on buying a fancy automobile.

6. Chicago. Finally, trial dates were set for the judges in Chicago who were accused of taking bribes. This was the shortest report, as the more public part of the process is just now getting under way. We got no interesting details, and we only got to see a picture of a court house which, I assume, was somewhere in Chicago. Clearly, we will hear more about the alleged crooked judges.

To be assaulted by these tales of trials all at once is almost too much to take. What makes them of interest in this context is that not very far beneath the surface are issues that could easily be considered personal or political, but which we choose to call legal and then become spectators to the spectacles.

Miami, for example, is a multiracial metropolitan area with real hatreds, hardened criminals, and lots of drugs and a huge cash supply. That a white policeman killed a black youth in a racially tense area is much more than a legal problem. What needs to happen is that, politically, people will have to learn to live together. That does not mean that it is merely a leadership problem. It does mean that unless communities within the larger community can get more real power, the tensions will continue.

Fall River, an ethnic community in Massachusetts, lets us watch again. Part of the trial was a lesson about how society has stereotyped women who have gotten raped. You know, they somehow encourage it. . . . so the stereotyped story goes. The fact, of course, is that to think that way is nothing short of a license to rape. Something as clearly criminal as rape, then, may revolve in part around issues which have not been resolved either socially or politically.

There is the strange (it seems to me) fact of the violence which followed the guilty verdict in Fall River. What was that about? It was about, at least it was partially about, people in a close community not being able to handle what they believed to be a local matter locally. While I am uncertain we would want all activities to be handled locally, there is something to be said for having a process where individuals have a choice of accepting something quietly or going to jail.

What is there to say about fornication, God's Law, and Tulsa, Oklahoma? I happen to be from Tulsa, and I must admit that the whole thing seems bizarre to me. One lesson seems clear: God's Law and man's law both seem to be in people's most private business. It appears that while the law may not be able to enforce morality, it does have the power to force people to pay a penalty if they violate procedural rights.

And rich people get videotaped toasting cocaine as being better than gold (it is easier to smuggle), and then get good lawyers to put the video in a kinder perspective. And people on the public payroll can be as crooked as people who make cash deals for drugs. Ah, America.

The amazing part of this particular "Week In Review" is that the "politics" was mostly about what the Democrats who were running for president had to say. Politics was Fritz Mondale saying, "Where's the beef" (and ruining a perfectly good ad); it was Jesse Jackson saying Jews were all right; it was Gary Hart showing people that he had written a book. But the real politics, it seems to me, the politics which affect our lives but which are denied us, were in those court cases.

We could only watch as personal, social, and political issues were melted into legal arguments.

JUSTICE AND POLITICS

Thus far, we have struggled with justice but have not really gotten much closer to it; we have worked through some of the problems without getting much closer to the solutions. We have done something. We no longer need trouble ourselves with the idea that law (our "justice") is impartial. No law is impartial; probably justice is not, either.

Laws are set up to help and protect certain people and certain things. Police make sure that some of the violators are caught, and our judicial system enforces the laws. Now, if one is white and middle-class, that may sound a great deal like justice. Police protect "us" against "them." Laws are designed to help "us," not "them." It may be with that us-them formulation, in that space between security and terror, that we might begin to understand justice.

While it is not terribly successful to argue that there are social classes in America (almost everyone considers himself or herself part of the middle class), it is undeniable that there are those without power, status, or wealth. If not a lower class, at least a class apart, a class outside the benefits of society. This group of people includes, roughly, the blacks, Chicanos, native Americans, white poor, and those who "drop out." Possibly most dropouts don't count; after all, they can drop back in. The white poor, the white dropout, may "miraculously" reach the middle class. But the others are outside, subject to a "justice" that does not seem to include them.

The police are ultimately thought of by the white middle classes as friends. Indeed, they are. Police catch criminals, control traffic, and in many ways help people. More exactly, white people. The police are the "thin blue line of protection," so the saying goes. And certainly they are. But they are much more than that. An example of ghetto justice may help show why.

James Baldwin writes of a black salesman in Harlem. One day, after he had left a customer, there seemed to be a great deal of activity in the street. People

> were running from the police. Other people, in windows, left their windows, in terror of the police because the police had their guns out and were aiming their guns at the roofs. Then the salesman noticed that two of the policemen were beating up a kid: "So I spoke up and asked them, 'why are you beating him up like that?' Police jump up and start swinging on me. He put the gun on me and said, '*get over there.*' I said, 'What for?' "

> An unwise question. Three of the policemen beat up the salesman in the streets. . . .

> As of my last information, the salesman is on the streets again, with his attache case, trying to feed his family. He is more visible now because he wears an eye patch. . . . His tone is simply the tone of one who has miraculously survived—he might have died; as it is, he is merely half-blind. . . . It is a dishonorable wound, not earned in a foreign jungle but in the domestic one—not that this would make any difference at all to the nevertheless insuperably patriotic policeman—and it proves that he is a "bad nigger."[11]

It is not easy to find justice in this example. Whites expect the police to protect them—and this generally happens. The person in business expects to carry out his or her white-collar crime, or illegal gambling, uninterrupted—and this generally happens. Anything beyond that is of little concern; beyond that is someone else's problem. So the police are left to deal with the problems of poverty and race hatred and decaying cities. Somehow whites expect social injustice to be solved by force, stopped by violence. Between the "us" and

---

[11] James Baldwin, "A Report from Occupied Territory," in Laurence Veysey, ed., *Law and Resistance* (Harper & Row, 1970), pp. 318–319. Originally appeared in *The Nation*, 203 (July 11, 1966), pp. 39–43.

the "them," the white middle class and the black ghetto, justice does not seem to exist. There is security for the whites, injustice for the blacks, and in the impossible middle—unrestrained and powerful—stand the police.

The black is colonized in white America. The black is trapped. How can he or she act "justly"? Maybe justice is treating a person the way he or she deserves to be treated. If that is the case, one can understand the logic of Frantz Fanon. Fanon writes of the colonized black in Africa. He writes of violence, and the justice of it.

> For the native, this violence represents the absolute line of action. . . . The group requires that each individual perform an irrevocable action. In Algeria, for example, where almost all the men who called on the people to join in the national struggle were condemned to death or searched for by the French police, confidence was proportional to the hopelessness of each case. You could be sure of a new recruit when he [or she] could no longer go back into the colonial system. . . . To work means to work for the death of the settler. This assumption of responsibility for violence allows both strayed and outlawed members of the group to come back again and to find their place once more, to become integrated. Violence is thus seen comparable to a royal pardon. *The colonized man finds his freedom in and through justice.*[12]

Perhaps violence not only is necessary but may even be justice in the case of the American black. But possibly justice is more than treating a person the way he "deserves" to be treated. Justice may involve more than that; it may be a reflection not only of the action of the one, but also of the action of the other. What I am suggesting is that a "punishment" may reflect the one doing the punishing. One does justice, but also loves mercy. It is possible that forgiveness is as much a part of justice as violence. Both may be doing justice, and both may involve freedom for the individual.

POLITICAL TRIALS AND PEOPLE

Part of what I am suggesting is that there are many elements in justice, which at their core have little to do with laws. These ele-

---

[12] Frantz Fanon, *The Wretched of the Earth* (New York: Grove Press, 1965), pp. 85–86.

ments have to do with people trying to live together in some sensible manner. I am not saying that there should no longer be judges or juries or laws. What I am suggesting is that we examine these things and try to figure out a better method of getting at justice.

We Americans seem hesitant to believe that any—much less many—trials are political ones. In fact, scholars in this field are trying hard to reach agreement on just what a political trial is. Let us stay on the fringes of scholarship and seek some common sense understanding of what political trials are and what they might mean.

In the most obvious sense, a political trial involves people who have been charged with treason against the state, or some such crime. We have very few of these. We can understand the desire of a state to protect itself. There is a history of political trials as old as the history of trials. Both Socrates and Jesus were perceived as great enough threats to the state to be brought to trial. In a sense, political trials have a noble past.

Yet we deny political motivation. When one is arrested for antiwar or antipoverty activity—and those things are surely political—the likelihood is that the charge will involve something like marching without a permit, or disrupting traffic. In other words, we require trials that never get to the issues involved. People intensely involved in acting on what they believe to be right are denied their validity as moral beings. They are denied any chance of having their principles dealt with justly.

There are, of course, even less appealing kinds of political trials. In some cases, police, prosecutors, and judges can conspire to frame—arrest—and try a politically "dangerous" person. The case of Eldridge Cleaver seems to indicate that this can happen.[13]

Being Blind

By the time Patty Hearst walked into the courtroom, we Americans knew a whole lot about her. Even a *Tommy*—deaf, dumb, and blind—would have had a hard time ignoring personal and private

---

[13] For an example of the problems involved, see Kenneth Dolbeare and Joel Grossman, "LeRoy Jones in Newark: A Political Trial?," in Theodore Becker, ed., *Political Trials* (Indianapolis: Bobbs-Merrill, 1971).

details about the woman. Not only was every outrage reported; at least three experts told us what they meant.

We all got caught: At one level the trial was about myths: a symbolic public display of our most recent past. *Politics* v. *Law; Patty* v. *the Public Prosecutor.* What the hell does "equal justice" have to do with a Symbol of the Rich being Kidnapped and Terrorized and her, very likely, Getting Into It and Seemingly Liking It?

At another level, Patty Hearst is a person. You know. Hands and eyes and feet and skin. A person. Feeling. Imagine yourself and you have a sense of, essentially, what/who Patty Hearst is.

So we got caught: Both the myth and the person are real. What to do? Can a law—a rule—give us the answer, show us the way?

It never made sense to me that she was guilty or innocent. Those are the categories that were forced on her, and wrong ones as far as I can tell. What the blindfolded Mother Justice couldn't see was that P. Hearst was probably *both* guilty and innocent.

In a strange way, all of us were.

But the law doesn't allow for the examination of that kind of truth.

Finally, there are trials that on the surface seem to have nothing to do with politics. The prostitutes who periodically get arrested, the tenant who refuses to pay his or her rent until something is repaired, and the foreigners, gays, and minorities are automatically guilty. The law is the law. What I want to suggest is that these cases could be handled differently, in such a way that they would take on a political meaning. If this were done, there might even be a chance that justice would emerge.

The People's Courts in Cuba seem to me closer to a just method than what we have been discussing. An idealized description may help. Essentially, these courts are neighborhood centered. The people in the area choose the judge. The judge is a respected, well known member of the neighborhood, though not necessarily a lawyer. The judge must simply be a fair, just person who understands the aims of society, the aims of a revolutionary people.

The cases that come before the judge are local ones. They are heard in public; in essence, this means that those neighbors who know of the case or the defendants or those who were close to what happened attend. Often, many attend and are part of a case. The catch is this: The audience may be somehow guilty of the crime of the defendant. Guilty for not stopping an argument, guilty for not helping right a wrong, guilty for not helping someone who needed help.[14]

Maybe that is what justice is about. Midway between "an eye for an eye" and "turning the other cheek," we are groping for justice. But the point might be that we should not necessarily wander alone. The People's Courts are one way to begin to understand that to be part of society is to assume some responsibility for what goes on, and that this responsibility reaches into the realm of justice. Not a justice of lawyers and complex legal procedures, but somehow of the doing of justice.

Focus Eight

The central theme of this chapter is that justice, and one's sense of it, involves more than laws, courts, and lawyers. Doing justice should be akin to doing politics; that is, it should be an activity that recognizes a role for the ordinary citizen. While politics concerns living together freely with dignity, justice, as understood in this chapter, concerns remedying known wrongs.

The argument shows the biases of the current American justice system. The system is based on ownership of private property and has come to favor the rich over the poor. Lawyers usually are needed to do anything within it; hence, the ordinary citizen feels helpless without them. Its adversarial dynamic presumes that one party is right, the other wrong; thus, mutual fault tends to be overlooked. The history of the Supreme Court and a contemporary exposé remind us of the system's human fallibility, hence

---

[14] The analysis of the Cuban system is meant to be more suggestive than exhaustive. It might be helpful to understand one of the things I am outlining. Not too many years ago, a man stabbed a woman in New York City. That wasn't news. That he stabbed her repeatedly with several scores of people watching *was* news. Under the system now being discussed, those people who watched—or who shut their windows and pretended nothing was happening—would be guilty of doing injustice.

undermining, in part, the sanctity we associate with the law and courts. As a consequence of all of the above, the decisions of the court system are not always fair, even when they are legal.

In spite of the reminders of human fallibility, this chapter advocates recognition of the human qualities of those involved in the justice system—rather than increased efforts at impartiality and objectivity—as the basis for further steps toward doing justice more fully. The justice advocated is not other-worldly and perfect, but earthly and imperfect— yet better than we are doing. The goal we should pursue is more fairness. The primary inadequacy is our tendency to believe that doing justice should be left to the court system and always be done within a narrow legal framework. In other words, although court rulings are awesome in their power to affect individual lives, neither they nor the laws behind them are moral principles. We still have to decide for ourselves the difference between the merely legal and the morally just, then accept some responsibility for carrying out moral measures.

Hence, this chapter criticizes the legal system from a positive perspective. The argument is shrewd about dangers to the court system from the extreme right and left ends of the political spectrum because those groups seem willing to ignore legal protections of civil liberties in order to impose their political ideologies as the only conception of justice. Therefore, the chapter proposes continuation of the current safeguards plus additional good sense efforts at moral judgment about justice within society.

The essential point here is that reliance solely on the court system for justice is much like acceptance of voting as sufficient political activity. Law and courts can distract from real justice if they are believed to be the entirety of doing justice. We all have some additional responsibility for a just society and should be prepared mentally to acknowledge shortcomings evident within the system and to experiment carefully with alternatives. Our sense of justice should encompass more than the existing legal institutions.

9

ABOUT GROUPS

It was my destiny to join in a great experience. Having had the good fortune to belong to the League, I was permitted to be a participant in a unique journey. What wonder it had at the time.

. . . we League brothers traveled throughout the world without motorcars or ships; as we conquered the war-shattered world by our faith and transformed it into Paradise, we creatively brought the past, the future and the fictitious into the present moment.

—*Hermann Hesse*

"There are going to be times," says Kesey, "when we can't wait for somebody. Now, you're either on the bus or off the bus. If you're on the bus, and you get left behind, then you'll find it again. If you're off the bus in the first place—then it won't make a damn." And nobody had to have it spelled out for them. Everything was becoming allegorical, understood by the group mind, and especially this: you're either on the bus . . . or off the bus.

—*Tom Wolfe*

GROUPS, AND SOCIAL SCIENCE PAST

There are times when we want to settle back, when we want to be surrounded by a kind of primordial ooze of companionship. We want the ease of wine or religion or dope. Sometimes we want the womblike comfort of a group.

Groups have a long—if not noble—history in American politics. From the time James Madison wrote of factions, group theory has tried to mirror the group action in America. We know, too, that Alexis de Tocqueville wrote of groups, of "voluntary associations," which to him seemed the backbone of the republic. Because groups seem to have something to do with our reality, we should try to understand them both as a social science discovery and for what they mean in the real world.

At one time or another small groups have been seen as the basis of just about everything. The king had his advisors, the pope his inner councils of close friends, the president a kitchen cabinet, and, most recently—but for rather different reasons—the heavy rock people have had their groupies.

But even with all those groups around, even knowing that they have had something to do with why things happened as they did, it is hard for us to truly understand the nature of groups. It is difficult mostly because we do not really want to hear about them. As students, we seem to shy away from an understanding of groups because it might be painful. In the end, it may turn out that we are all "groupies" of one kind or another; yet we do not know a thing about groups.

It seems reasonable to approach this section historically so as to better understand ourselves as an extension of what was. Around the turn of the century, groups were rediscovered in American society, this time by an academic named Arthur Bentley. A seductive theory, his. The idea, in a somewhat bastardized form, was that small groups were the oil that kept society running smoothly. One could look around—casually or carefully—and see that neighbors and corporate executives, army generals and important senators all formed themselves into groups. It was thought that all that was needed was to understand how people were brought together, what they did when they were together, and how the different bunches of them interacted—then we could understand all the important things about society.

Just think group, think small, and all answers become clear.

The understanding of groups did not stop there; indeed, it has been continued, updated, revised, and revitalized by those people who study large organizations. What the investigators found, while a bit of a surprise to them, should be no surprise to us. They found that people who worked in organizations tended to gather in groups. That people in these little groups did things pretty much alike. That they worked at about the same speed, thought about the same thoughts, said about the same things. In sum, members of groups became almost indistinguishable to those outside the group.[1]

In terms of historical importance we can shift from the 1930s to the 1950s, from groups in organizations to groups in society, from the Hawthorne studies to the studies of David Truman.[2] It is through Truman that we can begin to understand some of the basic issues of groupist ideology.

IDEOLOGY AND GROUPS

It is clear that when any "reality" is described, when any theory is presented, it carries with it a bias. Sometimes more pronounced than others; sometimes involving a whole world view, other times simple prejudices. Those who write about groups are certainly carriers of bias; they surely have a particular view of society to present.

The point is not that group theorists have biases—that is quite normal; the point is to understand what those biases are. We need to examine the implications of their views to know whether we can share them. We must compare what the roles of groups in society are said to be with what they really are; we must know whom groups help, and how; finally, we must try to figure out where

---

[1] These were the Hawthorne studies. One major finding resulting from them was that people being studied were more productive than people not being studied. For a first-rate article on modern working groups, see Elinor Langer, "The Women of the Telephone Company," *The New York Review of Books,* March 26, 1970.

[2] See David Truman, *The Governmental Process* (New York: Alfred A. Knopf, 1951).

group theory might be leading us. Maybe then we can begin to make sense out of our group selves.

Groups, according to the writings of David Truman, represent the multiple interests in a society. Our diversity is reflected—indeed, represented—by the groups to which we belong. Further, if there is a "national interest," it is only the sum of the interests of these groups. In other words, an individual belongs to a group, the group represents the interests of the individual in the public sector, and the sum of the interests of these groups is the "national interest."

Now certainly that makes sense. Indeed, it is wholly reasonable until one begins to think about it and question it. What I want to argue is that Truman fails us in very basic ways, and to understand his failure is to begin to understand one of the meanings of groups.[3]

One "sin" of Truman is simply this: He assumes unquestioningly that leaders do in fact represent the group interest. He does not ask how they do, or to what extent they do; he just assumes that leaders represent their groups. If Truman is correct, then the system of groups seems fair enough. It means that we can join a group and have a voice in what goes on. Regrettably, however, Truman does not appear to be right.

Theoretically, the internal workings of groups, and therefore the interests they come to represent, are complicated. Groups (for example, labor unions) inevitably come under the leadership of people who are insulated from the rest of the members. Worse, leaders begin developing interests of their own: the desire to stay in power, the desire to form friendships with other group leaders or with powerful, prestigious persons. Much behavior can be understood in bureaucratic terms.

In other words, the desires of the leader are often different from, or even in conflict with, the desires of the membership he or she represents. The leader has aims and goals that, in the last analysis, are conservative. His or her vision becomes limited to a particular position in the system, so that the key to policy must be to

---

[3] This is similar to the analysis in Mike Rogin's "Nonpartisanship and the Group Interest," in Philip Green and Sanford Levinson, eds., *Power and Community* (New York: Vintage Books, 1970). To get a clearer view of the traditional arguments, one should see Rogin's article.

keep the system stable. There is no reason to believe that stability is the goal of the membership of the organization; there is little evidence to show that the interests of the group are represented by the leadership.[4]

Group theory in the 1950s, then, was interesting but certainly not democratic. What Truman described was a system run by an elite of group leaders. The elite was responsible for the safety of the system and for its stability, but did not really concern itself with the democratic workings of the group. By definition, the interests of the leadership were thought to be the interests of the group, but that assumption was only partially correct. As defined by the leadership—by the elite—group interests were represented only if they did not endanger the smooth workings of the system, only if they did not endanger the security of the elite.

When viewed in this light, two things become more understandable. First, at the level of the example itself, it is clear that business and labor *can* agree on many things, because business leaders and labor leaders perceive that they have much in common. The dynamic that pushes the one pushes the other.

Second, it becomes obvious that Truman's theory of groups contains a particular view of the individual. The view is impersonal and material. The individual is to be materially taken care of by the group. That is in the person's interest and the public interest. Yet, in an important sense, a political sense, the individual is not much better off than he or she was before joining the group. The individual is not really represented by anyone, is not a member of a group that democratically decides the interests of that group; is not in control; is powerless.

In addition to the elite "sin" of the traditional analysis, there are other ways to view the problems and shortcomings of group theory and action.

For example, there is a real question about what the activity of joining a group really means. In an earlier chapter there was a list that compared how often Americans joined groups with how often people from other Western nations joined groups. What we

---

[4] Ibid., pp. 132–133.

saw was that Americans joined more groups. At least one underlying question went unasked: Can we count all those groups as political?

Do the Moose count as political? Or the Elks? And what does it mean to be *forced* to join a group? Lawyers must join the state bar association. Doctors must join medical groups. Workers in places that are unionized must join the union. Many of these groups do not seem to fit the definition of the "political" group.

How do the answers to these questions affect our statistical superiority in joining? Could it mean, when we make the necessary and appropriate subtractions, that we are not as politically active—even in groups—as it appears?

There is a good probability that this is exactly what it means. We simply cannot equate random group joining with political action.

There are other examples of group theory problems. We know that group leaders and group staffs have a disproportionate amount of power to define issues and negotiate solutions. But still, there is some power in the membership itself. That, it seems, is where the average citizen has his or her say. Certainly that is true in principle.

But average is not really the most accurate word to use. Let me tell you three traits of those people who are most likely to join a group. They generally have a higher than average income; they have a better than average occupation; they have better than average education.

So, we have a kind of dual elitism. First, the leaders and staffs both represent power and have their own power. And second, the more well off—the higher-status folks—are more likely to have their interests represented than others. It really should be no surprise. If you have time to devote, and money to spend, it is not unreasonable in our society that you will use some of each to organize to push your own interests.

There is another term, used by those whom we may think of as group apologists, that needs to be mentioned. The term is "vicarious representation." The idea is that, even without joining a group, an individual's interests will be represented.

I remember my first reaction to the notion of vicarious representation. What I thought about was certainly not political. How would I feel, I thought, if someone took a vacation for me or made love for me? In neither case was vicarious representation at all interesting. That holds true in more public things as well.

For example, I am against high gasoline prices, but there is really no group I can join that deals with this issue. There are, though, people for windmill power. If they are successful, then there is a chance that gasoline prices may drop a little. The theory goes that my interests are vicariously represented by the windmill lobby.

Realistically, it seems like a poor deal in a couple of ways. Given a choice based simply on power, I would much rather have the strength of the oil lobby than the righteousness of the windmill lobby. If the choice were based only on being right, I would be happy with the windmills.

Second, and certainly equally important, the whole theory revolves around my *not* being active, my *not* being political. The theory—group theory in general and vicarious representation in particular—assumes that politics should be handled by others. Either handled by those who are paid by my contributions or dues, or handled by those who happen to have some issues in common with me.

Vicarious, in the final analysis, is the right word to use. It is all vicarious—which is not political at all.

Such are the individual costs of this group theory, of this "public interest." They represent, in part, the social and political costs of our system of groups.

NEW GROUPS FOR CONTACT

David Truman was the 1950s; these are the 1980s. Life has become faster. We have to take speed to stay even. Organizations have become bigger. We have become smaller cogs in bigger machines. Much smaller. And much, much bigger.

Somehow society has tried to push us apart organically—and together mechanically. By that I mean that we are less and less able to understand ourselves as human beings, but more able to define ourselves as pieces of social machinery. We are more tool-like; we are more machinelike; we are more pieces of production than ever before.

Where does that leave us? Surely our social science theories would not consciously deny us our own humanity.

Of course they don't. No, social science would not do that. What it does do is what it has tried to do for years—tie us neatly together in little groups of powerless people. It happens at two levels: personally and organizationally. In one sense, this theory of small groups makes the world very recognizable. The United States is made up of millions of little groups. These groups—in car pools, at work, at school, in the neighborhood, while hunting or playing bridge—give humanity and, finally, a kind of self-definition to an individual.

In a sense the theory might be right. We seem to yearn for our own close groups. Yet even these groups have been changing and so too has our involvement in them. Groups in the brave new Now seem to have two distinct qualities: temporariness and great intimacy. Together these traits can be tyrannizing.

We Americans are a cross-section of generations. There are sets of people who, for one reason or another, live through a time which is of overwhelming importance to them. For example, Ronald Reagan never got over a kind of violent reaction to communists and probably millions of people never got over being hippies. One phase—still going strong in places—has to do with how we use groups over a short period of time. Or, to be more accurate, how groups use us in a limited amount of time.

America was, not long ago, an odd sideshow of Hollywood. Everyone "loved" everyone else. We were friendly to all because we knew that we would never see them again. We would pledge allegiance to the group, which in turn would demand great conformity and intimacy, and in a month or a year we would move on to be tyrannized again.

Groups seem to have reached their logical conclusion in becoming plastic, wholly artificial, and temporary. For a flat fee, one can buy instant identity, constant attention. One can join an encounter group. As therapy, encounters may be helpful. As contributions to any political change, to any substantive action, they seem to influence nothing. These groups provide human contact, which is an important neglected need of our times.

NEW GROUPS FOR SPEED

It is important to develop in greater detail some of the themes we have mentioned before. This and the following sections will deal with the coerciveness of groups, with leadership and participation in groups, and finally with magical groups. Coerciveness seems to be the most reasonable place to begin.

In the above there is the suggestion that there are at least two ways in which groups can limit one's power. By studying the setting of groups—how they are arranged and managed—and group dynamics, we will get closer to understanding how an individual group member may become powerless. First, the setting.

If I understand the trend correctly, we are moving toward a society in which work groups, and hence, all others, are becoming temporary.

(As we saw earlier, time has gotten down to fifty-nine seconds in boss/worker relationships. Stop-watch human-relations.) There is another book, *The Temporary Society*, which focuses on moving itself.[5]

The argument of the future is roughly this. Society, especially the technical one, is experiencing more and more problems. To get to these problems quickly, to solve them fast, we must change our living patterns. We must be able to move around quickly—move to the problems—meet new sets of coworkers, and form together to solve the problem.

Then, move again to the next problem.

This is more than just a way to organize (or to reorganize); it is a whole ethic, a whole way of understanding ourselves and society. We become people without a home, without permanence. We become a permanent part of an ever-changing environment, perpetual strangers in a group of strangers. To meet the new requirements, we must continually change homes, towns, work groups, and friends. Above and beyond what was discussed in connection with the Open Road, the implications of this style are enormous.

---

[5] Warren Bennis and Philip Slater, *The Temporary Society* (New York: Harper & Row, 1968).

First, and most obvious, power under such a system lies in the ability to move people around. In other words, there is somebody at the center finding problems and replacing people. Those who move become wholly dependent upon their bosses. They have no other stable reference point. It is possible that the military is the forerunner of temporary America. Every year or two the military family moves. From city to city, from base to base. They are thrown into new work groups and a new social life. Only if they are lucky do they see old friends, that is, people from other one-year stays at other bases. The military person is loyal to—and dependent upon—the United States Government (whoever that is). Loyalties are rarely to the location from which he or she is about to move.

The point is clear: In a world of temporary groups, power flows to those who control the moves.

We can approach it in a different way with this question: Where do we look to for strength if not in our phenomenal surroundings? While I am not certain there is an agreed upon answer, let me suggest one which seems reasonable. As we are less attached to the real (material) things around us, we become more attached to the ever present symbols which are common to us all. We rely on our committment to symbolic values we carry with us rather than those things we know in our immediate surroundings.

The second point about temporariness involves the kind of person who will fit. The question is this: Who will people the Temporary Society? Who will survive? We can speculate.

The young will survive the moving and adjusting. They are healthy enough for all the hassles. But the survivors must be more than young; they must be technical experts, too. A young person with technical expertise might not merely adjust to such a regimen; he or she could possibly thrive on moving from place to place, continually solving problems of a technical nature. The young could somehow handle the ever-changing groups of people, as long as there is work to do.[6]

---

[6] One particularly vivid and depressing forecast of the future is that it will be like Fort Lauderdale when students are there over spring vacation. See Alvin Toffler, *Future Shock* (New York: Bantam Books, 1970). Also, of course, see Christopher Lasch, *The Culture of Narcissism*, cited earlier.

They will survive, but for how long? "Young" is not a permanent condition; neither is technical expertise. In these days of new knowledge, an engineer of thirty may be out-of-date—may be an old-fashioned toolbox with old-fashioned tools.

There are some odd and horrible losses in this temporary world. We both grow "old" too quickly and stay "young" too long. We can't really *be* young and adventuresome. Got to get going—moving and dealing and making it, right out of college. The cream of the crop have the *new techniques,* the *stamina* to survive, and are *unformed* enough to continually adapt.

So there is the constant fear of being old. Being out of technological date. Being too slow to move and too much of a person to adapt to every silly change.

The temporary world robs both the rush of being young and the true pleasure of aging.

There is an amazing curse put on the young—a curse that goes with our age. It's called potential, and young people almost always have it. One could easily call it a social disease. I'm pleased not to be in college, or even in my twenties. I'm just beginning to glimpse the horrors we put on the young. The weight of the word potential.

There is a denial of personal power, a taking away (a not granting) of a sense of self. Sure you're whole, but empty. Young and hollow. *What does it mean?*

At least two things.

First, all ages seem to have been corrupted. Everyone wants to be young, and young people are denied the essences of life.

Second, in our temporary world, emotions get *democratized* and *discounted.*

Let's go back to groups, encounter-type groups, and look at them in a little different way. The real trap in our pop-psychological-instant-intimacy groups is something like this: To be "healthy," one must "express one's own personal feeling." To apply a good social science concept to that, a lot of it is just bullshit.

There are many things that are really unimportant . . . even some of your very own emotions. To make all emotions equal means you will never be able to see what's important and what's unimportant.

When another person or an event really *is* an intrusion into your life—really does affect the who-you-are in the world—what do you do if you've just been to an encounter group and have let it "all hang out"? Been "up front." Been "honest" and are "emotionally spent"? What do you do for something important? Chill out, as the expression goes.

We've made love/hate/anger/joy all silly and meaningless by elevating petty moods into important events of our personal lives. We seem all too willing to throw away empathy and care and probably a great deal of our politics and humanity for a cheap version of self-indulgent, childish whimpering.

We democrats go to encounter groups and vote on emotions. What a place we've gotten to.

The temporary society makes no allowance for the very young, for the old, for those not involved in technology. Part of the glue it uses—groups—seems systematically to take us away from our emotional self by flooding us with "emotion." What does it mean? To quote Kurt Vonnegut:

> The problem is this: How to love people who have no use?

> In time, almost all men and women will become worthless as producers of goods, food, services and more machines, as sources of practical ideas in the areas of economics, engineering, and probably medicine, too. So—if we cannot find reasons and methods for treasuring human beings because they are *human beings,* then we might as well, as has so often been suggested rub them out.[7]

Rub them out? Is *that* the ultimate solution of the temporary society? Probably not, but it is an idea.

Eternal moving affects us in less obvious but equally real ways. When you were a child and you went away for a vacation, did you ever say "good-by" to your house? (Do you still?) That simple, seemingly childish thing to do is an emotion which is tied to our constantly moving. Our house, our block, our neighbors form a

---

[7] Kurt Vonnegut, Jr., *God Bless You, Mr. Rosewater* (New York: Dell Publishing Co., 1965), p. 183. It should be noted that "doing away" with people is not Vonnegut's message.

good deal of our everyday reality. It is exactly that reality which we need to better understand.

Our world, at one level, is made up of millions of sense impressions. We take those impressions, sort out the important ones and give attention and meaning to them. If we stay in the same place for a period of time, the things in that place take on a collection of meanings. Also, if we stay in the same place long enough there is a certain kind of stability which we simply take for granted.

From the very beginning of white people settling in America, this kind of stability has been forsaken for moving West. The discussion of moving was one of the central points in the freedom chapter. I understand that to say there is a certain kind of stability in living in the same place sounds very un-American; but, because our moving has changed once again, we must look at it once again. After all, a hundred years ago there was land to move to, an environment in which people could create what they wanted, an openness of opportunity.

Change today is from city to city; from set environment to set environment; from bureaucratic role to bureaucratic role. What has happened is that moving disorients us in some ways, and stabilizes us in others.

The worker, the person who is getting transferred, is best off. He or she still has job stability. Although everything else has changed (except for family members), the job is essentially the same. Same product, same basic set of rules, same basic characters with whom to deal. While the building is different, the basic phenomenon of an eight-hour work day remains the same.

The worker's family, however, has lost all stability (except immediate family members). New everything: home, room, friends, schools, stores, social pressures, interests, neighbors. There is a tremendous effort to take everything in, sort out what is important and give it meaning. After enough of these moves, loyalty to a place, loyalty to neighbors and community, is not much of a possibility.

We become familiar *not* with everyday physical things in our life, but with constantly changing social pressures reported by the ever vigilant popular press, magazines, and electronic media.

Do not think that I am ignoring the remarkable bigotry and ignorance that can develop in places where people never move. Our history is rich in examples of the intolerance of wrongheaded communities. Our history is also full of stories about how individuals moved, and changed for the better. But, to constantly give up a familiar environment in order to escape the possible narrow-mindedness of some communities is foolishness.

To give up the familiar is to give up, in a strange way, meanings you have given the world. Until those meanings are replaced, it is difficult to be as active and vital as you once were.

When we were kids, and we said good-by to our house, we were saying that we were leaving a source of our strength, but that we would be back. We were leaving the easiness of familiar surroundings. Now, think about that everyday dynamic/emotion in organizational and political terms. As a leader, wouldn't it make you more secure if your workers or citizens were made to periodically say "good-by" to a source of their strength, never to see it again?

While it may sound silly to think that merely living in the same place may well be a source of power for the citizen, to believe it should be considered. One of the points of the book is that there are too many everyday things we are willing to ignore (or, to put it less kindly, unwilling to look at). Maybe it would help if what I've been saying is presented in a more formal manner.

How about this for a dynamic to be discussed: As individuals move, power tends to centralize. That holds for organizations and government . . . at least in the United States.

COERCION

Enough about the setting of groups. What about the workings of the group itself, the interactions of those who compose the group? For several reasons—not the least of which is that they are manageable—many empirical studies have been done on the behavior of small groups. The conclusions of the studies are not surprising. In a small-group setting, the pressure to conform to group norms is great. In a simple, now classic study, S. E. Asch demonstrated how powerful group pressure could be.[8]

---

[8] S. E. Asch, "Effects of Group Pressure upon the Modification and Distortion of Judgements," in Bernard Hinton and H. Joseph Reitz, eds., *Groups and Organizations* (Belmont, Calif.: Wadsworth Publishing Co., 1971), pp. 215–223.

The experiment involved eight persons seated in a room. They were shown lines of various lengths and were asked obvious questions about the lines. The whole "test" was very easy and monotonous.

As the "test" progressed, one individual began to find himself being contradicted by the rest of the group. His "right" answer did not correspond with the answers given by the other seven. What had happened, of course, was that seven members of the group had been coached to give incorrect answers.

In this very simple exercise involving the judging of lengths of lines, the results were "clear and unambiguous. There was marked movement toward the majority. One third of all the estimates in the critical group were errors identical with or in the direction of the distorted estimates of the majority.[9] The reasons why a person would contradict what he or she had visually perceived are instructive. When each subject was asked why he had responded to the "test" the way he or she had done, the most common explanation was that the group had answered that way. The majority of the group seemed to be acting without hesitation, indeed, with confidence; so the outsider assumed they were right.

Being in a minority seemed to make things hard on the individual. Asch writes that the "principal impression" of the subject was that he was "so caught up by immediate difficulties that he lost clear reasons for his actions, and could make no reasonable decisions."[10]

All of that is a little abstract. There are, regrettably, less abstract examples. Let me offer an example that, if it had not happened, would have been very difficult to imagine.

The example is Jonestown. It is an example of many things, only one of which is groups.

Do you recall Jim Jones? He was a cult leader who, in the late '70s, led his group of followers to commit suicide. His is an interesting/sick story because, in many ways, he was an authentic do-gooder. He encompassed some of America's best ideals. He really seemed to believe in equality, in justice, in the races living in harmony. He worked hard, he had a certain gift of persuasion, he was

---

[9] Ibid., p. 216.
[10] Ibid., p. 217.

charismatic. In a move that seemed insightful and full of good sense, he and his followers moved to a place where they could be left alone to establish their community.

There was one real shortcoming, one real shame: Jim Jones had some serious psychological problems along with his high ideals. The problems got increasingly worse.

We know how the story turns out. Jones's charismatic paranoia, along with the enormous amount of group pressure that was multiplied in the jungle, turned out to be a deadly combination. Kool-Aid will never be the same. The children died first. Jones died yelling the word *mother* over and over.

While it is a fact that not all groups end this way, it is wrong to ignore or dismiss the power of group pressure.

We have, in a sense, extremes in which we are literally given our choice of poisons: To be isolated is to be totally without power. It is to be lonely, alienated, desperate. Giving yourself entirely to a group may well be giving yourself entirely. Jonestown shows us that is not always such a good idea.

If the Asch experiment and the Jonestown example are any indications, it is not difficult to conclude that small groups are potentially very coercive. But it would be wrong to stop with that obvious insight. It would be equally wrong to suggest that all groups are evil or that all groups are bad for their members. In order to begin to understand groups as something other than coercive, we must try to envision changes in our attitudes.

GROUPS RECONSIDERED: PASSIVE AND ACTIVE

This may sound like a paradox, but I do not think that it is: For groups to be less coercive, we must become more involved in them. Let me try to explain briefly.

Small groups are potentially very important to the way we act and the things we do. We know that. Further, we know that we are constantly involved, to a greater or lesser degree, in groups. Whether it is a sorority or fraternity, a bridge club or basketball team, or just some snobby little social group, we are involved. The problem is that we are not *consciously* involved. Too often we passively accept membership while never actively taking part in the direction of the group. We accept coercion without accepting participation; we are acted upon without acting.

To put it a little differently, to be a part of a group is to be subject to its rules. This is true whether we accept it or not; it is true whether we actively engage in the group decision making, or feel we are different from the group, or not really a part of it at all. In part, our identities stem from these small groups. What is necessary to understand is that the group is part of you no matter how you feel about it. To belong to a group and not take it seriously is to limit the power you have over who you are.

What I am arguing is that groups are important to one's self and, as such, should be treated importantly.

LEADERSHIP AND POWER; AN INTRODUCTION

To get at the problem of living in groups—the problem of participation—is a complicated task. It involves leading and following and membership. Also involved are ideas about democracy and authority and all those themes political scientists should be concerned with. But a discussion that considered all these ideas would be misplaced here. We are, after all, trying to make sense of groups. We are trying to figure out how we can make groups—an everyday fact of life—a more meaningful, everyday fact of life. We are trying to understand how to free ourselves from current group practice by becoming conscious of the benefits groups have to offer.

It is important to realize that people who join together—in groups, or politically, or whatever—must come to some kind of understanding of how they will behave. I am not talking about a strict code of rules, or law and order, or even order; I am just suggesting that we made an effort to shape our groups toward common interests and goals. We should be aware that power and leadership exist whether we acknowledge them or not.

If that is so, if leadership and power do exist in groups, then their forms should be understood and agreed upon by the members of that group, if they are not to be tyrannized by them. An example may be useful. It is the example of the group living of the people in the Haight Ashbury during 1966 and 1967. It was an interesting time, a good one to learn from for a couple of reasons. First, there was a great deal of energy for change. Second, even with that energy there was failure. Given history, it is only appropriate that we learn from failure. The hippies accepted a different lifestyle during this period and by example tried to change society. Their dealings with groups point up questions with which we must deal. John Howard explains:

> Stated simply, the argument is as follows. The hippies assumed that voluntarism (every man doing his own thing) was compatible with satisfying essential group and individual needs and with the maintenance of a social system in which there was an absence of power differentials and invidious distinctions based on, for example, wealth, sex, or race. That assumption is open to question. Voluntarism can work only where the participants in the social system have a sufficient understanding of the needs of the system to be willing to do things which they do not want to do in order for the system to persist. . . .

Howard asked one of the Diggers why they were no longer distributing food in the park and received this answer:

> "Well, man, it took a lot of organization to get that done. We had to scuffle to get the food. Then the chicks or somebody had to prepare it. Then we got to serve it. A lot of people got to do a lot of things at the right time or it doesn't come off. Well, it got so that people weren't doing it. I mean a cat wouldn't let us have a truck when we needed it or some chick was grooving somewhere and can't help out. Now you hate to get into the power bag and start telling people what to do . . . but without that, man, well. . . ."[11]

The point that is important to make is that the "power trip" is not, by definition, a bad thing. What is essential is that power be understood and then used when and how the group wants it used. Back to the hippies:

---

[11] Reprinted from "The Flowering of the Hippie Movement" by John Robert Howard, Professor of Sociology, State University of New York, in volume 382 of *The Annals* of The American Academy of Political and Social Science. Copyright 1969 by The American Academy of Political and Social Science.

We had all kinds of people there at first and anybody could stay if there was room. Anybody could crash out there. Some of the motorcycle types began to congregate in the kitchen. That became *their* room, and if you wanted something to eat or a beer you had to step over them. Pretty soon, in a way, people were cut off from the food. I don't mean that they wouldn't give it to you, but you had to go on their "turf" to get it. It was like they had begun, in some very quiet and subtle way, to run things.[12]

In sum, for a group to fulfill the intentions of each individual, elements of the relationships among the members—like power and leadership—must be understood and agreed upon. If that is the case, the chances of the group's becoming a good or even an extraordinary experience are greatly increased.

OH MY GOD . . .

They are playing a game. They are playing not playing a game. If I show them I see they are, I shall break the rules and they will punish me. I must play their game, of not seeing I see the game.

—*R. D. Laing*

Because there is no public place to be political, no space in which we may be citizens, we are forced to make each of our actions a political statement of one sort or another. From our diet to our dress we make ideological choices. There are lots of serious folks who really do live their politics.

To be fair (not a terribly noble aim, but adequate enough in this case), at least something should be said about religion. In an important way, believers are taking their actions almost ponderously seriously: Their day is a reflection of His Day or Her Day, and theirs is a "politics" of True Belief.[13]

---

[12] Ibid., p. 207.

[13] If it makes any difference, I can remember fairly accurately my last "encounter" with God. When I was nineteen my mother and I were talking. We were discussing religion and she said: "It's too bad we don't believe in God. I suppose it would be a comfort." I said something like: "Yeah, it's too bad." Enough of True Confessions.

I don't want to push this "fair" thing too far. There is much more about religion that I will not discuss than I will. If your God is real and not mentioned and vengeful, you don't have to worry. I'll get what's coming to me for the oversight.

We are, when we get down to it, Americans. That rates pretty high on a Simple-Minded-Scale, but it is a fact that is fairly helpful to remember. Some of us, and I mean a *very, very few,* are able to un-Americanize ourselves. The rest of us are Americans, and it gets into and influences just about everything we do. From hamburgers to God, we are red, white, and blue.

Ain't a bad thing; in fact, there's something good and noble about it.

The problems really don't appear while you are being yourself; the real trouble starts when you start being one or another kind of an unself.

But this is about religion. We know, in our very beings, about lip-service religion. A Sunday morning in church if you happen to be with your parents, or two days a year in temple, or catching up on a busy week of sinning in a confessional. Check in *as if* there were a god for an After-Life Insurance policy. Not all that pure of motive, but it's good just to be sure.

A comfortable eternity is worth a few boring sermons.

For some years now, there have been people who were willing *not only to say* that's silly, but actually to do something about it. There are chanters and freaks and preemies and an amazing variety of orthodox Christians and Jews and believers in the Buddha and different kinds of Zen.

Many of these people are making serious and impressive efforts at making sense of the world they didn't ask to be born into; they are trying to live a good life. A life that takes into account the problems of our society and compels them to do something differ-ent. I'm not really concerned if they are right- or wrong-headed; I am much more concerned in the statement they make and what we have to learn from them.

There is some sense in starting with what we (mostly) are, and ending up with what we are not. The biggest turn-on, the fastest growing and most popular new nonreligion religion, is TM. The transcendental meditationists. TM'ers. Ommmm. Hummmm.[14]

If we—a committee of us—were to invent a business for our fellow Americans, there are some obvious sorts of things we would want. In order to make lots of money, we could offer a product easy to make and use; promise it would help all sorts of things (reduce crime in the streets, improve sexual performance, make dull work happier, help you get better grades, help you make more money, and bring about world peace); make it religious/nonreligious popculture exotic, and let people still smoke, drink, be junkfood junkies; and sell it with something close to a scientific guarantee.

Why, if we did it right we'd be rich.

We could start a university, sell to 30,000 new people a month, have $12 million a year in revenue coming in. Fat City.

We could also be sued by the World Plan Executive Council-US (the TM central office) because they already *do* these things and *make* those claims, and *have* that income. (We can learn a whole lot about ourselves by learning about Transcendental Meditation in America. It may turn out that we are what we hum.)

One might want to argue, probably very rightly, that what I wrote is not true. It is wrong in particular, but not in spirit. What seems most wrong is the fact that no committee could invent such a wonderful business. I apologize.

The TM'ers have an impressive list of "up your" promises.[15] For example: Up Your Recall, or Up Your Productivity, or Up Your IQ.[16] And there are lots more. The point—if it's possible to over simplify—is that the world is going at an out-of-control pace, and we poor people can't cope. Who can argue with that?

---

[14] Of course I have a mantra, but I can't tell you. I'mmm sworn to secrecy. Also, I have no doubts that TM'ers who report fantastic results are telling the truth.

[15] The source of much of the following is Denise Denniston and Peter McWilliams, *The TM Book: How to Enjoy the Rest of Your Life* (New York: Warner Books, Inc., 1975).

[16] Ibid., pp. 79, 93, 74.

In order to make sense and keep up, what we need to do is relax (to be precise, it only takes forty minutes a day) and get in touch (in *direct contact*) with the source of thought. We have to tap into the pure energy in the mind.

Step Right Up. Buy Into Your Own Mind.

Anyone can do it. It is easy to learn and effortless to do, and it actually takes only hours to learn.[17] The magic mantra gives you a rest deeper than sleep (there is Scientific Proof) and can make you more creative and even give you a faster reaction time (there is Scientific Proof).

With the stress off your nervous system, you can avoid those nagging heart attacks, and your mind can reach its full potential. You can lick this tense twentieth century and reach Enlightenment.

(Let me interrupt this commercial with some clarification. Upon investigation, we find that enlightenment is a fairly heavy-duty concept that comes from many of the Eastern religions. For TM it means having 100 percent of one's potential available for use. More curious still, it is claimed that enlightenment is *everyone's birthright*. Should we now say "Life, Liberty, and Enlightenment"?

Back to our commercial.)

TM technique is "a great scientific discovery." It "makes suffering in life a thing of the past." Not only that, there is nothing to believe in (even an atheist can do it), no special clothes to wear (not even sandals), no change of lifestyle. You don't even have to concentrate. But there will be changes: *"Some will find calculus a breeze. Others will have no difficulty writing epic poems before breakfast."*[18]

All that, and you can still eat McDonald's hamburgers.

And, as a footnote, if just 1 percent of you in your community do this, the *whole* community will "suddenly . . . increase its efficiency, orderliness, and productivity."[19]

All this for less than $200.

---

[17] Most of these words are from *The TM Book,* not from me. These, for example, come from ibid., p. 51.

[18] Ibid., p. 116.

[19] Ibid., p. 336.

IT MIGHT BE HARDER THAN THAT

If I don't know I don't know
I think I know
If I don't know I know
I think I don't know

—R. D. Laing

Crowned with garlands, the three-year-old child plays the
drum; The eighty-year-old man plays with a balloon.[20]

As a treat to myself, I was reading a skinny book—*Zen and the Art of Archery*—before trying to sleep every night. It was written by a German who went to Japan and tried to learn Zen through a Master who taught archery. I would read a few pages, do some thinking about it, and was enjoying it.

I even flattered myself into thinking I understood some of it.

Somewhere around the middle of the book—somewhere around the second or third year of archery/Zen—the Master introduced the concept of the target and how the arrow and the target should meet at a certain point.

To tell you the truth, I had been aiming at the target since page one. Oh, American me.

The Zen life is one that we seem to be trained and taught not to understand. To grow up in America is to grow up with a set of instincts that close us off from the essences and meanings of Zen. If that is true, and I have to admit I believe it is, it would be silly for me to write in an authoritative way about what Zen *really* is.

There are a couple of obvious things that might give us the proper distance on those people—and those groups of people— who study Zen. The fact seems to be that one is not "taught" Zen, nor does one actually "study" Zen. Two quotes may be helpful:

> One would not even be able to talk about teaching it since Zen cannot be taught, that is, taught through symbols; it passes directly from master to student, from "mind to mind." The image

---

[20] Thich Nhat Hanh, *Zen Keys* (Garden City, New York: Anchor Books, 1974), p 164.

employed here is a *seal* imprinted on a mind; not a seal of wood, copper, or ivory, but a "mind seal."

and

But Zen is not the study of Zen; Zen is life. Zen is direct contact with reality. . . . Zen can only be lived and experienced. As Master Tue Trung Thuong Si said, "This marvelous piece must be played." What is the good of discussing a musical masterpiece? It is its performance that counts.[21]

Let me try another way of getting at not getting at Zen. There are certain Zen monasteries where, upon entering, the novice is given a book called the *Little Manual*. It is a small book, and a famous one. The instinct of the Western mind would be to think of the book as one of philosophy. After all, it is the first book people trying to learn Zen are supposed to read.

In the *Little Manual* there is no Zen philosophy.

The book, basically, is about how to control your mind and concentration, what the required discipline and behavior of life is in the monastery, and an essay encouraging Zen disciples to "take to heart the fact that their time and life are precious and should not be vainly dissipated." The book is used by all monks no matter what their age or the amount of time they have studied Zen.

The essence of Zen is found in the *Little Manual* in part because it suggests an individual focus on each thing he or she does; this action leads to the "Awareness of Being." As I understand it, one would be ill advised (unless he or she wants to prove stupidity) to write much more. It takes a full lifetime of considered acts by serious and good people with a different mind-set to truly understand the Awareness of Being.

There are few if any actions taken that are not subject to self-awareness and meaning. From the closing of a door to the washing of one's hands, a student of Zen must be conscious and understanding. There are "acts of majestic behavior" and "subtle gestures."

---

[21] Ibid., pp. 31, 131. Emphasis in original.

"It is said that in Buddhism there are ninety thousand 'subtle gestures' the novice must practice."[22]

That's a fairly serious project, a lifetime worth. Certainly not the *only* kind of serious project; in fact, it seems remarkably out of our grasp. But it serves as a fine example of how taking the quality of your life seriously can easily be a full-time job. There is something almost magical about those people, but there are equally magical—if not totally different—examples of a more recognizable kind. Before doing them, it seems right to end with a story about enlightenment.

> Little Toyo was only twelve years old. But since he was a pupil at the Kennin Temple, he wanted to be given a *koan* to ponder, just like the more advanced students. So one evening, at the proper time, he went to the room of Makurai, the master, struck the gong softly to announce his presence, bowed, and sat before the master in respectful silence.
>
> Finally the master said: "Toyo, show me the sound of two hands clapping."
>
> Toyo clapped his hands.
>
> "Good," said the master. "Now show me the sound of one hand clapping."
>
> Toyo was silent. Finally he bowed and left to consider this problem.
>
> The next night he returned, and struck the gong with one palm. "That is not right," said the master. The next night Toyo returned and played geisha music with one hand. "That is not right," said the master. The next night Toyo returned, and imitated the dripping of water. "That is not right," said the master. The next night Toyo returned, and imitated the cricket scraping his leg. "That is still not right." said the master.

---

[22] Ibid., p. 25.

For ten nights Toyo tried new sounds. At last he stopped coming to the master. For a year he thought of every sound, and discarded them all, until he finally reached enlightenment.

He returned repectfully to the master. Without striking the gong, he sat down and bowed. "I have heard sound without sound," he said.[23]

MAGICAL GROUPS

It may occur to you, sooner or later, that there is very little "hard," empirical objective information—not much social science data—on magical groups. In my searchings of the literature on small groups, I have encountered none indexed under "magical." That should not disallow my using the designation; all it means is that some kind of definition, or at least explanation, should be given.

Up to now, we have been involved with what we know, with ordinary groups doing those things to individuals that ordinary groups generally do. But it seems to me that there is another kind of group, one in which the members are somehow transformed, somehow special, somehow engaged in an enterprise different from the rest of us. The examples of this come from fiction, and something close to it: Hermann Hesse's *The Journey to the East* and Tom Wolfe's *The Electric Kool-Aid Acid Test*.[24]

The point of these books and the point I shall try to make is this: Far from the common uses of groups we are generally taught, far from the "normal politics" view of American groups, some groups may actually point the way to different kinds of relationships and to a different kind of politics.

To begin at a common beginning point of political scientists, let us start with power. There are some bad feelings about power. If understood in the conventional way, the misgivings are very

---

[23] Excerpt from *Zen Buddhism: Stories, Parables and Koan Riddles of Zen Masters* (Mount Vernon, N.Y.: Peter Pauper Press, 1959), pp. 24–25. Reprinted with permission of Peter Pauper Press.

[24] Hermann Hesse, *The Journey to the East* (New York: Farrar, Straus & Giroux, 1970); Tom Wolfe, *The Electric Kool-Aid Acid Test* (New York: Bantam Books, 1969).

understandable. Power is dominance over; it is—to use the common definition—the ability of A to make B do something B would not otherwise have done.

In that sense, power is in part negative. The definition may be both limiting and harmful; it may influence us to act in certain ways. First, as students or as citizens, we can well understand what B feels like. We can understand what it means to be made to do something we otherwise would not have done.

Second, while A has power, he or she is also caged by the relationship. The person holding power is limited to his or her own imagination. There is little chance that A can become different, can qualitatively change, can get beyond his or her own thoughts. Seen from that point of view, from the point of view that has A making B do something B wouldn't otherwise have done, we can understand why power seems limited and abusive.

The conventional definition of power prescribes "reasonable" ways to behave. Given the definition as a guide to action, we could be expected to "hoard" power, to "spend" it only when necessary. There would be no sharing or spreading of that kind of power: only spending and losing it. But power need not be like that; there can be a different view of power, a different definition of it that might alter the way we act. There might be a view of power that would make it creative.

In order to redefine power so that it would apply to a "magical group," we need change only one word: Power is the ability of A to make B do something he or she *could* not have done before. Power then becomes a source of creative energy, an ability or skill that will help induce someone to take an action, to strike out anew, to do something that was impossible in the past. Just as significantly, power becomes a shared commodity, something that *increases* when used, not decreases.

The most obvious place for this to take place is in a small group, but it must be a group that is stable, not temporary, one that understands power, not one that ignores it; finally, it must be a group that is working for something in common, not one in which there is little coincidence of interests.

The idea of leadership must also change. In a bureaucratic world, leadership is pictured as involving a supervisor/subordinate relationship. The leader is at the top, the rest of us at the bottom. That seems natural enough, and it is certainly an adequate description of everyday life. To envision being a leader is to envision being at the top of something and possessing a good deal of power. It is, in a sense, to assume responsibility for all those underneath you. A plantation owner "took care" of his or her slaves, a school principal "takes care" of his or her students.

Of course that view of leadership depends on a repressive view of power. It may be important to understand leadership as being not on an up-and-down scale with followership but rather on a continuum with it. Leadership and followership are two ends of the same line. One is not "over" the other. One person may have some qualities or traits or skills that make that advice or those directions more acceptable than the others'. In those areas, that person leads.

What is important to understand is that a leader is also a follower. That it is a relationship in which sometimes one leads, sometimes another. If one has the ability to lead a group of people to do things collectively that they could not do individually, and if the members of a group want that to happen, then one person should "lead." But this important fact remains: The relationship between leader and follower is an essentially equal one. From that relationship, the creative powers of the people individually—and of the group as a whole—are increased.[25]

That has the makings of a magical group.

The essence of this discussion—at least the point *I* am most interested in making—is that we are foolish to take groups and group theories at their face value.

Involved in what we think ordinary and obvious are a whole set of assumptions that need to be examined. Such terms as *power* and *leadership* really do mean something, and the way we define them may have an influence on the way we act. It would be at the

---

[25] Just as it seems harmful always to be private, always alone, so it seems harmful always to be public, always open. The tension comes in being open yet retaining some sense of privacy, some sense of that part of us that makes us individuals. What is important is that privacy does not make much sense without publicness. One needs the other to set boundaries and to give meaning.

far reaches of silliness to suggest that by changing the way we define words, the whole world will automatically change. I am not suggesting that. I am trying to make the point that we are tied to concepts and activities we rarely try to understand, to ones we seldom challenge.

There do seem to be other ways to see the world—and maybe that other vision is a better one.

> *They had all voluntarily embarked upon a trip and a state of consciousness that was "crazy" by ordinary standards. The trip, in fact the whole deal, was a risk-all balls-out plunge into the unknown. . . . Stark Naked had done her thing. She roared off into the void and was picked up by the cops by and by and the doors closed in the county psychiatric ward, and that was that, for the pranksters were long gone.*
>
> *—Tom Wolfe*

Focus Nine

There has been a great deal of emphasis in this book that people should act together with others. An obvious contemporary forum for doing so is a group of some sort. Many authors have characterized America as a nation of joiners. We have groups for almost everything: living groups, fraternal groups, private and public interest groups, self-help groups, travel groups, entertainment groups, therapy groups. Name an area of life and Americans probably have a group for it. The central question in this chapter is whether our groups enable us to act together politically in the best possible way. Crucial to the answer is our notion of power. Does the essence of power consist of making someone do something which that individual would not otherwise do, or should power be understood as enabling someone to do something he or she could not do without the help of others?

The answer is a matter of emphasis. Politically, groups usually want to create both kinds of power: They want to enable their members to do something they could not do alone and usually the goal of the group is to make people other than themselves do something they would not have done without the prodding. In other words, usually groups form in order to make their members more efficacious in the world.

This chapter outlines two ways a group may become powerful. The first is normal: The group forms a hierarchy within itself of leaders and followers. The leaders decide the best way for the group to accomplish its objectives while the followers provide suggestions and assist the leaders in reaching the goals; but, mainly the followers do what the leaders outline for them. The leader-follower positions are fixed even though the leaders occasionally change. This first type of group may be "democratic" in the sense that the followers elect leaders and hold them accountable for their actions. It is powerful when the sheer number of followers is large enough and the leaders are shrewd about the choices of what to do; that is, when the leaders find tactics strongly supported by members and most compelling to those outside the group who they wish to influence. As this chapter shows, these leaders, in turn, will encourage the group to do only those things which will keep them in leadership positions. The leaders, then, are conservative or self-interested in this particular way.

The chapter exemplifies the second route to power with "magical" groups. The "magic" here is that all members are both leaders and followers. No hierarchy is presumed; different members lead at different times depending on their capabilities. This type of group is "democratic" in the sense that each member has an equal chance of formulating the plans with which the group as a whole can most strongly agree. People join not only to accumulate sheer numbers and to press their self-interests, but also to exercise their intelligence in the common endeavor. The group is powerful because it is more flexible about what it can do, better able to actively tap the greatest potential of each member in its internal workings, and, when able to agree, more dynamic since the common endeavors contain a part of everyone's thinking.

These magical groups are much rarer than the other type, especially in our era of complex, bureaucratic organization. Yet, they are not theoretically impossible. Human beings still have the potential to mutually join their rightfittingnesses, when publicly articulated, in complementary ways. Furthermore, while the country today seems too vast and populous for effective grass-roots, non-hierarchical organization, high quality leadership did arise during the revolutionary and constitutional eras and was able to wage a war of independence against a militarily superior motherland, then found political institutions of such lasting value that we still use them today. So, while magical because of their creativity, this second type of group can be the base of efficacious political organization. Once we understand the idea of them and take active roles in the groups of which we are members, the quality of our political lives and of the world can improve.

9½
FRIENDSHIP

Friendship, friendship: Just the perfect blendship
When other friendships have been forgot
Ours will still be hot.

This is not really a whole chapter. It is a part of one, a piece of a whole. The ideas that follow are most closely tied to the preceding discussion of groups. The group chapter is incomplete. There is something basic to, as well as prior to, small groups. Friendship is an ingredient of groups, and it is a topic that deserves some attention.

It is important that at least two things be said before we begin to work through the idea of friendship. First, it is a fantastically complicated topic, one that is possibly impossible to fully understand. In order to make our effort more reasonable, more manageable, we will limit the discussion to friendship in America.

Second, the effort is worth making because it might give us insights into our social and political environment. If we *are* the system, if we carry a miniature version of the system in our heads—and act as the system would have us act—then we need to think about how we act.

FRIENDSHIPS: AMERICAN MYTHS

Our first myth is somehow true, and somehow not. The kind that we do not want to believe but for some reason act as if we do. The myth involves women. It seems to me that the first myth we may share is this: Men make better friends than women.

The myth is amazingly degrading. It assures us that two women are rarely true friends—rarely friends who honestly share, who honestly give, friends who are able to stay close for years and years.

But why? Lurking in us is the thought that the essence of women's failure to be friends with other women lies in their jealousy. In a male-chauvinist-pig sort of way, men seem to believe that each woman is too insecure to be the friend of another woman. The idea is that what a woman needs is a strong male, someone to whom she can talk, someone on whom she can lean.

Americans seem to believe that women together are either hens or bitches, but never friends.

I am always in search of new social science laws. The following "law" fits enough cases so that it should be remembered: For every wrongheaded action, there is an equal and opposite wrongheaded action. The law seems to hold here.

As just suggested, our collective myths about women's friendships have been both wrong and destructive. The sustained attack on those myths carried on by the women's movement has done much to change all of that. Nothing wrongheaded about wanting to change something bad.

But there is something not right about this equal but opposite reaction: Only women can be friends with women. The theory goes that men (oppressors) are at war with women (fighting for their freedom), and enemies cannot be friends. The theory denies the possibility of men doing good or of women doing evil. The theory is silly.

Martin Buber writes that when you deny humanity—the potential for both good and evil—to another, you deny your own humanity.

Martin Buber was right.

The whole men/women thing is difficult to sort out. Certainly some men have been, and continue to be, "pigs." Surely our myths are harmful. But it seems that neither sex is without sin. As we will soon see, the myths that have to do with men are really no better than those that have to do with women.

The problems of this half-chapter are centered on friendship. In this section, the question is: Can men and women truly be friends? Again, our vision is clouded with doubt. We know that men and women can *like* each other; but is that friendship?

The stereotype thought is obvious to all. They can be lovers, or they can be "just like sister and brother," but the idea of being friends with someone of the opposite sex seems just plain foolish. We are in a strange time: a time when we realize men and women *are not* the same, yet *are* the same. It is a time when we must not assume that women doing "men's jobs" is a sign of liberation, or that men doing "women's jobs" is a sign of weakness. In the flux of all of us having an identity crisis, friendship is tough to find.

For men, women are okay to sleep with, but it is foolish to try to be too friendly with one.

Friendships between men—so goes our myth—are also limited. The first obvious limitation—obvious indignation—concerns black men and white men. The myth is that for a white, the black man is everything but a friend.

For two hundred years, we were taught to believe that the black was a "boy." A grinning, happy boy. Tough to be best friends with a boy.

Then there was the myth that black men were sexually superior. Tough to be best friends with a rival. A rival who was better.

Finally, in enlightened, liberal circles, the black man became a status symbol. Whitey had to have one at every party. But the black was not there as a friend; he was there to be on display.

So blacks hated whites and whites hated blacks; and friendship was limited in yet another way.

The results of all this are limiting. White men end up being friends with white men. Given that one is not too much richer than the other, two white men seem to be able to be friends in America. They can drink together, tell dirty jokes, and sometimes even talk about important things. The only limitation is that they cannot love each other. For males to be friends, they have to prove to society that they are more attracted to women than to men. They can neither cry nor comfortably kiss in public.

Friendship—or, as I understand friendship in America—makes little sense, does little good. We fail to take seriously the sometimes special world of women or of men; we fail to grant the trait of humanness to most of those who are black or red or yellow or brown.

In doing so, we seem to define the world as violent—as unemotional and masculine, as unsentimental and white.

TOWARD THE LAST CHAPTER

He swallowed a whole lot of wisdom, but it seemed as if all of it had gone down the wrong way.

James Thurber wrote that a moth never burned its wings by flying toward the stars.

There is little reason for one to bother reading this "Toward," as it does not rightly belong to the preceding chapter or to the one that follows. It has to do with some of what goes into—but rarely comes out of—writing.

Like many endeavors, writing consists of a series of traumas; with a book, these traumas are numbered in chapters. I suppose a ten-and-one-half chapter book is not so traumatic. It is hard to imagine a twenty-three chapter book. But that is not the whole point. The point is that The Last Chapter is somehow different from the others. It is (or maybe should be) different for a number of reasons.

The Last Chapter is the final chance to make whatever point one has been trying to make throughout the book. It is the last, best, and only chance one has left. It is the obvious place in which to sum up, to make clear, and to explain precisely. That should be pressure enough, but there is more.

The Last Chapter is the place to right all the wrong things that have been implied, to apologize for the tricks employed, or the shoddy arguments, or whatever. Some of that is easy enough to do, if one is so inclined.

It seems to me, though, that there is a great urge to come up with The Final Answer in The Last Chapter. To write is often to make up both the answer and the question (the order is not terribly important) and to create an illusion that things are thereby better, or that they soon will be. This book is probably in that tradition. The only problem is that I am still not quite sure about either the answer or the question.[1]

Certainly there have been "answers" in almost every chapter. Just by dealing with this particular set of problems, I have assumed much. But it seems unlikely that this textbook should end with a neat series of solutions, or have a Last Chapter that

---

[1] To be truthful, I just completed a book in which I asked a question and offered an answer. Of course, it was not quite that simple. In fact, the answer was really answers that suggested new sets of questions.

contains "strategies" for completely renewing society. It is not that I believe that all is well; indeed, complete renewal may be the minimum we need. The problem is: I do not know of a neat plan to solve our problems.

The *real* problem is this:

I do not believe in neat plans.

The last chapter does a little of all those things I have mentioned. There is a summing up, a final point making, and some apologizing. For certain, it does not reflect the wishes I had for it, which is my last apology.

> Today is gone. Today was fun.
> Tomorrow is another one.
> Everyday,
> From there to here
> From here to there
> Funny things are everywhere
> From there to here
> From here to there,
> Funny things
> Are everywhere.[2]

---

[2] From Dr. Seuss, *A Cat in the Hat* (Random House, 1957). Reprinted by permission.

10
THE LAST
CHAPTER

There was once a company of six dancers who were part of a circus in the local village. Five of the dancers could leap about three feet. The villagers followed these five closely, knowing just how high each could jump. They would applaud enthusiastically at the dancer who would leap just a few inches higher than the others.

The sixth dancer could leap almost six feet. The villagers ignored him, wishing to reward the others in his company. When asked why he continued to leap so much higher than the others, while being unappreciated, he replied simply: "Because the other dancers understand."

—*Sören Kierkegaard*

"Either do not attempt at all, or go through with it.

—*Ovid*

[He] had nothing to protect him against the world but his splendid laughter, and the immense naked courage behind it.

—Hannah Arendt

HAPPINESS

"We are all happy, if we but knew it."

—Dostoevski

It seems fairly obvious that if we had our choice, we would choose to be happy rather than unhappy. We want to be happy; we aim at it and plan for it and sometimes even strive toward it. But it seems to me that we have more of a passion for happiness than we have knowledge about it. As with so many seemingly important things, the greatness of our wants is equaled only by the greatness of our ignorance.

Happiness seems a reasonable topic to discuss when one considers the preceding topics. Maybe *all those other things* really do have some relationship to the ways we act and to how we feel. Maybe those things can make us happy, or unhappy, without our even knowing it. Maybe not. But happiness is a subject that should be explored.

Happiness is not *the* goal of humanity, or even of politics, and I do not want to argue that it is. I would simply like to suggest that to begin to think about how we think about happiness may help us to understand not only what we have but possibly what we don't have. By exploring happiness we may be able to see more clearly how to get what we want, and we may also be able to ask ourselves if what we want is worth getting. To begin with, we should try to understand a little of what happiness consists of in ourselves and in our relationship with society.[1] Then we will explore different ways of dealing with society.

There is no obvious beginning point to a happiness discussion.

---

[1] The following discussion is based, in large part, on an unpublished article by John Schaar, entitled ". . . And the Pursuit of Happiness." The overstatement of the case is my, not his, doing.

No point that is so natural a place to begin that it cannot be ignored. Dictionaries may help; so too may Aristotle or Augustine or Jesus. But a discussion that thorough may serve to confuse as much as to make clear.

For a laugh, we could start at an unlikely place—with the Puritans. They serve as models for many things, but I doubt that they have ever been a model for happiness. H. L. Mencken once wrote that Puritanism was the gnawing feeling that someone somewhere might be happy.

So much for the Puritans.

By the time of the Constitution, we had already decided that happiness—at least the pursuit of it—was something "originally" guaranteed. The apocryphal story goes that when Thomas Jefferson was drafting the Declaration of Independence, he wrote about the right to life, liberty, and property. That is said to be the true phrasing of the thought, but it was not much artistically. So Jefferson rewrote. He changed it. Instead of pursuing property we were to pursue happiness. The point is an obvious one: In many American minds there is no difference. Any subtle distinctions are unclear. They are the same—property is happiness is property is happiness.

But what does that mean now? What does it mean to us? One could easily imagine that it means something like this. Before, to have property was enough. An individual was thought to be more or less happy if he or she owned things. But times have changed. We have changed. We have sophisticated our tastes, modified our styles; now, we consume. Maybe happiness is no longer just the pursuit of property.

Maybe happiness in America means buying things we won't use, using things we don't need, and wasting things we don't want. To consume is to destroy, yet our happiness is in the consumption. Our credit revolves as our purchasing power increases, and the dynamic is supposed to bring smiles to our faces and happiness to our hearts.

Of course, as middle-class, cared-for, mostly pampered college people, we think the consumption formulation vulgar and offensive. "No," you think, "that is for the others. *They* have to buy to be happy. Not me. Not us. No sir. For us to be happy, we just have to have fun."

So that is what you do: run after fun. Have a drink, smoke some dope. Now that is fun. Or you might ski. Or you might play bridge. Or you might go out and kill animals. Now that is really fun. What *more* could we want? Aren't we all happy now?

But is happiness just fun? Fun is cheap. Fun may be little more than a way to fill empty hours, or it may be a way to achieve status and social approval. In the final analysis, fun may have about as much to do with happiness as buying things does. Buying and having fun may simply be methods of display, motion, and instant reward.

If we look around for happiness, or even for fun, it is reasonable to assume that we will continue to be disappointed. The fact seems to be that society gives us few choices. We watch dull television, or the beautiful people in movies, or read *Penthouse* or *Mademoiselle*. And we think that is cool, and so we accept it and think ourselves happy. But that is little more than a sophisticated, societal lie.

The Madisonian man or woman in us will be content with new dresses or pictures of naked men and women, and we shall feel a little guilty and a little good, and go harmlessly on our way.

We somehow squander our right to pursue happiness for the security of mindless, inoffensive fun. We confuse internal pursuits— beauty, nobility, excellence—with the pursuit of happiness understood as the fulfillment of desire. We are too well trained in our own evilness and too used to our own self-interest to accept the task of trying to be happy while living with other people or while seeking values that do not have an obvious, tangible reality.[2]

Maybe there is no such thing as happiness in our society. The harder we look, the more hopeless we become. We grow further apart and pretend somehow that loneliness is happiness. We consume, and we kill, and we read and watch things that only limit our perceptions, dull our imaginations.

To begin to think hard about happiness is to begin to feel cheated. It is to feel that there is an empty space where fullness should be. The more we pursue happiness in a society based on the

---

[2] I would like to share a curious fact in the form of a question: Why are so many people so willing to share unhappiness but unwilling to even acknowledge happiness? Curious, huh?

presumption of our own evilness, the less well off we are as human beings.

But to end "happiness" in great despair does not make much sense, at least not much good sense. If I really agreed with Archbishop Whately that happiness was no laughing matter, I should be forced to believe that happiness was probably not worth the trouble of figuring out. No, what I want to say is the obvious: I have seen people happy, and have even felt it, and have certainly enjoyed it. Not only that, happiness might be important. It was Hawthorne who suggested the likeness of happiness to a butterfly, which flits away when chased but which may come and light on your hand if you will only sit quietly, occupied with something else.

It is wholly possible that we have been searching in the wrong place, pursuing the wrong question. If we take Hawthorne seriously, it may be best to occupy ourselves with that "something else."

BEYOND BUTTERFLIES

I have no desire to set out a reasoned and reasonable argument about what one should do, about what that "something else" would look like if we wanted to have the butterfly light on our hand. Indeed, the implication of my remarks up to now is that happiness may simply be a nice by-product. It may not be worth pursuing in its own right.

Nor do I wish to agree fully with Hawthorne. While his insight into the chase seems a good one, his analogy is not quite accurate. Just sitting may be good for butterfly landings, but I am not certain that it is the best condition for happiness. Indeed, happiness may be, in part, the connections between one's self and others and society. It may have to do with how one thinks and sees and acts, not with how well one sits still.

If what has been said so far is right—if a portion of happiness is both personal and societal, and if our society is more limiting than fulfilling—then we must consider some general notions of what might be done. No plans (specifically); no Final Answer; nothing that hasn't already been suggested. Certainly each chapter has contained ideas about how we might begin to politicize our politics and possibly take our public selves and actions more seriously. No need to repeat that.

It is important to understand a little more about how to deal with what is going on now. If the preceding chapters have been at all successful in defining the present—and how we got here and where we are logically heading—then something should be said about the ways in which this "reality" might be confronted. It seems clear that almost everyone can get along, that most can cope, and that many can even "succeed" according to the present rules. But, if what has been said is correct, then that seems a surprisingly self-defeating option to take.

What we must do is to talk about the different ways of facing the problems of now, of the different options for everyday life, and make those ways free from the conventional definitions of "success." There are at least four ways.

WAY ONE: DO NOT DO IT

There may be a point, for some people, when it seems impossible or unlikely that what has been going on can keep going on. A point at which all seems hopeless or insane or inane, wicked or vile or cruel. A point when they just cannot continue doing whatever it is they have been doing. There are those who believe that nothing they do is getting them anywhere, yet who cannot quite figure out the next move.

One next move might be this: Stop doing those things that are not helping. Begin to understand—and don't do—the things "they" do.

What follows is an elaborate story that helps illustrate the point. It is suggested as an obvious move if what you are doing doesn't seem worth much. It is just a suggested move, not a stance toward life or an ultimate political action. It is simply a story of breaking away. The story is about Ken Kesey and a speech he once gave to protest the war in Vietnam. It is also a good historical example. This is the story about how a great many people defined themselves by how they acted.

Before beginning, a word about Kesey. He is a fine American author. *One Flew Over the Cuckoo's Nest* and *Sometimes a Great*

Notion are beautifully written, powerful books. Kesey was heavily involved with LSD, and now writes and farms and does politics in Oregon. To understand his acid lifestyle of the mid-sixties, read Tom Wolfe's *The Electric Kool-Aid Acid Test*. But that is, mostly, beside the point. One can learn from Kesey without using heavy drugs. He can conceptualize important things fantastically well. Enough background.

In 1965, Ken Kesey was invited to a teach-in held by the Vietnam Day Committee at Berkeley. According to Wolfe, no one was sure just why he was invited, but he was and he accepted the invitation. So Kesey and his friends dressed up in funny war costumes, painted themselves and their big old school bus in bright Day-Glo colors, took horns and electric guitars, and went to Berkeley.

When they arrived, a whole series of speakers was talking about "genocidal atrocities" and the need for great marches in the streets. Pretty soon it was Kesey's turn, and this is what he had to say.[3]

"You know, you're not gonna stop this war with this rally, by marching . . . that's what *they* do . . . they hold rallies and they march. . . . They've been having wars for ten thousand years and you're not gonna stop it this way . . . ten thousand years, and this is this game they play to do it . . . holding rallies and having marches . . . and that's the same game you're playing . . . their game."

Kesey stopped talking. According to Wolfe, he reached "into his great glowing Day-Glo coat and produced a harmonica and start(ed) playing it right into the microphone, '*Home, home on the range, hawonking away on the goddamn thing—Home . . . home . . . on the ra-a-a-a-ange hawonkawonk. . . .*' "

And his friends behind him began to play their guitars, and dance, and blow their horns. But the crowd—the serious Berkeley people—could not quite understand. This was a serious thing: the teach-in before the march. Home, home on the range? "We know about that *home!* We know about that *range!* That rotten U.S. home and that rotten U.S. range—" Maybe that is what the audience

---

[3] As reported by Tom Wolfe in *The Electric Kool-Aid Acid Test* (New York: Farrar, Straus & Giroux, 1968).

was thinking; but they just misunderstood. Kesey stopped playing and began to speak:

"I was just looking at the speaker who was up here before me . . . and I couldn't hear what he was saying . . . but I could hear the sound of it . . . and I could hear *your* sound coming back at him . . . and I could see the gestures and I could see his jaw sticking out . . . and you know who I saw . . . and who I heard? . . . Mussolini . . . I saw and I heard Mussolini here just a few minutes ago . . . Yep, you're playing their game. . . ."

Most of the crowd simply was not with Kesey or his friends. Some booed; most were just confused. That changed nothing on the stage. There was more music and more talk, more guitars and more "Home on the Range." The message was always the same: You're playing their game. And then another message:

"There's only one thing to do . . . there's only one thing's gonna do any good at all . . . and that's everybody just look at it, look at the war, and turn your backs and say . . . Fuck it. . . ."

"—hawonkawonkawonkawanka—"

Then the music got louder and madder and the Day-Glo crazies were really into playing and dancing and strutting to variations of the old classic "Home on the Range." And the Berkeley people weren't ready, and were a little shocked, and maybe a little drained of their desire to march, of their desire to "be like them." And Kesey repeated his message—and our first way out:

"Just look at it and turn away and say . . . Fuck it
—hawonkawonkawonka blam
—fuck it—
hawonkafuckit . . . friends. . . ."

WAY TWO: DO IT

It is not at all difficult to imagine some people's unhappiness with the above advice. For a whole group of individuals, both the style and the substance are potentially as distasteful as they are disagreeable. The style is a matter of taste, which is important—but not necessarily to this discussion. To walk away takes a good deal of understanding and nerve; but it is not necessarily the way for everybody. Some people want to know where they are going, just what they are getting into. They ask the naturally conservative (but reasonable) question: Will it be better than what we have?

To cling to that question is to limit what will be to what one is sure of, to what one knows. While Kesey's advice is precise, it is limited. He has no thoroughgoing view to offer us. It seems to take a certain kind of person to leave what is, without really knowing what will happen. In part, it takes an individual who knows that what is is not enough, is lacking something, is wrong; and who, because of that, is willing to try to create something else. Leaving—or not doing—something that seems wrong is not necessarily a negative act.

But it is clear that most of us, most of the time, need more than the advice to leave. We need some kind of direction. Moreover, we want that direction to be built on a rather explicit view of the world. Given that, Kesey is not our man. Possibly, Georges Sorel is.[4]

In order to get any meaning out of Sorel, in order to understand his politics and his influence, it is necessary to talk about some of his ideas of society. Basically, Sorel believed that societies ebb and flow; they are founded and destroyed, they decay and are renewed. There is no permanent answer, no state of peace. There are just continual cycles of change.

Europe, at the turn of this century, was in what Sorel believed to be a state of decline. Indeed, he thought the people bland, compromising, and corrupt. The institutions were as bad: Both Church and State seemed to him decadent. We are familiar enough with more contemporary versions of this kind of analysis to see why Sorel may be of some use, why he may illuminate some points.

The problem in Sorel's view—to oversimplify—was this: How can things be reformed and renewed? How can the decadence and the old ways of acting be cut out, be changed? His goal was a new style of being, a new way of acting. He wanted people to involve themselves in creating new societal forms, and he wanted this done in a new atmosphere of liberty. These were no modest aims.

What Sorel tried to do was involve the majority of the people—in his term, the proletariat—in the change. To his way of thinking,

---

[4] See Georges Sorel, *Reflections on Violence* (New York: The Free Press, 1950).

there was a slave morality and a master morality. It was only the master morality that was noble enough to cause heroic action. It was the master morality that the people had to acquire. Moreover, this morality had to be shared, had to be public, had to be political. If society was to be renewed, there had to be a collective force stronger than society. There had to be political action of a great mass of people.

Sorel proposed that people be reeducated—but with a difference. People were to be taught through a concept of their own hope. They were to be given a new myth, a new ideal of what might be, a new vision to do battle for. It should be made clear that this myth cannot be characterized as single idea, or as a series of small changes, or as a blueprint. It isn't logical or rational or open to critical analysis. The new myth is a complex of pictures and images of what we believe. It contains what we hate and what we want and what we will fight for.

We have a myth of America. It may or may not be worn out. If it is old, out of date, decadent, then, according to the teachings of Sorel, we must create a new myth. The new one will be built on our hopes, on our own best thoughts.

The idea of the myth is important in understanding Sorel, and in understanding what we must do. For at the heart of his myth is a commitment to violence, a commitment to starting afresh. Through this commitment, people begin to take action, to reeducate others by their example, and to develop a sense of the master morality. In the creation of the myth and through commitment to it, an individual will turn more and more to the interests of the community and to the fate of his fellows.

In the end, the state is destroyed and a new one is created. But according to Sorel, the individual is not only creating a state: he or she is also creating virtue. To take it to the next step, the individual is achieving a remarkable aim: By creating virtue the individual is also helping to create himself or herself.

The themes of Sorel are instructive; he is able to help us understand that the state and politics are beyond the rational, the routine, the bureaucratic. The whole idea of remaking—indeed, of creating—through political action enables us to glimpse an important vision we now lack. It is, in part, to begin to know that change is connected with the creation of, and then the substitution of, one way of looking at the world for another, of one myth for another myth. Finally, Sorel teaches us that there is a close tie between the development of the political and the individual, and that ultimately, the virtue of the one is tied to the virtue of the other.

For those who do not want to walk away but who believe that the state of the state is beyond repair, Georges Sorel might point the way. Certainly his arguments are too powerful to simply ignore, his aims too grand to put aside. Sadly, he may have been wrong about us: It is possible that we are *all* corrupt, all bland and compromising. Maybe we are slaves to a morality that effectively blocks us from the new myth—from the Myth of the General Strike.

But that is off the point.

WAY THREE: RETURNING

As the sixties and seventies burned themselves out, as acid eroded brains and revolts got torched (for instance, the SLA in Los Angeles), Ways One and Two began to seem not quite right for these times. This is a quiet, try-to-be-happy regrouping time.

There is not a vast literature about such times. Yet there is one book—one story—that is just about right. It has to do with American virtues, happiness, know-how, and family. If there is any one drawback in the book it is the size of the family it describes, since we live in a militantly zero-population time. You see, the size of this family is impressive: There were a father, a mother, and a dozen children.

The name of the book is *Cheaper by the Dozen,* and it was written by two of the children.[5] It was published in 1949 and records events from 1910 to 1924 or so. Way Three is fun; or at least it sounds fun.

There really were a dozen children:

"How many would you say we should have, just an estimate?" Mother asked.

---

[5] Frank Gilbreth, Jr. and Ernestine Gilbreth Carey, *Cheaper By the Dozen* (New York: Bantam, 1975).

"... an even dozen," said Dad. "No less. What do you say to that?"

"... a dozen would be just right. No less ... Boys or girls?"

"Well, boys would be fine," Dad whispered. "A dozen boys would be just right. But ... girls would be all right too. Sure. I guess."

"I'd like to have half boys and half girls. Do you think it would be all right to have half girls?"

"If that's what you want," Dad said, "we'll plan it that way." He took his memoranduam book and solemnly wrote: "Don't forget to have six boys and six girls."

So they did—they being Lillian and Frank Gilbreth. In seventeen years they had six girls and six boys. And there was something uniquely American about the plan and the planners. Lillian and Frank, interestingly enough, had the same vocation: They were industrial engineers. They were early advocates of efficiency, just like good ole Frederick Winslow Taylor.

The Gilbreths were true believers: "... Mother the psychologist and Dad the motion study man ... believed that what would work in the home would work in the factory, and what would work in the factory would work in the home."

The house, according to the book, was fun to live in ... and very well organized.

There was a chart in the bathroom where each child old enough to write had to sign in after he or she had taken a bath, brushed his or her hair and teeth, and made the bed. Also, each child had to plot a graph showing his or her weight, progress in homework, and the like. Everything was done regularly—and routinely—and was done in the most efficient way. Frank Gilbreth buttoned his vest from the bottom up instead of the top down because it saved him four seconds.

The children were organized so that each older child was responsible for one of the younger ones. Lillian took care of the baby, and Frank took care of himself.

There was, not surprisingly, a division of labor in the house. The boys would cut the grass; the girls would sweep and dust. Tall girls would dust table tops; short girls would dust table legs. And it was all like that. When there was an extra job, the children would submit bids for it, and the lowest bid won.

Clearly, the parents were extraordinary. The book documents the amazing interest Frank had in efficiency—how he saw so much of the world as inefficient.

For example, there was the time when several of the children needed to have their tonsils taken out. Frank understood surgeons to be simply skilled mechanics, and decided to improve on their efficiency. He talked the doctor into doing the surgery in the Gilbreth home, and into having each operation filmed.

The plan was easy enough to understand: By comparing six operations of the same kind, Frank believed he could find the least wasted motion in every phase of the procedure and in the end make everything more efficient.

There were some problems (one healthy child had her tonsils removed by mistake), and some funny things happened, but all the while the cameraman was in the operating room with his camera going.

Can you imagine living in a house where one of the adults wanted to reform the world by making it faster? Can you envision the mass removal of tonsils as a wonderful way to collect data to save time? Isn't it *American* to think that way? Don't we want efficiency in our lives, and in government, and even when we buy tickets to a movie?

It is fair to tell you how this particular venture in efficiency turned out: The cameraman forgot to remove the lens cap from the camera; so naturally there were no pictures.

The cameraman quit before Frank could fire him.

The world—or at least the part of the world in which people deal with physical objects—was understood in terms of Therbligs. (The term *Therblig* is Gilbreth spelled backwards, almost.) A Therblig is a unit of motion or thought. Time and motion studies in a factory or in a home concerned trying to reduce those dreaded Therbligs. Frank and Lillian were really good at it.

In the last chapter of the book we are told that Frank had a weak heart and knew he would die young. In spite of that, in spite of the fact that he would leave a widow with twelve children, he wanted those dozen kids. His children seemed to think that "one of the principal reasons" why "he had organized the house on an efficiency basis" was so that things would be easier for Lillian when he died.

Maybe that is so. I'm not convinced, but it's a nice thought.

What Frank could not have counted on was Lillian's reaction after his death. After being "taken care of" all of her life, first by her parents and then by Frank, she simply came into her own. She sat in Frank's chair, was no longer a weepy, frightened woman, and assumed a great deal of authority.

She was, to use today's word, liberated.

She became, in an odd way, just like Frank.

Way Three, then, is an American way. It is the mix of fun-family and efficient-factory. It is warm, without wasted motion.

It's home . . . the Way we want to return to.

WAY FOUR

There is a Way Four, which is not obvious enough to sum up in a catchy phrase. In a sense, this fourth way counsels us to do the best we can, no matter what. Although it might seem pessimistic (it counsels that, no matter what, we all die and rot), I do not believe it is. While not as obviously political as Sorel or as direct as Kesey, this way does provide a basis for action. While it comes from the Bible, from Ecclesiastes to be precise, it certainly is not religious. Indeed, it pretty much ignores the God problem. It involves what we should do, if anything, and why. It involves the same questions raised in the discussion on happiness and by Kesey and Sorel.

Vanity of vanities, all is vanity.

Ecclesiastes was written by the son of David, the king of Jerusalem. The best guess is that Ecclesiastes was written by King Solomon, a person reputed to be wise, just, wealthy, and virtuous. An impressive combination. It is from this vantage point that he writes his advice, that he tries to explain their merits in accordance with what he understands to be the human condition.

First, Solomon explains that we cannot count on being different than we are; we cannot count on having something new. All has happened; all will happen again. We will continue unsatisfied, unfulfilled, if we continually expect something new. "I have seen all the works that are done under the sun; and, behold, all is vanity and a striving after wind."

But there are goals other than trying to be different. There is wealth: "I made me great works; I builded me houses; I planted me vineyards. . . . I acquired me man-servants and maid-servants, and had servants born in my house. . . . I gathered me also silver and gold and treasure. . . . So I was great . . . and whatsoever mine eyes desired I kept not from them; I withheld not my heart from any joy, for my heart had joy of all my labour; and this was my portion from all my labour.

"Then I looked on all the works that my hands had wrought, and on the labour that I had laboured to do; and, behold, all was vanity and a striving after the wind. . . ."

Verses can be repeated, about wisdom and about virtue, and the conclusion is always the same: All is vanity, a striving after the wind. That is a part of our condition we cannot ignore. It is a part of our condition, in part, because we all must die.

". . . There is one event to the righteous and to the wicked; to the good and to the clean and to the unclean; to him that sacrificeth and to him that sacrificeth not; as is the good, so is the sinner . . . there is one event unto all . . . the heart of the sons of men is full of evil, and madness is in their heart while they live, and after that they go to the dead."

And when we "go to the dead," that is it.

"For to him that is joined to all the living there is hope; for a living dog is better than a dead lion . . . the dead know not anything, neither have they any more a reward; for the memory of them is forgotten. As well as their love, as their hatred and their envy, is long ago perished; neither have they any more a portion for ever in anything that is done under the sun."

No heaven, no hell: just vanity and chasing the wind. Then, no more a portion forever in anything. But this fourth way—this advice of Solomon—is not depressing. These are not grounds for despair. The advice is twofold: First, enjoy life. "Eat thy bread with joy, and drink thy wine with a merry heart . . . let thy garments be always white; and let thy head lack no oil. . . . Enjoy life with a wife when thou lovest . . . whatsoever thy hand attaineth to do by thy strength, that do; for there is no work, nor device, nor knowledge, nor wisdom, in the grave, wither thou goest."

Second, be with people. "Two are better than one . . . if two lie together, then they have warmth; but how can one be warm alone? And if a man prevail against him that is alone, two shall withstand him; and a threefold cord is not quickly broken."

Enough Bible. Maybe too much. But the points are sufficiently important to be made explicitly. For some, Kesey's advice was obvious and good; for others Sorel or the Gilbreths were good. Yet there are many who cannot quite make blind leaps, who are not ready for an ideological stand, who just have to think things through as far as possible. That is the point here: To understand vanity and death is not to be immobilized, is not to despair, is not to avoid action. It is to do all these things—to act, and to move, and to accept happiness. It can easily be the basis of politics, for it is all we have; and if Solomon is right, we only have one chance at it.

So the fourth way is the most vague of all, but maybe also the most urgent.

WHERE TO BEGIN: WHAT TO TALK ABOUT

> *Freedom is fire, overcoming this world by reducing it to a fluctuating chaos, as in schizophrenia; the chaos which is the eternal ground of creation. There is no uni-verse, no one way.*
>
> *We are always in error*
> *Lost in the wood*
> *Standing in chaos*
> *The original mess*
> *Creating*
> *A brand-new world*
>
> *Thank God the world cannot be made safe, for democracy or anything else.*
>
> —*Norman O. Brown*

There is one topic which should be thought about before ending this chapter. The topic is this: Where do we begin to talk about politics. By that I mean to ask what the logical entry point is when we want to know about those things that are political.

As you have seen, this book is not about those things that we normally think of as being "political." The "real" concerns that we read about in the newspapers do not necessarily form the central concerns of what has been written. There are many political scientists who militantly focus on immediate issues: schools, health care, income distribution, and the like. It is not so much that they focus on these areas; it is that they believe these are the only legitimate concerns of politics and political science.

To those political scientists, it is all wrong to focus on the kinds of issues of this book. To them, privatization, aloneness, groups, friendship and the like, are simply not topics. Worse, to discuss these things in everyday language just makes a mistake all the worse.

There are some ways in which those people are right. Although they are dead wrong about everyday language, there is a point about discussing everyday issues. Who, after all, would want to argue that better schools and food for those who are hungry are not the point? Of course, they are the point. These are the concerns of our political system, and the ways we handle them are who we are. Yet, to limit our discussion to the topics, without seeing what is behind them, is to limit ourselves to both our questions and our answers. It is to limit ourselves to failure.

The idea can be explained in a different way. If we concentrate entirely on issues like housing, food, health, and the like, part of what we are assuming is that a government is like a huge household. We automatically limit our public activities—what is called politics by the press—to the issues of running a house. We are like a very big, impersonal family. Somehow, we all want the best bedroom, our own telephone and television. One of the things this book has been about is that there is more to politics than merely family affairs.

There are, to put it another way, a number of fundamental questions we must learn to discuss and come to terms with before we are able to answer the "better health" problems of everyday, obvious politics.

In order to ask a different—and I would claim more essential— kind of question, we must first ask what we can expect from politics and our political system. We have been taught to make unnecessary distinctions. We separate the tensions between the "cultural" problem of aloneness from the "political" problems of food and money. The separation is there because of the way we were brought up. We learn a very narrow view of politics, and that view limits what we can understand. It would be far better to see that a more inclusive idea of politics and political action can help resolve the natural tensions between individual and societal virtue.

Until we are able to see that everyday discussions take place in a context loaded with meaning, and until we see that the context contains a definition of politics which carries qualitative values that absolutely influence everything said, and until we realize that, the only solutions to problems will be "tricks," will be variations of the themes contained in the definitions that form the context of the problems. They will be variations on the very themes that helped bring about the problems in the first place.

The two suggestions I am making are these: First, we must redefine politics in such a way that it helps us to define who we are. We must understand politics as a creative process—both for ourselves and our society. Second, with that definition firmly in mind we must try to solve the critical problems around us. But the order, in this instance, is critical. We cannot do the second until we have done the first.

It is necessary to understand that to talk about politics is to talk about both the process and the problem, about both the individual and the outcome.

One of the results of this is to take us into the area of political theory. Norman Jacobson writes that "the genius of all great political thinkers is to make public that which is of private concern, to translate into public language the more special, idiosyncratic vocabulary of the inner man in hopes of arriving at public solutions which might then be internalized by each of us."[6]

This book, in large part, has tried to get at our "normal" context of politics, and to suggest that there are many ways in which this context is inadequate. An effort has been made to make

---

[6] Norman Jacobson, *Pride and Solace* (Berkeley: University of California Press, 1978), p. 100.

explicit the implicit ideology which we were born into and which dominates our thinking. With that in mind, we can go to the last topic and get an overview of what has gone on.

ON TRYING TO UNDERSTAND THE WHOLE BOOK

This is meant to be an introduction to politics, some ideas that may lead one to begin to understand a few important problems.

What was done seems reasonable enough to do at a beginning level. An effort was made to try to understand the elements of politics. Pretty obviously, the book has been concerned with much more than how a bill becomes a law or how to be elected mayor or president. Simply and reasonably and logically, we have found that politics is prior to and more important than our governmental apparatus.

In many ways, politics is a function of how we think of each other and of how we relate to the whole. It is us and them, and we and me, and I and thou, in all combinations. To understand that, we began at the beginning.

The beginning was a simple search into how we related to each other, into how society wanted us to understand ourselves, and—somewhat closer to the root of the matter—into how much we counted. So we read *Federalist* No. 10 and tried to figure out what it means and how we have acted according to it. The conclusion was unhappy, but fairly accurate: Madison's account of society—of us—was true. We Americans built a society on the evilness of us all. Somehow we chose to emphasize those things least desirable in ourselves. We discovered that we believed each other to be evil, and that our belief had become a self-fulfilling prophecy.

Larry Spence gives us a wonderful description of this whole way of thinking. He calls it *the principle of the fewest sons of bitches*. "Since it is the nature of men to steal, kill, cheat (that is, increase chaos) at every opportunity, the chances for survival are enhanced if a few men are designated a government with certain rules as to where, when, and how the cheating, killing, and stealing are to be done. The supposition is that getting robbed and beaten by a few men at designated times and places is better than getting it from all sides at all times and at any place."[7]

There was the whole question of how we know things, of what things are real. The conclusion was rather an odd one: We found that we believed knowledge was something that could be touched, or physically felt, or seen. We believe that we know things by rationalizing them, by objectifying them. So there is little opportunity to think about "unreal" things, about knowledge that is neither wholly objective nor rational.

A world in which all things were rational and objective would be a world without humans; it would be mute testimony to our own stupidity.

So we hunted hard for our own humanity. We began to realize that the political state was more than laws and elections, that politics had something to do with who we were. So we tried to be free but saw that we were made to be alone; we tried to understand justice but could only talk about being judged.

There were depressing times for me doing some of the work. To consider some of the problems, and then to think about how they were currently being solved and how they *might* be solved was often no fun. But no fun is really no criterion for measure. It seemed right, to make sense to begin the study of politics by studying what politics was doing to each of us. Just as importantly, it is necessary to know about what you are allowing to happen to you simply out of ignorance.

Everything means something (or many things); nothing is wholly obvious. So we tried to understand what was happening and how it happened. There were discussions about how groups could pressure you, freedom isolate you, voting degrade you, and happiness sadden you. It was no mistake that we reached the conclusions we did.

What was discussed, much of what was decided, are real, hard, true facts. They are, to some degree, the facts with which we have lived up to now. They seem imprecise simply because they are

---

[7] Larry Spence, *The Politics of Social Social Knowledge* (University Park: Pennsylvania State University Press, 1978), page 17.

difficult to measure; but, in the long run, they are much more important than most things easily quantifiable.

The study of political science—of politics—can be the study of these facts. I think it can, at its best, be an attempt to understand how to relate to our society in a public, open—indeed, political—manner. My bias is obvious: It seems important to understand what is happening, which things must be kept, and which things should be changed. We are free to study any aspect in any manner; but it seems a great loss when we fail to relate what goes on to our human condition. To discuss politics without people seems as silly as discussing economics without goods and products, or history without the past.

There is a possiblility that there are some of you who find this a little depressing. Vanity? Violence? A dozen children? Who needs any of that? Who needs another set of seemingly silly or disappointing choices? It is just too much like presidential elections: It is like trying to pick the least bad candidate.

The book was not written to depress you. I promise. A little outrage, anger, insight—whatever—but certainly *not* for depression.

Earlier there was a discussion about A Plan and An Answer; a discussion in which both seemed wrong. I was serious about that. What I am not against is doing things: I am for action. It is clear that politics is much too important to be left to the politicians, to the bureaucrats, to the technicians. We are better than that.

Now the rub.

The difficulty is figuring out the best thing to do, finding people to do it with, and then doing it. What do you believe? What do you do? Until you begin to think about the world and act in it, "they" have you. Just knowing the critique of society is not enough; constant looking in the mirror does not count as a political act.

Odd as it may seem, it does matter—on one level—if you choose any of the suggested "ways" in this chapter, or if you choose something else. What matters is that you choose and that you do. What I want to argue is that there is something in the very nature of political belief and action that is necessary and important for the human spirit. Equally important, belief and action are needed to resist the quiet, deadening tyranny of our times.

When you do something—when you act—you affect the world; you add to the sum of stories about trying to make the world better. Maybe it *is* having a huge family, maybe it *is* getting involved with Day-Glo. The choice has to do with what you know and believe and enjoy. It is a matter of knowledge and taste. Maybe what is best is just turning your back at just the right time, and doing it in public.

The thing that matters most is that you act. Be smart. Do something.

The remarkable aspect of the human spirit is that each of us has the capacity to act.

So, there you have it—it is not depressing at all.

Once there was a flock of geese. They were kept in a wire cage, by a farmer. One day, one of the geese looked up and saw that there was no top to the cage. Excitedly, he told the other geese:

"Look, look: There is no top. We may leave here. We may become free."

Few listened, and none would turn his head to the sky.

So, one day, he simply spread his wings and flew away— alone.

—*Sören Kierkegaard*

Focus Ten

This book has been about thinking about political action in America. The last chapter analyzes the reward for taking action—happiness, more accurately, public happiness. Happiness is the result of other accomplishments, a by-product of doing well something other than directly seeking happiness. One may anticipate being happy, hence want happiness; yet, according to the chapter, happiness befalls one when engaged actively in carrying out other projects. In other words, happiness happens to one rather than being directly created. Among the inalienable rights of Americans, the Declaration of Independence tells us, are life, liberty, and the pursuit of happiness. The argument of the book might be summarized as the following variation on this traditional American statement: Life is rightfully given human beings in the mystery of birth, liberty earned rightfully by those in political action, happiness pursued rightly by using life to keep liberty alive. Public happiness will befall those able to live together freely with others in a public way.[8]

If you will permit us a sweeping generalization, there are two kinds of happiness: public and private. To see the difference between the two, review the entire book by focusing on the main American myth of each chapter and the alternative guiding idea or assumption proposed by that chapter. The following list will assist the review.

	Enduring Myth	**Suggested Alternative**
Chapter 1	Evil people	Sufficiently trustworthy
Chapter 2	Scientific objectivity	Rightfittingness
Chapter 3	Bureaucratic souls	Unique distinctiveness
Chapter 4	Meaningless work	Essential work
Chapter 5	Passive voting	Action and voting
Chapter 6	Voluntary uniformity	Joint individuality
Chapter 7	Freedom from	Freedom to
Chapter 8	Legal justice	Moral justice
Chapter 9	Hierarchical groups	Magical groups
Chapter 10	Private happiness	Public happiness

The left-hand column adds up to private happiness. If a person believes that others with political power always are self-interested, that only science can tell us about the world, that a bureaucratically formed soul is sufficient, that work is inherently meaningless and must be endured, and that voting once every two or four years is the primary activity of a citizen, then he or she is well on the way toward living a life of voluntary uniformity, avoiding action with others, accepting only legal definitions of justice for society, being

---

[8] For the best recent working out of this idea in American terms see Hannah Arendt, *On Revolution*, Chapter 3.

bored in hierarchical groups, and, if blessed with comfortable surroundings, enjoying private happiness. He or she will lead a typical American life. And that life will not be so bad; typically, the American way of life is felicitous.

On the other hand, America offers more political promise for the citizen than the current myths emphasize. Add up the right-hand column. If a person assumes that other people with power can sometimes care enough for the good of the community over their self-interest to share power, that rightfittingness can be good judgment, that effective organizations can foster individual moral habits, that some work is worthwhile for its own sake, and that citizen activity in grass-roots arenas is a political right primary to voting, then he or she is well on the way toward the ability to see individuality as possible together with others and freedom as an activity that creates power for everyone who may want to do justice actively, perhaps in magical groups without a fixed leader-follower hierarchy. His or her reward will be public happiness—praise for effectively acting together with other people to keep alive the American tradition of active citizenship. Ideally, a life would have an ample measure of both public and private happiness. We Americans almost by nature pursue private happiness. The point of this book has been to remind us that public happiness also is part of our heritage.

The assumption of this book has been that we give guidance to our lives in part with distinctive, enduring American beliefs or assumptions about the political world. The overall dynamic of this book has been to scrutinize these myths in order to see whether they encourage citizens to political action. Thus, the chapter ideas complement each other in showing how better to think in order to be prepared for acting.

In sum, the book argues that politics is more and harder than government, that there are many avenues for being one's best self while also genuinely caring about politics, and that the first priority of government and politics should be the encouragement of citizen activity. Furthermore, while the argument criticizes the conventional myths of American political life, it advocates thinking in a way that inspires one to be one's own solid, thoughtful, courageous self rather than an eccentric. Simply stated, the point is to have reasons for what you do and the courage to do other than the expected when necessary. Not least, expect direct exercise of political power as a right, privilege, and American heritage, so that, if an opportunity arises, you will know why to take advantage of it. Some even will attempt to create opportunities; the rest of us now will have a reason for joining them.